D1474040

THE JOINT EXPEDITION TO
CAESAREA
MARITIMA

Volume I

Studies in the History of Caesarea Maritima

THE JOINT EXPEDITION TO

CAESAREA
MARITIMA

Volume I
Studies in the History of Caesarea Maritima

BULLETIN
OF THE
AMERICAN SCHOOLS OF ORIENTAL RESEARCH
Supplemental Studies
No. 19

Edited by
David Noel Freedman

THE JOINT EXPEDITION TO

CAESAREA
MARITIMA

Robert J. Bull:
D. Larrimore Holland: General Editors

Volume I
Studies in the History of Caesarea Maritima

Charles T. Fritsch, Editor
Glanville Downey
Gideon Foerster
Harry W. Hazard
Irving M. Levey

SCHOLARS PRESS
Missoula, Montana

THE JOINT EXPEDITION TO

CAESAREA
MARITIMA

Volume I

Studies in the History of Caesarea Maritima

Charles T. Fritsch, Editor
Glanville Downey
Gideon Foerster
Harry W. Hazard
Irving M. Levey

Published by
SCHOLARS PRESS
for
The American Schools of Oriental Research

Distributed by
SCHOLARS PRESS
University of Montana
Missoula, Montana 59801

THE JOINT EXPEDITION TO

CAESAREA
MARITIMA

Volume I

Library of Congress Cataloging in Publication Data

Studies in the history Caesarea Maritima.

(The Joint expedition to Caesarea Maritima ;
v. 1) (Bulletin of the American Schools of Oriental
Research : Supplemental studies ; no. 19)
Bibliography: p.
1. Caesarea—History—Addresses, essays, lec-
tures. I. Downey, Glanville, 1908-
II. Fritsch, Charles Theodore, 1912-   III. Se-
ries. IV. Series: American Schools of Oriental
Research. Bulletin of the American Schools of
Oriental Research : Supplemental studies ; no. 19.
DS41.A55 no. 19, vol. 1 (DS110.C13)   930s (933)
ISBN 0-89130-034-1   75-29059

The coin represented on the cover of this volume is a Sestercius minted in
Caesarea during the reign of the Emporer Hadrian. The original coin is at the
Museum at Sdot Yam, Israel.

The cover design is by Kay Wanous of New York City who served as artist with
the Joint Expedition to Caesarea.

Printed in the United States of America

1 2   3   4   5

Printing Department
University of Montana
Missoula, Montana 59801

In Memory of
G. Ernest Wright
Who was as a father to three generations
Of Archaeologists in the
Middle East

Contents

General Introduction

This is the inaugural volume in a series of studies on the magnificent Syro-Palestinian Caesarea on the coast of the Mediterranean Sea planned by the Joint Archaeological Expedition to Caesarea Maritima. Caesarea Maritima is the city Herod the Great constructed between 21 and 10/9 B.C., the city which for half a millenium enjoyed the status of being effectively the capital of Palestine. It is a city whose history has been neglected too long. Our purpose in this series, thus, is to write the history of Caesarea as completely as possible and to do this by drawing upon all of the literary and archaeological data available. Hence these volumes will contain essays drawn from extant ecclesiastical and civic records, the various chroniclers' reports touching upon the city and its inhabitants, archaeological reports from the Joint Expedition's various digging seasons in the field and other archaeological data, and, finally, synthetic interpretive studies which will attempt to integrate all of our data into a full-scale history of the city.

Therefore, Volume I contains essays on various facets of Caesarea's history drawn almost exclusively from the literary remains. Volume II will present the preliminary archaeological field reports from the 1971 and 1972 seasons of the Joint Expedition. Volume III, on current plans, will present essays based upon both literary and archaeological sources.

Volume I presents four major essays on Caesarea's history. Gideon Foerster of the Israeli Department of Antiquities and Hebrew University, Jerusalem, has contributed an essay on the early history of Caesarea. In it he recounts the known information concerning Strato's Tower, measures Josephus and the classical authors against archaeological data, portrays Roman Caesarea vividly, and surveys the civic and cultural history of the city down to the Byzantine period. Glanville Downey of Indiana University has enhanced his justly broad fame as a student of the histories of ancient Near Eastern cities in his essay on Caesarea and the Christian church. Something of the importance Caesarea enjoyed within the larger Christian community comes to light through Downey's chronicling the data of the New Testament, Eusebius' writings, and the Byzantine records. Irving M. Levey of the Princeton University treats Caesarea and the Jews in his lengthy study and delineates the major role the city's Jewish community played for over four hundred years in the history of Palestinian Judaism. The economic, social, and political conditions of the Jews in Caesarea are described. The roles the city played during the period leading up to the First Jewish Revolt (A.D. 66-73) and as the "Metropolis of Torah" in the Amoraic period are highlighted. And the hatred of the Jews for Caesarea, the immoral "daughter of Edom" (Lam. 4:21), at whose Gentile hands they had suffered such cruel persecution, which is so plain in Talmudic literature, is treated. Finally, Harry W. Hazard of Princeton has written definitively on Caesarea during the Crusades when the city was partially rebuilt and fortified. An expert on the Near East and the Crusades, Hazard has thoroughly perused the chronicles of the Crusades and sketched out a careful history of Caesarea during that period. The four essays are accompanied by a preface and an introduction by Charles T. Fritsch of Princeton Theological Seminary, their original compiler.

As the reader will observe, these essays occasionally overlap in their coverage and differ in their interpretations. That is of the essence of a good symposium, and the documentation is rich enough to aid the reader in forming his own opinions on most contested points.

These essays are almost a decade old, and the reader deserves a word of explanation concerning their publication. They were originally contributed for a symposium volume planned by Fritsch in the early 1960's (see his preface, *infra*) which, thanks to unforseen complications, never was published. The question then automatically arises: why publish these studies now after so long an interval? The answer is a twofold one. Although these essays are necessarily dated by the ongoing stream of scholarly research and publication during the past decade, each is written by a distinguished scholar and each makes a notable contribution toward filling in the lacunae in our knowledge of Caesarean history. To date there has been no truly full-scale study of Caesarea, and the available shorter works fail to provide the sorts of information to be found in this volume.[1] Hence the editors opted to print the essays as they stand and to provide the interested public with at least this much information on Caesarea as quickly as possible.

A special sort of caveat must also be interjected, however, explicitly to protect the authors from undue criticism in failing to accommodate the scholarly advances of the past ten years. There are, of course, specific points treated in each of these essays which have come under scholarly review in the intervening years, and there is an abundance of other literature touching more generally on various aspects of these essays which has also been published. This means, to take a single essay as an example, the views recently espoused by R. M. Grant respecting the reliability of Eusebius' historical information and interpretations[2] cannot have been assessed by Downey. Nor can he be held accountable for recent attacks on the consensus view concerning Eusebius' role at the Council of Nicea.[3] Moreover, the reissue of Walter Bauer's *Rechtgläubigkeit und Ketzerei im ältesten Christentum*[4] in 1963, to say nothing of its recent English translation,[5] was too late to catch Downey's attention. Had Bauer's book enjoyed the focus of scholarly attention at that time which it is now receiving, it would have been incumbent upon Downey to take into account its views (e.g., with respect to the role and importance of Demetrius' expulsion of Origen from Alexandria for the history of the church at Caesarea, to cite only one example). But, with the possible exception of the last work which was available in its first German edition, these are merely examples of the sorts of research which were unavailable when Downey's essay was written. The same sorts of information could be adduced for each of these essays in its respective field. The time which would have been required for these contributors to update their research and revise their essays was deemed by the editors to be an unwarranted additional delay in publication in light of their intrinsic worth as they currently stand, however, and each now appears in its original form.

Despite these caveats concerning the age of these essays, each stands as a significant survey of Caesarean history from a particular vantage point, and together the essays contribute importantly to our understanding of the ancient Palestinian capital. Hence they deserve publication and careful study.

The General Editors tender their thanks to each of the contributors to this volume and especially to Mr. Fritsch for making these essays available for publication in this form. Our sincere appreciation also to the American Schools of Oriental Research for their support of this project and for their incorporating Volume I into Supplemental Studies of the Bulletin of the ASOR.

R. J. Bull
D. L. Holland,
General Editors

Madison, New Jersey and Brookfield, Wisconsin
Advent I., 1972

Notes:

[1] The book by Avraham Negev, *Caesarea* (Tel Aviv, 1967), is a good but very brief, survey of the history of the city, and it illustrates the point.

[2] Robert M. Grant, "Early Alexandrian Christianity," *CH*, 40 (1971), pp. 133-144, among other places.

[3] E.g., in the studies of D. L. Holland, "Die Synode von Antiochien (324/25) und ihre Bedeutung für Eusebius von Caesarea und das Konzil von Nizäa," *ZKG*, 81 (1970), pp. 163-181, and "The Creeds of Nicea and Constantinople Reexamined (An Article in Review of Giuseppe Luigi Dossetti's *Il Simbolo di Nicea e di Costantinopoli*)", *CH*, 38 (1969), pp. 248-261.

[4] Walter Bauer, *Rechtgläubigkeit und Ketzerei im ältesten Christentum* (Tübingen, 1934, 1963²), second edition edited and with accompanying essays by Georg Strecker.

[5] Walter Bauer, *Orthodoxy and Heresy in Earliest Christianity*, edd. Robert Kraft and Gerhard Krodel (Philadelphia, 1971).

Preface

In the summer of 1960 Mr. Edwin A. Link brought the first underwater archaeological expedition to Israel for the purpose of exploring the long vanished port of Caesarea Maritima and charting the circular breakwater which enclosed the harbor. The expedition was sponsored by Princeton Theological Seminary and the American-Israel Society, and I was asked to serve on the staff as "field" archaeologist.

In preparing for this assignment I soon came to learn that most of the material written on Caesarea was limited to the description of the city found in the works of Flavius Josephus, the Jewish historian of the 1st century A.D. Haefeli's monograph, *Caesarea am Meer* (1923), for instance, the standard work on the subject, devotes seventy-one pages to the building and history of the city as described in Josephus, and the last six pages to the period between the fall of Jerusalem (A.D. 70) and modern times.

It is astonishing that the most important city in Palestine for six hundred years—from the 1st to the 7th centuries A.D.—has been so lamentably neglected by modern historians. Rich in the religious traditions of Christian, Jew and Moslem, and in the cultural remains of the Graeco-Roman, Byzantine, Moslem and Crusader periods, Caesarea Maritima reflects, as no other city does, the vicissitudes of Palestinian history for thirteen hundred years. Although some important archaeological work has been done there on a limited scale in recent times, Caesarea Maritima still awaits a well-organized, systematic and extensive archaeological campaign to uncover the many valuable treasures which lie there under the sand. It is good to report that a full-scale excavation of the site has begun in 1971 under the auspices of the *ASOR*, with Professor Robert J. Bull as director.

The purpose of this volume is, therefore, to present several studies covering the important periods in the history and life of Caesarea.

To the authors who have contributed to this scholarly venture I am most grateful. Their definitive studies on various aspects of Caesarea's history and culture contribute significantly to a fuller understanding of Caesarea's pivotal role as Palestine's leading city for most of the time from its construction by Herod the Great to the end of the Crusader period.

To Professor Frank E. Brown, Director of the American Academy in Rome, and the library staff of the Academy, I would like to express my gratitude for their warm hospitality and helpful cooperation during my stay in Rome in 1963 when I began working on this project.

For this project Mr. E. A. Link and Mr. Sol Feinstone gave substantial gifts which are deeply appreciated.

For my wife and children who have waited so patiently for this moment, I reserve my last special word of grateful thanks.

Princeton, New Jersey   Charles T. Fritsch
June, 1973

Introduction

From the writings of Flavius Josephus, the Jewish historian, we learn more about the plan and construction, the architecture and statuary of Caesarea Maritima than we know of any other city in the ancient world. Built at the site of Strato's Tower by Herod the Great, it became the most important city in Palestine for six hundred years. It was the center of Roman administration, the official seat of the Roman procurators in Palestine, and the headquarters of the Roman army in the province. Its importance was recognized by Tacitus, the Roman historian, who called it *JUDAEAE CAPUT* (*Hist.* II, 78).

Herod's magnificent buildings were crowned by the temple dedicated to Augustus in which was placed a statue of the Emperor larger than that of the Olympic Zeus on which it was modeled. The harbor, called Σεβαστός, with its colonnaded promenade and colossal statuary, was a tribute to the skill and daring of the Roman maritime engineers. The whole city was built in a style worthy of the name it bore.

The fame of the city soon spread far beyond the borders of Palestine. An interesting reference to Caesarea is found, for instance, in a letter to the councilors of Caesarea from Apollonius of Tyana who lived in the first century, A.D. He described Caesarea as "the greatest [city] in Palestine, excelling all others there in size and in laws, and in institutions and in the warlike virtues of ancestors, and still more in the arts and manners of peace . . ."[1] Centuries later, Moslem geographers and travelers described Caesarea as a most beautiful city with well-watered gardens and groves of orange and citrus trees.

Caesarea throughout its long history was truly a cosmopolitan city, a center of religious and cultural currents flowing from east and west. Oriented geographically toward the west, its main contacts from the beginning were with the Graeco-Roman world which deeply influenced every phase of life. Archaeological evidence, as well as literary sources, indicates the important role which the large Jewish community played in the political, religious and cultural life of the city. Christianity quickly took root there (cf. Acts 10) and flourished with such vigor that by the third century Caesarea had become one of the most important Christian centers in the Mediterranean world. After the Arab conquest of the city in A.D. 640, Moslem culture and religion held sway for more than four centuries. During the period of the Crusaders (1099-1265) life once again changed dramatically in Caesarea. It was now a much smaller town than in Roman days, with a population that was mainly European. Surrounded by massive Crusader walls which once

---

1. The text of the letter is found in *Philostratus, the Life of Apollonius* with an English translation by F. C. Conybeare (Loeb Classical Library) II 417-19, 417. I am indebted to Prof. W. C. van Unnik, of the University of Utrecht, for this reference.

again stand clear of engulfing sands, Caesarea was a formidable bastion of Western Christendom in the Moslem World. Temporal power was wielded by fuedal lords and ladies, and ecclesiastical authority was vested in a long line of archbishops appointed over the see of Caesarea.

It has been our purpose in this volume to present this variegated picture of Caesarea's history as fully and clearly as possible. By diligent research and thorough analysis of the source materials, the authors have not only given us a new conception of the importance of Caesarea itself throughout the thirteen hundred years of its history, but they have also shown how the study of a city like Caesarea increases our knowledge of ancient and medieval history in general.

The description of Caesarea in most handbooks and encyclopedias is usually based upon the well-known source material found in the Book of the Acts, Josephus and Eusebius. In these studies we have broadened this historical perspective to include the Moslem and Crusader periods, as well as studies in depth of Christian and Jewish life in the city.

The last phase of Caesarea's history belongs to very recent times. At the end of the 19th century the Turkish government settled a group of Bosnians on the site of the Crusader town where their mosque and abandoned houses can still be seen. In 1940 a kibbutz, known as Sedot Yam (Fields of the Sea), was established just south of the Roman theater. Today Caesarea is one of the main tourist attractions in Israel, with a beautiful golf course, magnificent hotel and comfortable tourist accommodations. During the summer evenings the restored Roman theater by the sea reverberates to the music of the world's greatest artists. The excavated areas are well preserved and clearly marked to lead the visitor through the various phases of Caesarea's colorful history.

—Charles T. Fritsch

THE EARLY HISTORY OF CAESAREA

Gideon Foerster

Strato's Tower, the deserted village where, according to Josephus, Herod the Great erected Caesarea, his principal port-city, has a history little shorter than that of its much more splendid successor.

This site is first mentioned in the papyri comprising the archives of Zenon, the chief assistant of Apollonius, treasurer to Ptolemy II of Egypt (285-246 B.C.). These archives include a number of letters and documents which describe Zenon's visit to Palestine in 259 B.C. Among the places where he stopped to obtain food he mentions Strato's Tower. Here he obtained five artabas of wheat-meal.[1] We also learn from this 3rd century B.C. source that there was an anchorage for ships at this site.

A later source from the 1st century B.C.,[2] Artemidoros of Ephesus, who is quoted by Marcianus of Herakleia, states that Strato's Tower was a settlement near Dor.

Strabo,[3] writing in the days of Augustus, again indicates, though in a more detailed manner, that Strato's Tower was located between Acre and Jaffa, and emphasizes the fact that there was an anchorage there.

It would seem then that the site was already settled in the 3rd century B.C., although this does not mean that it was founded at this time. Even though the name Strato was quite common during this period, especially among generals and high officials,[4] it is more probable that the Strato who founded this town lived when Palestine was under Persian rule, since we know that the Ptolemies usually gave dynastic names to newly founded towns.

Strato is the Greek form of the Semitic name 'Ashtart, found in the phrase *Abd Ashtart* (servant of 'Ashtart-Astarte) which was applied to at least two Sidonian kings; one ruled in the days of Artaxerxes II (404-358 B.C.) and the other in the days of Alexander the Great.[5]

The settlement of the Phoenicians along the coast of Palestine, which was expedited by the establishment of trade routes of the Phoenician merchants in the Persian period, was the result of certain economic factors, and was aided and abetted by the Persian rulers. The Persian forces themselves received support from the strong Phoenician fleet which formed the major part of the Persian naval force; in return, Tyre and Sidon were granted extensive lands along the coast of Palestine, which served as an agricultural belt for the narrow and less fertile Lebanese coastal plain. Its produce was essential for the Phoenician trade-centers, which were in a stage of rapid development, and the coast provided necessary anchorages for their ships. Settlements of this sort undoubtedly existed at Dor and Athlit, as well as at

Strato's Tower, during this period.

In the *Periplous*[6] ascribed to Scylax, and composed in the 4th century B.C., there is a gap in the place where Strato's Tower should be mentioned. After Sidonian Dor a Tyrian town is noted, which was situated on the bank of a river. This description does not fit that of Strato's Tower in two points. First of all another Tyrian town, Ascalon, is mentioned immediately after the Tyrian town referred to above. According to the normal order in Scylax, however, a Sidonian and Tyrian settlement are given in alternate succession. It would appear then that a (Sidonian) town is missing between the two Tyrian towns.

In the second place, Strato's Tower is not situated on the bank of a river, as the Tyrian town is said to be. This may refer to Tell-Melet—the Krokodeilon Polis of Strabo at the mouth of the Zerqa River. The order of towns in this 4th century B.C. list should have probably been: Sidonian Dor, Tyrian Tell-Melet, Sidonian Strato's Tower, and Tyrian Ascalon.

This Sidonian phase of settlement in the Persian period, which was soon influenced by the new Hellenistic culture, became very actively involved in trade with the Hellenistic world: on the one hand, with the Greek islands (especially Rhodes and Cnidus) whence wine was imported, and on the other, with the southeast, through Nabatean Petra.

The later history of the site is known from less obscure sources. The town passed from the Ptolemies into the hands of the Seleucids on two occasions: in 218 B.C., at the time of the conquest of Antiochus III, and finally in 198 B.C.

The Seleucid Empire, which was on the decline and actually decaying, hardly possessed the power to defend the Greek settlements in the face of the rising anti-Hellenistic movement. At the head of this movement stood the Hasmonean kings, who aspired to restore the kingdom of David, and considered themselves the rightful heirs of that realm. Dor, Strato's Tower and its vicinity were governed towards the end of the 2nd century B.C. by the tyrant Zoilus, a local ruler, of the Hellenistic type. When Alexander Janneus besieged Acre-Ptolemais, Zoilus sent a force to relieve the beleaguered city. Both Zoilus and the inhabitants of Ptolemais, who were concerned for the future of their lands, appealed to Ptolemy, King of Cyprus, who at the time had landed at Sycamona with the intention of intervening in the war over Ptolemais. However, Janneus, with the help of a bribe of some 400 gold talents, won him over to his own side. As a result, Dor and Strato's Tower came under Janneus' control,[7] and Zoilus fell into his hands. Thus was Strato's Tower first annexed to Judea, and it would seem that at that same time a Jewish community was founded there.

At the time of Pompey's campaign Strato's Tower was among the towns which were freed,[8] and it was rebuilt afterwards by Gabinius. It appears that the town had not been destroyed by the Hasmoneans, but had merely been reduced from its status of an autonomous *polis*, which Pompey later restored. Its position from then on did not change. It was first ruled from Syria;

later it was granted to Cleopatra by Antony, and finally, after the latter's defeat at Actium, it was given to Herod the Great by Augustus.[9] Herod turned this delapidated village into a metropolis which he named Caesarea after the Roman Emperor.[10]

Caesarea[11] was founded by Herod in 13/12 or 10/9 B.C.[12] A Jewish King by the will of the Romans, he was hated by his subjects. He was forced to secure his regal position mainly by founding new cities which would support his unpopular rule and serve the economy of the country without being dependent upon the existing cities which did not favor him. Shalit's opinion[13] that Herod also wished to promote the political and cultural ambitions of the Romans in the East seems well founded. The importance attached by the Romans to the founding of new Hellenistic cities in this region is well known, and Herod saw in himself an extension of Rome in this regard. He[14] saw in Caesarea a military colony like the one at Samaria, which is described by Josephus.[15] The rebuilding of the latter city by Herod, which was completed some four years before the building of Caesarea began,[16] made it possible for him to carry on more efficiently the construction of the largest port in Palestine at that time.[17] In the overall plan of this magnificent city emphasis was placed upon the port, which, according to Josephus' detailed description, was equal in size to that of Piraeus and included a breakwater, docks and sailors' quarters. In the city itself were a temple dedicated to the Caesar and a royal palace, a theater, an amphitheater, and other public buildings. Josephus also mentions the construction of parallel streets and a sewage system which was as well constructed as the buildings above ground.[18]

In Herod's twenty-eighth year as King, when these extensive building projects were completed, the city was inaugurated with much pomp, and named after Augustus.[19]

On this occasion Herod founded the quinquennial games, aimed to provide both intellectual and physical enjoyment.[20] In these competitions valuable prizes were awarded to the three winners; these were provided in part from the coffers of Julia, the wife of Caesar. Gladiators were brought in, as well as many wild beasts, and horse races were also held. The festivities, which Herod dedicated to Augustus, were equal to those of Rome, and according to Josephus even surpassed them. This was probably no exaggeration. Numerous foreign representatives and masses of the local population attended the festivities. These traditional games were continued and expanded, and we have much additional information concerning them.

Though Caesarea was soon to replace Jerusalem as the geographical, economic and political capital of Palestine, Jerusalem continued to be the official capital of Herod's kingdom. There is little doubt, however, that Herod's family spent much time in the new palace at Caesarea. We know, for instance, that Herod evidently brought Alexander and Aristobolus to Caesarea after their trial in Jerusalem and shortly before they were put to death at Samaria. Their supporters in his court were eliminated after he had summoned the public assembly in Caesarea and the masses had stoned them to death.[21] Most interesting is our knowledge of the visit of Marcus Vipsanius Agrippa to Caesarea, during his tour of the East in 15 B.C., i.e. before the official inauguration, and of the splendid reception accorded him there.[22]

With Judea, Archelaus inherited the Hellenized Caesarea upon the death of Herod in 4 B.C. After his removal in A.D. 6, when Judea fell under the rule of Roman procurators, Caesarea became the official capital. The praetorium, built by Herod and mentioned in the New Testament, was undoubtedly used by the procurators.[23] A short time after Herod's death, we hear of an occupation force, comprising "Caesareans and Sebastians" ($Καισαρεῖς$ $καὶ$ $Σεβαστηνοί$) in the service of the procurators and the other rulers in Judea. This set its stamp on the events of most of the 1st century A.D. In this same period we know of the support given by these auxiliaries to Sabinus, the procurator of Syria, when he came to supress the disturbances in Judea at the time of Archelaus' removal.[24]

The cavalry was commanded by Rufus and the infantry by Gratus. The garrison was composed of a cavalry *ala* of 500 men and five cohorts of infantry, each of 500. At this time Caesarea is mentioned as the principal harbor for exports and imports.

The first procurator related by Josephus to have resided at Caesarea was Pontius Pilate, who governed from A.D. 26 to 36 for Tiberius,[25] in whose honor Pilate erected a Tibereium in the city.[26] Josephus tells us of another aspect of his activities[27] when he reports the demonstrations which were conducted by the Jews of Caesarea before the procurator's house in the city after the transfer of the standards to Jerusalem; these the demonstrators demanded be removed from Jerusalem. After their rally on the sixth day in the great stadium of Caesarea, Pilate threatened to put them to death unless they agreed to leave the standards in Jerusalem. The Jews persisted in their refusal and Pilate, capitulating, returned the standards to Caesarea.

Significant Christian activity had begun at Caesarea as early as the 1st century. The deacon Philip came from Ashdod to Caesarea[28] and established his home in the city, and we hear of his four virgin daughters prophesying there.[29] Some three hundred years later their house was still shown.[30] After the dismissal of Pilate on account of the clash with the Samaritans, Marullus arrived in his place; in his time the first pagans, the Roman centurion Cornelius and his family, were baptized by Peter.[31]

Herod Agrippa I, like his fathers, dwelt permanently in Jerusalem, but spent a considerable part of his time in Caesarea.[32] He struck coins at Caesarea with non-Jewish symbols as part of his general currency. Great celebrations were held in the theater at Caesarea in A.D. 44 on the occasion of the return of Claudius to Rome. In these games delegates from abroad also participated. Agrippa was attacked by pains on the second day of the festivities and died suddenly.[33] Immediately after his death disorderly rejoicing broke out among the city garrison,[34] which was composed of local recruits who detested him on account of his great friendship for the Jews. The troops burst into his palace, took from it the statues of his daughters and set them on the roof of a brothel.[35] Claudius wished to punish the garrison by sending them to Pontus,[36] but the decision was cancelled due to the intervention of the Emperor at Rome; later under Vespasian they were transferred from Judea.[37] These events sowed the seed of the disorders which reached their height on the eve of the First Revolt.

Herod Agrippa I's death brought his kingdom again under the direct control of Rome and her delegates, the procurators. Ventidius Cumanus, who governed for four years between A.D. 48 and 52, used the garrison of Caesarea—four cohorts and a unit of cavalry from Sebaste—to attack the Jews, and caused numerous casualties among them.[38] Antonius Felix, who arrived in the country after his predecessor had been removed due to Jewish complaints, was a brutal man whose policy was no less harsh than that of Cumanus. During his administration Paul passed through Caesarea on a number of occasions and was confined there between the years 58 and 60 and subsequently taken by sea to Rome.[39] Under Felix disorders broke out among the Gentile and Jewish populations of the town over the matter of the privileges demanded by the latter, on the plea that Herod had been a Jew and had built the city.[40] In these riots the Jews gained the upper hand, but Felix suppressed them and destroyed a number of houses belonging to rich Jews with the help of his troops who were, as stated, local levies. Following the disorders two deputations were sent to Nero to ask him to settle the dispute between them,[41] but Felix was dismissed from his post in A.D. 60 before the matter was decided.[42]

Porcius Festus was sent to Palestine before the Emperor's verdict had been given on the claims of the two deputations from Caesarea. Shortly after he had taken up his post Nero's judgment was delivered against the Jews, thanks to a bribe which was given to one of his ministers. As a result of the adverse decision Jewish rights remained ungranted.[43] This decision constituted a new peak in the Roman policy of discrimination. Tension increased between the Jews, who had been denied their rights, and the Gentiles who now felt that the authorities were on their side. After two years of Festus' administration and two years of Albinus' knavery, Gessius Florus, a native of Clazomenae, in whose time the First Revolt broke out, was sent to the country. The events which took place in connection with the synagogue of Caesarea under the administration of Florus, the last procurator, were in fact part of the disorders preceding the First Revolt; the violence wrought upon the Jews coming to the synagogue and its desecration[44] led to serious clashes between the Jews and the Gentiles in Caesarea. The streets to the synagogue, which was in the Gentile quarter, had to be blocked because of the erection of workshops on a vacant lot surrounding the synagogue. Thanks only to the intercession of influential Jews, among whom was Yohanan, the tax-collector, the work was halted. But this created even greater tension, and the Greeks and Syrians desecrated the synagogue by sacrificing birds on its threshold.[45] Simultaneously the treasure of the Temple in Jerusalem was plundered by Florus' troops. This led directly to open hostility between the Jews and the Romans. Florus compelled the Jews of Jerusalem to welcome two notorious cohorts of the Caesarean garrison into the city. After wreaking much slaughter among the Jews, Florus sent one cohort back to Caesarea.[46] These events in Jerusalem served as a signal for the beginning of the rebellion, for at the same time as the Jews attacked the Roman garrison in that city, nearly the entire Jewry of Caesarea, some 20,000 in number, composing a considerable portion of its population, was butchered.[47] A similar massacre of Jews was carried out in many other mixed cities after the Jewish acts of retaliation.

Since Florus had failed to restore quiet in the country, Cestius Gallus, governor of Syria, left Antioch with the XII Legion and vexillations of other legions to put down the insurgents. His first base was Acre, whence he marched forth to operate against Galilee. He then made his headquarters at Caesarea. From here he continued his operations against Galilee, and also later set out through Antipatris, Lydda, Beth Horon and Gibeon, where he prepared to storm Jerusalem. His attack on the Temple Mount was repulsed, and after suffering a resounding defeat near Beth Horon, Gallus returned with his defeated forces to Caesarea.[48] An inscription on a tombstone or altar found at Caesarea in 1946, inscribed under a legionary eagle and mentioning Julius Magnus of Legion XII F(u)lm(inata), has been quoted by its publisher in proof of the participation of that legion in the fighting of the Second Revolt.[49] But it is more likely that this refers to the encampment of the legion at Caesarea at the beginning of the First Revolt. The victorious forces of Vespasian, including the 3000 troops of the garrison of Caesarea, established their base at Caesarea at the end of the summer of A.D. 67, and from there operated in all directions to suppress the Jewish uprisings. Josephus himself was then probably at Caesarea and married a woman who was one of the prisoners. The V and the X legions wintered at Caesarea, and prepared to attack Jerusalem, while the XVth was sent to Beth Shan.[49a] In the spring of A.D. 68 Caesarea was the base for Vespasian's forces, which were then overrunning Jewish Transjordan;[50] later it was the base from which Lydda, Antipatris and Javneh were captured,[51] as well as the mountainous country of Samaria as far east as Beth Shan, and southward to Jericho, where the news reached Vespasian of the death of Nero in June of the same year.[52] Vespasian thereupon broke off operations and stayed in his headquarters at Caesarea to await the course of events in the Roman Empire as a whole, and in Palestine in particular. But the success of Simeon bar Giora in Judea compelled him to leave his base and to undertake the suppression of the nests of rebels in Mount Ephraim and Judea, namely, Gophna, Akkrabatene, Bethel, and Hebron, which were captured by Cerealis after a stout resistance.[53]

A situation was therefore created whereby, on the eve of the siege and capture of Jerusalem, only Herodian Masada and Machaerus remained in Jewish hands. In July, 69, Vespasian was proclaimed emperor by Julius Tiberius Alexander, Prefect of Egypt, and the proclamation was confirmed by the legions in Judea, Syria and other places. In Caesarea itself the event was probably celebrated more than elsewhere, as Vespasian was there when he was made emperor.[54] Before setting out for Rome, he handed the command of the legions to his son Titus, who was then in Alexandria. The latter marched thence to Caesarea, which was the gathering point of the legions, and Josephus seems to have been personally present on the march.[55] Here were assembled legions XV and XII, the latter having been severely mauled two years previously, as well as numerous local auxiliary forces from the Syrian cities.[56] Titus brought Legion X from Beth Shan; V was then encamped at Emmaus. In the spring of 70 Titus moved on Jerusalem and at the beginning of Nisan stood before the city's walls.[57]

Jerusalem fell after a siege of five months, and Titus returned to his base at Caesarea with the remnants of the population of the Jewish city and its fighters; after a short stay there he went to spend some time at Caesarea Philippi.[58] Returning to Caesarea, he held various festivals and games in which the Jewish prisoners fought each other, over 2,500 of them forfeiting their lives.[59]

In the same period the notorious garrison of Sebastians and Caesareans was transferred from the city.[60] Josephus' last mention of Caesarea concerns Flavius Silva, who returned to the city after liquidating the last point of Jewish resistance of Masada in the summer of 73.[61]

After the destruction of Jerusalem, her rival Caesarea usurped her place finally and completely. Caesarea became the capital of Palestine and continued so till A.D. 375; she remained the official capital of part of the country from that same year till the end of the Byzantine period and the Arab conquest in the middle of the 7th century.[62] Her convenient location from a geopolitical point of view, on the coast at the center of the country, was highly appropriate to the requirements of the Roman and Byzantine administration, and was much superior, economically and politically, to the inland situation of Jerusalem.

In the rest of this chapter we shall present a brief account of Caesarea's flowering as a Jewish and Christian center in the following centuries, of her contemporary economic prosperity, and of her central position in the history of Palestine. Caesarea's role during the First Revolt as a base of the Roman forces in the country earned for her the gratitude of Vespasian, who granted her the title of Colony;[63] her full appellation was now "Colonia Prima Flavia Augusta Caesarea" or "Caesarensis." She did not obtain full *ius Italicum,* but received from Vespasian exemption from the poll-tax, and later, from Titus she received exemption from *tributum soli.*[64] Tacitus calls her "Judaeae caput,"[65] and Talmudic and Midrashic literature describes the status of Caesarea after the fall of Jerusalem in the most pointed manner as "Caesarea, daughter of Edom"[66]—Edom being Rome or "little Rome."[67] "Hillel son of R. Berakhia said . . . till Jerusalem was destroyed there was no

(other) town of importance; when Jerusalem was destroyed Caesarea became the metropolis;"[68] the position was summed up by Tractate Megillah[69]
in the words: "If anyone tells you that both Caesarea and Jerusalem have
been destroyed, do not believe him; that both are standing—do not believe
him; that Caesarea has been destroyed, Jerusalem is standing, or that
Jerusalem has been destroyed and Caesarea is standing—believe him."

Caesarea's status also finds expression in its independent coinage,
which began in the fourteenth year of Nero,[70] ceased under Vespasian and
Titus,[71] and was resumed under Domitian.[72] The character of her coins is
demonstratively pagan, and they tell us much of the cults common at
Caesarea and throughout the east in the first centuries of the current era
down to the termination of independent issues in the middle of the 3rd
century.[73] The deities who appear on the coins of Caesarea represent a fairly
broad repertoire of the cults accepted in Rome and the orient in those
periods. Kadman in his book has drawn up a statistical table of incidence
with regard to the appearance of the deities on the coins, and we may avail
ourselves of his conclusions.[74]

The commonest appearance, with 33% of the "reverse" types, is that of
the Tyche of the city. Kadman, following Hill and others, identifies her with
the Semitic Astarte.[76] After her comes the Egyptian Sarapis, with 11%; at
this period he was worshipped even at Rome and throughout the east.[77] The
"imperial trinity"[78] appears from the reign of Antoninus Pius, and included
Dionysus, Demeter and Tyche in the center, pictured in the facade of a
temple. Isolated appearances may be ascribed to the Olympian gods such as
Poseidon,[79] Apollo,[80] and, from the time of Trajan Decius till the end of the
coinage, also to Zeus,[81] Helios,[82] Ares,[83] and Hygeia.[84] Nike is represented
on coins not as a goddess in her own right, but in Kadman's opinion as an
attribute of the imperial victory.[85] Dea Roma, of whose cult at Caesarea we
hear from Josephus[86] in association with the cult of Augustus, appears on
coins of Caesarea only from the beginning of the 3rd century.[87] This is not,
indeed, the same Dea Roma with the lineaments of the Argive Hera, described by Josephus;[88] her form is that of Roma Aeterna as portrayed by the
colossal statue erected in the Temple of Hadrian at Rome.[89] The coins also
contain evidence of the imperial cult[90] from the time of Trajan.

Before we go on to discuss other evidence relating to the cults of
Caesarea, we may sum up the chief cults of which the coins inform us. We
see that the worship of Tyche-Astarte (?) and Sarapis, and perhaps also of
Dionysus and Demeter, were, except for the worship of the emperors, the
principal cults of Caesarea, which are reflected by the coins. We hear of the
cults of Sarapis and Isis in Palestine from the Tosefta;[91] we also learn of the
worship of Isis at Caesarea from a papyrus known as the *Prayer of Isis*[92]
which belongs to the 2nd century A.D.

Besides the Temple of Augustus and Rome, which have already been
mentioned, we know of a Tibereium at Caesarea,[93] also of a Hadrianeium.[94]
The descriptions on coins of tetrastyle[95] and hexastyle[96] temples, appear to
be somewhat schematic, and represent, on the whole, the usual type of
temple found in Syria. Among the statues of gods found at Caesarea, not all

of which have been published, we may note one of the Ephesian Artemis,[97] a head of Dionysus,[98] and part of the torso of a Genius.[99]

We return to the history of Caesarea after the First Revolt; information is scanty. A notice of Malalas, a chronicler of Antioch, tells of the erection by Vespasian of an Odeium on the site of the synagogue, with plunder taken from the Jews; this appears side by side with the report of the erection of a theater at Daphne, also on a synagogue site, and with materials looted from the Jews.[100] It would appear that the economic ruin which overwhelmed Judea following the First Revolt,[101] and which took the form of the confiscation of lands and various heavy taxes, did not affect Caesarea, since at this time the city contained very few, if any, Jews at all. The city, which was the seat of the government and the chief entrepôt for export and import, appears to have flourished and grown in these years.

During Hadrian's reign the Hadrianeium, known from a Christian inscription, appears to have been erected.[102] It was built perhaps at the time of the Emperor's visit to the country in A.D. 129-30. Jerome reports, in connection with an earthquake that occurred in 128, that Caesarea and Nicopolis-Emmaus "collapsed"—to use his own term.[103] This report is further mentioned by late writers who were doubtless utilizing Jerome. Great damage to the port of Caesarea was attributed to this earthquake, and it appears never to have been repaired; it finally brought about the blocking up of a considerable part of the harbor. During the revolt of Bar Kokhba, Caesarea, now the capital of the country, probably served as the headquarters of operations against the insurgents, although there is no direct information to confirm this.[104] After the suppression of the rebellion, R. Aqiba was imprisoned and tortured, but the Talmud does not indicate that this took place at Caesarea, although this is possible.[105] Three inscriptions found near the aqeduct of Caesarea[106] inform us of its building or repair by units of the X and VI legions under Hadrian. Very probably these units merely supervised the carrying out of the work, which was done by Jewish prisoners who had fallen into their hands. These two legions are also referred to in a papyrus found in Egypt;[107] it is a copy of a petition and the governor's reply thereto. The petition is an appeal of twenty-two veterans of the X legion who had been transferred over twenty years previously (the petition belongs to the year 150) from the Misenum squadron of the fleet to the legion, apparently as a result of preparations for the suppression of various revolts; they request discharge-certificates from the legion, as in this period their legionary service had endowed them with privileges superior to those acquired by service in the fleet. Veterans of the VI legion sign as witnesses. The governor to whom the petition was addressed was Julius Cadus, who was resident at Caesarea and was hitherto unknown. The petition was exhibited in "the portico of Iunia Ba . . . at Caesarea,"[108] and a copy was sent to the Prefect of Egypt. After the Second Revolt Caesarea became the capital of the province of Syria-Palestina, and the governor was now of consular rank as a direct result of being in command of two legions, the X and the VI.

Considerable doubt must be attached to the report that Antoninus Pius visited Caesarea, but it may reasonably be supposed that he donated baths to the city.[109] It would seem that the period which lasted from mid-2nd to the end of the 3rd century was an era of growth and economic and intellectual prosperity at Caesarea, as it was throughout the Empire.

An inscription from Aphrodisias in Caria (Asia Minor), which dates from the reign of M. Aurelius, discloses the Gentile character of Caesarea in that period. The inscription speaks of Aelius Aurelius, a native of Aphrodisias, who was victor in a number of contests ($\dot{\alpha}\gamma\hat{\omega}\nu\epsilon\varsigma$) at Caesarea Stratonos,[110] including wrestling matches. Another inscription of A.D. 221 from Laodicea refers to the games held at Caesarea, Ascalon and Scythopolis.[111] These games were to be alluded to again in the coming centuries as one of Caesarea's distinguishing characteristics, even in the period when Christianity prevailed.

In A.D. 192, after the assassination of Commodus, the last member of the Antonine dynasty, a Libyan general born at Leptis, Septimius Severus, ascended the imperial throne simultaneously with the Roman governor of Syria, Pescennius Niger, who was also proclaimed emperor. In the civil war which was waged between the two in A.D. 194, Caesarea took the side of Septimius Severus, the victor, who awarded the city an additional title——Felix Concordia,[112] because of its support.[113] Kadman[114] connects the receipt of the title with the visit of the imperial family—Septimius Severus, Julia Domna and their sons Caracalla and Geta—to Caesarea in A.D. 201, whereas Avi-Yonah dates it in 199.[115] Alexander Severus granted the title "metropolis" to Caesarea about 230; her full title then was "Colonia Prima Flavia Augusta Caesarea Felix Concordia Metropolis Syriae Palaestinae." Kadman believes that Alexander visited Caesarea[116] during his eastern journey;[117] Philip Senior and his son Trajan Decius did so in 244.[118]

Caesarea's economic prosperity in the 2nd and 3rd centuries is described in sources from the Mishnaic and Talmudic periods. They describe Caesarea and her sister-cities as "the lands of life"—"a place of cheapness where there is plenty to eat"—and as the commercial and economic centers of the country.[119] "The parable is told of a man who went to Caesarea and spent 200 zuz."[120] We hear from Mishnaic sources of a Samaritan element at Caesarea after the Bar Kokhba revolt; this occupied a respectable position among the three elements of the population (the local pagans, the Jews and the Samaritans themselves)[121] until the time of Persian and Arab conquests. Other sources, such as Ammianus Marcellinus,[122] also describe Caesarea in the 3rd and 4th centuries as being at the head of the list of the country's chief towns.

Caesarea's economic wealth enabled the flourishing of such practices of the Roman rulers as the erection of temples, the fostering of cults and the holding of the annual contests already mentioned, and made it possible for other elements of the population of Caesarea to develop intellectually and culturally in the most varied directions.

Footnotes

1. F. Preisigke-F. Bilabel, *Sammelbuch griechischer Urkunden aus Ägypten*, III, 1, (Berlin 1926) No. 6777.

2. C. Müller, *Geographi graeci minores* (Paris 1876) 576. The information is repeated by Stephanus Byzantinus, *Ethnika*, (Graz 1958) 255.

3. Strabo, 16,2,27.

4. One of Zenon's men was thus named. *CPJ* I No. 6, 11.3,5.

5. "Straton," *RE* Zweite Reihe VII (1931) col. 273.

6. K. Galling "Die Syrisch-Palästinische Küste nach der Beschreibung bei Pseudo-Skylax," *ZDPV* 61 (1938) 66-69.

7. *JA* XIII, 12,2,4.

8. *JA* XIV, 4,4 = *JW* I,7,7.

9. *JA* XV,7,3 = *JW* I,20,3.

10. *JW* I,21,5.

11. In addition to Caesarea Palaestinae there were other cities of this name in Cappadocia, Cilicia and Mauretania, as well as Caesarea Philippi—all in the Mediterranean area.

12. In his article "The Foundation of Tiberias" in *IEJ* I (1951) 160-169, Avi-Yonah, in contrast to the accepted view of 10/9 BC, (*e. g.* Schürer, *GJV* I 272) suggests the year 13/12 as the date of the inauguration of Caesarea, thereby obtaining synchronization with an important event in Roman history, Augustus' fiftieth birthday and the thirtieth year of his imperium. Acceptance of this date requires a departure from Josephus' usual chronology of the history of Herod's reign, which began in 37 BC with the capture of Jerusalem, and not in 40 BC when his royal accession was ratified by the Senate. This finds confirmation from apocryphal sources. See the chronological survey of Herod's reign in Schürer, *GJV* I 360-75. Avi-Yonah's proposed date fits Josephus' dates if we accept what the latter says in *JA* XVI,5,1, that the building of the city continued ten years, and not twelve, as in *JA* XV,9,6. The reasonable possibility of course remains that Josephus was using here an official Roman source which reckoned Herod's reign from 40 B.C. Kadman *CC* p. 19, and Frova, in *CM* 10, accept Avi-Yonah's view.

13. A. Schalit, *King Herod. Portrait of a Ruler* (Jerusalem 1962) 100 (Hebrew).

14. *Ibid.*

15. *JA* XV,8,5. See also W. Otto, "Herodes," no. 14, *RE* Supplement II (1913) col. 80.

16. *JA* XV,8,5.

17. *Ibid.*

18. Principally *JA* XV,9,6; *JW* I,21,5-8. A detailed discussion of the building activites will be found below.

19. *JA* XVI,5,1; *JW* I,21,7; Καισάρεια *JW* I,21,7; also *Ammianus Maracellinus* XIV, 8,11 in contradiction of *Nov* 103 which erroneously attributes the title to Vespasian; in the 1st cent. on coins of Nero it is called Καισάρια ἡ πρὸς Σεβαστῶ λιμένι—Kadman, *CC* nos. 1-6; Καισαρέων, Καισάρεια Σεβαστή—ibid., nos. 16-18, and *JA* XVI,5,1; παράλιος Καισάρεια—*JW* VII,2,2,III,9,1; ἡ ἐπὶ τῇ θαλάττῃ—*JW* VII,1,3; 2,1; on Trajan's and Hadrian's coins, *Colonia Prima Flavia Augusta Caesarensis*–op. cit. nos. 23-24, 27-28.

20. *JA* XVI,5,1 "κατὰ πενταετηρίδα;" "κατηγγέλκει μὲν γὰρ ἀγῶνα μουσικῆς χαὶ γυμνικῶν ἀθλημάτων."

21. *Ibid.* XVI,11,5-7; *JW* I,27,6.

22. καὶ Καισαρεία περὶ τὸν λιμένα τὸν ὑπ' αὐτοῦ κατεσχευασμένον. *JA* XVI,2,1. This information lends some support to Avi-Yonah's belief that the city was inaugurated, not at the actual completion of the work, but at a later time because of external events—see n. 12.

23. Acts 23:35; *cf.* also 25:23.

24. *JW* II,3,4.

25. *Ibid.* II,9,2,—he was Judaea's fifth procurator.

26. The inscription dedicating the Tibereium was found by the Italian expedition in the excavation of the Roman theater in 1961. See Frova, "L'iscrizione"' 419-34.

27. *JA* XVIII,3,1.

28. Acts 8:40.

29. *Ibid.* 21:8-10.

30. Hieronymus, *Peregrinatio Sanctae Paulae*. Tobler, 31:" . . . where she saw the church of Jesus formerly the house of Cornelius, the house of Philip and the room of the four virgin prophetesses."

31. Acts 10:48.
32. *JA* XIX,7,4.
33. *JW* II,11,6; *JA* XIX, 8,2; Acts 12:21-23.
34. *JA* XIX,9,1.
35. *Ibid.* XIX,9,1.
36. *Ibid.* XIX,9,2.
37. *Ibid.* XIX,9,2.
38. *JA* XX,6,1; *JW* II,12,5.
39. Acts 24:27.
40. *JA* XX,8,7; *JW* II,13,7.
41. *JA* XX,8,9; *JW* II,13,7.
42. *JA* XX,8,9; *JW* II,14,1.
43. *JW* II,14,4; Schürer, *GJV* I 579.
44. *Ibid.* II,4-5. This synagogue is mentioned in various Talmudic passages which will be cited later.
45. *Ibid.* II,14,5.
46. *Ibid.* II,15,3,6.
47. *Ibid.* II,18,1; VII,8,7.
48. *Ibid.* II,18,9-11; 19,1,9.
49. B. Lifschitz, "Roman Legions in Eretz Yisrael," *BIES* 23 (1959) 64 and Table 10, no. 2. Another inscription is cited by Avi-Yonah, "Greek and Latin Inscriptions from Jerusalem and Beisan," *QDAP* 7 (1939) 54-61, also alluding to this legion.
49a. *JW* III,9,1; but see F. M. Cross, Jr., *The Ancient Library of Qumran* (N.Y. 1961) 62, n. 18 for the view that the V and XV wintered in Caesarea, and the X in Beth Shan (*JW* IV,2,1).
50. *JW* IV,7,3-6.
51. *Ibid.* IV,8,1.
52. *Ibid.* IV, 8,1-4; 9,1-2.
53. *Ibid.* IV,9,9.
54. Schürer, *GJV* I, 622 n. 78; *JW* IV,10,6.
55. *JW* IV, 11,5; V, 1,1.
56. *Ibid.* V,1,6.
57. *Ibid.* V,3,2.
58. *Ibid.* VII,1,3; 2,1.
60. *JA* XIX,9,1.
61. *JW* VII,10,1.
62. First the capital of Provincia Judaea, and afterwards, of Provincia Syriae Palaestinae.
63. Pliny, *Historia Naturalis,* 13,69; on the coins, Kadman, *CC* nos. 20-25.
64. *Digesta* L, 15,8,7; *ibid.* L, 15,1,6.
65. Tac., *Hist.,* 78, and see further Schürer, *GJV* II 137 n. 175.
66. *B. Meg.* 6a.
67. *Seder Hadoroth*—Josi Bar-Kisma.
68. *Lam. R.* 5.
69. *B. Meg.* p. 6a.
70. Kadman, *CC* pp. 28f.
71. *Ibid.* nos. 1-19.
72. Nos. 20-21.
73. *Ibid.,* nos. 198-230; the coins of Trebonianus Gallus and Volusianus are the city's last independent issue.
74. *Ibid.* p. 50, fig. 3.
75. *Ibid.* pp. 50-53.
76. Kadman's belief, *CC* p. 53, deriving from the *Enc. Brit.* IV (1953) 526, that evidence of the cult of Astarte, popular at Strato's Tower, is to be found in the name of the town (which was called after a Sidonian king of the 4th century) is without authority. It is well known that the cult was very widespread in that period throughout the Semitic world. See G. F. Hill, *Some Palestinian Cults in the Graeco-Roman Age* (London n.d.) and Schürer, *GJV* II 35.
77. Kadman, *CC* pp. 56-57, nos. 36, 28.
78. *Ibid.* pp. 53-56, nos. 33,58,66,80.
79. *Ibid.* nos. 135,136.
80. *Ibid.* nos. 133,134.
81. *Ibid.* no. 132.

82. *Ibid.* 177.

83. *Ibid.* 137.

84. *Ibid.* 142.

85. *Ibid.* nos. 24,43,54 etc. p. 63.

86. *JW* I, 21,7.

87. Kadman *CC* nos. 91,92,115,144.

88. *JW* I,21,7.

89. C. C. Vermeule, "A Hadrianic Representation of Rome on Coins," *Num. Circular* (London 1954) 485-86.

90. Kadman, *CC* nos. 55,87,94,95,149,150,180,181,227,228.

91. *Tos. 'Aboda Zara* 468.

92. *Ox. Pap.* XI, 1380, p. 197, col. v,1.94: Στρ [ἄτω] ν [ος] πύργῳ Ἑλλάδα ἀγαθήν It may be supposed that Isis, who in the Hellenistic period was still identified with Aphrodite, was identified also with Tyche-Astarte, as the Semitic 'Ashtart is subsequently identified with Aphrodite and Venus. (Isis was in fact identified with most of the goddesses of the Roman epoch).

93. See p. 6 and n. 26; this appears not to be a temple.

94. Germer-Durand, "Inscriptions Romaines et Byzantines de Palestine," *RB* 4 (1895) 75 f.

95. Kadman, *CC* nos. 33,58.

96. *Ibid.* no. 93.

97. A. Frova, "La Statua di Artemide Efesia a Caesarea Maritima," *Boll. d'Arte* IV (Roma 1962) 305-313.

98. Now in the Haifa Municipal Museum.

99. Found in the recent excavation of the Department of Landscaping and the Preservation of Historic Sites; A. Negev, "Caesarea Maritima," *CNI*, II (1960) Pl. ii, no. 4.

100. *Ioannis Malalae Chronographia*, X 261, 11. 13-16 (ed. L. Dindorf, Bonn 1831); although this source is generally of doubtful value, the above report appears to us to be correct. *Cf.* also the critical texts of bks. IX-XII, ed. by A. Schenk von Stauffenberg, *Die römische Kaisergeschichte bei Malalas* (Stuttgart 1931) 232, 493.

101. G. Allon, *A History of the Jews of Eretz Yisrael in the Period of the Mishnah and the Talmud*, I (Tel Aviv 1952) 25-53 (Hebrew).

102. See n.94.

103. R. Helm, *GCS*, Bd. 47, Jerome, (Berlin 1956) 200, "Nicopolis et Caesarea terrae motu conciderunt." Cf. *IEJ* 1 (1950-1951) 255, where 130 is given as the date of this earthquake.

104. Not as Kadman, *CC* p. 23.

105. *B. Ber.*, 61b, and not as Kadman, *CC* p. 23; according to *Mid. Prov.*, his body was brought to Caesarea and laid in a cave near the Tetrapylon.

106. Cf. Z. Vilnay, *PEFQS* 60(1928) 45-7; B. Lifshitz, *Fatomus* 19(1960) 110.

107. *Papiri Greci e Latini in Egitto, PSI* IX, (1928) no. 1026.

108. This is perhaps the eastern portico alluded to in *Tos. Ahil.* XVIII, 13, as pure, in contrast to all the other places—apparently due to its public functiòn as a place where the Governor's proclamations were made—see below.

109. According to Malalas he also erected baths at Laodicea, in Ephesus and in other places, following natural catastrophes, and perhaps at Caesarea, as a result of the earthquake of A. D. 128; see F. S. Schell, "Zur Gesch. des Kaisers Antoninus Pius," *Hermes* 65 (1930) 177, 208; Schenk, *op. cit.* 307-318.

110. P. Le Bas and A. H. Waddington, *Voyage Archéologique en Asie Mineure*, III (Paris 1870) no. 1620[a].

111. *CIG* 4472.

112. This title has not yet been found in inscriptions, but appears on coins, *cf.* Kadman, *CC* nos. 63, 68 and 70.

113. Lifschitz believes that "Fidelis Constans" is to be understood. See p. 54, n. 3 in his article cited in n.49 above.

114. Kadman, *CC* p. 24.

115. M. Avi-Yonah, *In the Days of Rome and Byzantium.* (Jerusalem 1962) 29 (Hebrew).

116. Kadman, no. 102, etc., and p. 24.

117. *Ibid.*

118. *Ibid.*

119. *Palestinian Talmud,* Kila'im IX, 32c.

120. *Sifre. Deut.* Sect. 306; the economic crisis would appear generally not to have affected the provincial capital, as we learn from the development and flourishing state of the Christian and Jewish communities in the period of crisis: the latter indeed resulted in the well-known contemporary persecution of the Christians.

121. Allon, *op. cit.* I, 84-85.

122. *Ammianus Marcellinus* XIV, 8,11.

CAESAREA AND THE CHRISTIAN CHURCH

Glanville Downey

The First Two Centuries

The known history of the Christian community at Caesarea begins, sometime after the martyrdom of Stephen, with the arrival in the city of the evangelist Philip, one of the Seven (Acts 6:5), who came to Caesarea at the end of a tour—"preaching in all the towns"—that had begun further south along the coast at Azotus (Acts 8:40). Pontius Pilate may still have been in residence at Caesarea at this time. If, as seems likely, Philip was a Greek-speaking Jew, it would be natural for him to settle in the provincial capital and cosmopolitan seaport; and this apparently is why we next find him in Caesarea about twenty years later, at the time of Paul's final visit to Jerusalem (Acts 21:8), seemingly a settled householder, with four daughters old enough to be prophetesses. It thus appears that Philip, so far as we know from our extant sources, represents the first continuous leadership in the Christian community at Caesarea.

Philip's arrival at Caesarea was followed by the vision of Cornelius, the centurion of the *cohors Italica,* as a result of which Cornelius sent for Peter, who was at that time staying in Joppa (Acts 10:1 ff.). The story of the conversion of Cornelius—like other centurions in the New Testament, a good man—illustrates the way in which certain Gentiles, on coming into contact with Judaism, could be attracted by its teaching. In this respect Caesarea, with its population of Greeks and of Roman officials and soldiers, played a distinctive part, comparable to that of Antioch, in the beginning of the Christian mission to the Gentiles.[1] Caesarea, as the capital and adminis-trative center of Palestine, was predominantly a non-Jewish city. Cornelius was not the only one of the Gentiles who had become interested in Judaism, for in addition to his family and household (Acts 10:2) he had an orderly who was a religious man (Acts 10:7); and when Peter came to Caesarea Cornelius gathered his relatives and close friends to meet him (Acts 10:24).

Peter's preaching at Caesarea was the first recorded preaching of the Gospel to the Gentiles (nothing is known of the preaching of Philip), and his discourse as reported, no doubt in summary form, gives a characteristic picture of the apostolic preaching (Acts 10:34-43). How many were baptized as a result, we are not told; but Peter stayed and taught at Caesarea "for some days" as a guest of Cornelius and his friends (Acts 10:48).

We next hear of the community at Caesarea in the account of Paul's passing through the city en route to Jerusalem at the end of his second missionary journey, when he had come by sea from Ephesus (Acts 18:22). Paul was already familiar with the city, for he had taken ship there for Tarsus after his visit to Jerusalem following his conversion (Acts 9:30).

Once more Paul visited Caesarea, this time on his final journey to Jerusalem (Acts 21:8-16). On this occasion he was in company with Luke, and the visitors stayed at the house of Philip the Evangelist. After several days, a prophet named Agabus arrived from Judaea, and prophesied Paul's being bound by the Jews in Jerusalem.

It was probably in Caesarea, from Philip's daughters, that Luke received information which he records in the earlier part of Acts; and Eusebius notes that according to Papias, Philip's daughters were known as sources of information on the early church.[2]

Finally, Caesarea played an important role in the closing chapters of Paul's career. After he had been arrested in Jerusalem and was threatened with murder by the Jews, Paul was sent for safekeeping to Caesarea, where he was put in the custody of the procurator Felix (Acts 23:23 f.) and imprisoned in the procurator's headquarters in Herod's palace (Acts 23:35). After a hearing before Felix, the conditions of Paul's imprisonment were relaxed and his friends were allowed to care for him (Acts 24:23).

Paul was thus kept in custody for two years, and it was said that Felix hoped that he might receive a bribe from Paul. At the end of this time Felix was succeeded by Porcius Festus; and Festus, wishing to gain favor with the Jews, left Paul in confinement (Acts 24:26 f.). The change of procurators seems to have taken place about 58 or 59.[3]

In a hearing before Festus, Paul appealed to Caesar (Acts 25:11). Some days later King Herod Agrippa and his sister Bernice arrived at Caesarea to pay a courtesy call on Festus. The procurator told Herod Agrippa about Paul's case, and Paul was allowed to speak before the king, in the presence of the prominent citizens of Caesarea, most of whom presumably were Gentiles (Acts 25:13—26:32). Those who heard him agreed that Paul was innocent. Nevertheless, having appealed to Caesar, he had to be sent to Rome, and it must have been very soon after this that Paul went on board ship and sailed from Caesarea on his famous voyage.

During his two year's captivity in the Palestinian capital, Paul cannot have failed to be active in writing and in whatever teaching he was able to do. Luke was with him (Acts 27:1-2), as well as Philip and other friends. Caesarea as a headquarters offered many advantages for communication with the churches that Paul had established, and in this respect it must have been as convenient as Paul's former headquarters, such as Antioch, Corinth and Ephesus.

Following Paul's departure we have no reliable evidence for the history of the Christian community at Caesarea for over a century. As was the case with other Christian centers at this epoch, there was a traditional list of the early bishops of Caesarea, which is plainly fictitious. The first bishop was alleged to be the publican Zacchaeus, succeeded in turn by the centurion Cornelius, by a Theophilus who is otherwise unknown, and by a second Zacchaeus.[4] The sources in which these "bishops" are named date from the fifth century or later, and Eusebius in his *Ecclesiastical History* is silent concerning them. Eusebius' silence is in this case the more significant since the *Ecclesiastical History* was written in Caesarea, and Eusebius could have used whatever local sources were available. Such lists of the first incumbents of the prominent episcopal thrones represent an effort on the part of the ecclesiastical writers to draw up an unbroken episcopal succession, often making use of legendary sources.[5] Our first reliable notice of a bishop of Caesarea is found in Eusebius' *Ecclesiastical History*, in which is recorded the name of Theophilus, who occupied the episcopal throne ca. 189.[6] Along with Narcissus, bishop of Jerusalem, Theophilus presided over the council at Caesarea in 195 which was summoned to consider the "Paschal question," the widespread and acrimonious controversy over the proper date for the celebration of Easter.[7] On this question Caesarea allied itself theologically with Alexandria rather than with Antioch. Eusebius found the documentation concerning this council in the library at Caesarea.

The Third Century

With the opening of the third century, as our knowledge of the history of the church increases, Caesarea begins to occupy a position of prominence among the Christian centers of the eastern Mediterranean world. The distinction in scholarship and teaching for which Caesarea is best known in Christian history was apparently first brought to the city by Origen, when he found himself obliged to leave Alexandria. With his arrival, Caesarea became the intellectual center of the Christian world, and the formation of the celebrated library at Caesarea, which had its beginnings in the work of Origen, guaranteed the continuation of the scholarly tradition he established there.[8]

Caesarea thus took its place with the other coastal cities of this region of the Mediterranean—Alexandria and Gaza—which were distinguished for their scholarly activity. The existence of ready communications by sea gave all these centers a vitality and material prosperity which encouraged scholarship, as well as making it possible for them to keep in touch with intellectual activity elsewhere. It is significant that Caesarea was like Gaza in having its chief intellectual and theological connection with Alexandria rather than with Antioch or Constantinople.[9]

Origen first visited Caesarea in 215, fleeing Alexandria when Caracalla instituted his notorious massacre of the people of Alexandria in retaliation for their having satirized him for the murder of his brother Geta.[10] Alexander, bishop of Jerusalem (212-250), had been a fellow student with Origen in the school of Clement of Alexandria, and when Origen came to Caesarea, Alexander urged Theoctistus, bishop of Caesarea (217-258), to make use of Origen's remarkable and by now well-known powers as a teacher and exegete. Origen's work was so effective that although he was a layman the bishops took the unusual step of inviting him to expound the Scriptures, not only in a lecture room, but in the public worship of the church in Caesarea. When he heard that Origen was teaching publicly in a church, Demetrius, the bishop of Alexandria, wrote to Alexander and Theoctistus to protest that it was not canonically permitted for laymen to speak in church while bishops were present and listening. Alexander and Theoctistus in reply cited several precedents in Asia but Demetrius insisted that Origen return to Alexandria and resume his accustomed teaching there. Origen obeyed his bishop.[11] This was about the year 219.

With his remarkable gifts, Origen began to be invited to visit churches throughout the East to settle theological difficulties and arbitrate disputes. On one of these trips Origen allowed himself to be ordained at Caesarea by Theoctistus and Alexander, without the knowledge of his bishop, Demetrius of Alexandria.[12] Theoctistus and Alexander doubtless had it in mind that Origen's opportunities for teaching and preaching would be widened if he were ordained; but the action, in disregard of Demetrius, was a serious infraction of ecclesiastical custom and responsibility. When he returned to Alexandria Origen was condemned, deposed from the ministry, and exiled from the city. This is what brought him, in 231, to settle permanently in Caesarea.[13] He was forty-six years of age, and was to spend most of the remaining twenty-three years of his life in scholarly work and teaching in Caesarea.

Origen's life at Caesarea was a busy one. An excellent library began to be built up, composed both of Origen's own writings and of books he collected for use in his researches and teaching. Origen's friend Ambrose continued to supply him with shorthand writers and copyists, as he had done at Alexandria.[14] Distinguished pupils came to him from a distance; even Firmilian, bishop of Caesarea in Cappadocia (231-265), came to study with Origen, and Alexander of Jerusalem and Theoctistus of Caesarea were constantly with Origen, "as their only teacher," as Eusebius writes.[15] One of his distinguished pupils was Gregory Thaumaturgus, later bishop of Neo-Caesarea in Cappadocia (245-265), who wrote a singularly valuable account of Origen's personality and notable gifts as a teacher.[16]

Origen's scholarly work is so well known that it need not be described here in detail. Famous as "the first systematic theologian" of the church, he has been characterized as "the first great scholar, the first great preacher, the first great devotional writer, the first great commentator, the first great dogmatist."[17] His works were concerned with Scripture, doctrine, apologetics and pastoral theology. The establishment of the Hexapla of the Old

Testament is one of his greatest achievements, and his work played an important part in the establishment of the "Caesarean" text of the New Testament.

On several occasions Origen left Caesarea for travel and study, and during the persecution under Maximinus (235-238) he took refuge in Cappadocia with Firmilian, while others in Caesarea—among them Origen's friend Ambrose—did not succeed in escaping.[18]

However, Origen was not able to save himself during the following persecution, under Decius, in 250-251. His friend Alexander of Jerusalem, brought to trial before the governor of Palestine in Caesarea, was imprisoned. Origen was arrested and subjected to prolonged and severe tortures in prison.[19] He survived, but his health was broken and he died in 254, at the age of sixty-nine.[20]

The persecution, fortunately, did not affect Origen's library, and the collection was preserved and put in order by the priest Pamphilus, a man of wealth who devoted himself to the library until his own martyrdom in 309.[21] Pamphilus copied many of Origen's writings with his own hand and made a catalogue of the collection. He also increased the holdings of the library, assisted by his friend Eusebius, later the great church historian and bishop of Caesarea. According to Isidore of Seville, Pamphilus' library contained "nearly thirty thousand volumes." Isidore wrote in the late sixth or early seventh century, and we do not know what his source was, but the figure could be correct. Pamphilus, a true bibliophile, loved to give books, especially the Scriptures, to people who needed them. The church historian Rufinus notes, as something unusual, that Pamphilus gave books not only to men, but to women. In order to be able to supply the demand for books, Pamphilus established a *scriptorium* in connection with the library, and this must have become an important center for the diffusion of Christian literature, as well as for the transmission of carefully edited and corrected texts of the Scriptures.

Bishop Theoctistus of Caesarea seems to have escaped the persecution under Decius, for he is mentioned in a letter of Bishop Dionysius of Alexandria in which are enumerated the bishops of the churches throughout the East who were united and at peace following the persecution, and had joined in rejecting the schismatic Novatian.[22] Theoctistus died in 258, apparently before the next persecution, which was begun by Valerian in that year.

In the persecution of Valerian in 258 and 259, Domnus, who had succeeded Theoctistus in 258, likewise seems to have escaped.[23] Apparently the imperial decree was not rigorously enforced in Caesarea, for the only martyrs of whom we hear in the city were three countrymen who decided to come into the city and seek martyrdom, and a woman who belonged to the Marcionite sect and therefore was not counted as a real martyr by orthodox Christians.[24]

Domnus held the episcopate for only a short time and was succeeded,

ca. 260, by Theotecnus, whom Eusebius knew in person.[25] At the beginning
of his rule, Gallienus (260-268) issued a rescript of toleration, but during the
early part of his reign the usurper Macrianus, an enemy of the Christians,
was in power in the East, and we hear of a martyr in Caesarea, a Christian
soldier named Marinus.[26]

Theotecnus was one of the bishops who took part in the two councils
convened at Antioch in 264 and 268 to try the bishop of Antioch, Paul of
Samosata, for heresy of which he was finally convicted in 268 and
deposed.[27] At some time before the final council, Theotecnus consecrated
Anatolius, a scholar on the church calendar and on arithmetic, to serve as his
coadjutor and succeed him when he died. The consecration of a coadjutor
bishop might be taken as evidence for the growth of the church at Caesarea
at this time. For a while the two together ruled the churches of Caesarea and
its territory, but when Anatolius was passing through Laodicea-by-the-Sea
on his way to the council at Antioch, the people of Laodicea detained him
and persuaded him to become their bishop, in succession to one Eusebius,
who had just died.[28] After this, Theotecnus ruled alone for many years,
dying ca. 303. It was during his time that Eusebius, the historian, who had
been born in Caesarea ca. 263, became acquainted with Pamphilus, who had
extended his activities and had founded a theological school in Caesarea to
continue the tradition of Origen.[29] The work of the school was of course
greatly benefited by the proximity of the library. Eusebius assisted Pamphilus in the work of collecting and classifying Origen's writings, and later
composed a life of his master, under whom he had been introduced to the
life of scholarship. In this biography (now lost) Eusebius gave a list of
Origen's writings.[30] In honor of his beloved master, Eusebius called himself
"son of Pamphilus."

The Fourth Century

With the development of Eusebius' career we pass into the fourth
century. Of Eusebius' early life in Caesarea little is known. He must have
been catechized and baptized under Theotecnus, and ordained to the
priesthood either under Theotecnus or under his successor Agapius (bishop
ca. 303-312).[31] Beginning with Eusebius' lifetime, and with his recording of
events he himself witnessed, or concerning which he gained direct information, our knowledge of the history of the church at Caesarea becomes more
detailed.

It was during a visit of the Emperor Diocletian to Caesarea in 296 that
Eusebius first saw the prince Constantine, then about twenty years old, who
was to be the future emperor.[32] The following years, during which Eusebius
was busy with his studies in the library of Pamphilus, brought the last and

greatest of the persecutions (303-313), during which Eusebius escaped harm. He suffered a great personal loss when his master Pamphilus was imprisoned (autumn, 307), and finally martyred (February 16, 309).[33] With Pamphilus there suffered eleven others, some of them Egyptians who had happened to be passing through Caesarea and were arrested when asked questions concerning their identity. This was routinely done with all travellers. Others of the twelve were Christians who happened to visit Caesarea from other places just at this time.

The other martyrs of Caesarea are recorded in Eusebius' work *The Martyrs of Palestine*. As we read this book, we can hardly doubt that Eusebius himself witnessed the torture and death of the martyrs, or had first-hand accounts from eye-witnesses.

One of the most celebrated martyrs was Romanus, a deacon and exorcist of Caesarea, who happened to be in Antioch at the beginning of the persecution, and was barbarously executed there, becoming one of the major local saints of Antioch.[34]

In Caesarea itself, another martyr was Apphianus, a student in the theological school, who escaped from Eusebius and his companions, who were trying to restrain him, and ran to seek martyrdom. According to Eusebius' account, an earthquake occurred at Caesarea at the time of the martyrdom.[35]

In the fourth year of the persecution, the city was honored by a visit from the Caesar Maximinus, and one Agapius (not the bishop) was put in the arena to be devoured by wild beasts in honor of Maximinus' presence. In the following year, Theodosia, a maiden of eighteen from Tyre, was martyred. Eusebius' account indicates that an unusual number of martyrdoms took place in Caesarea because confessors from other parts of Palestine were sent to the provincial capital for trial by the governor. A number of confessors were also sent from Egypt to Caesarea to be tried. The trials, which were conducted in public, were accompanied by savage and ingenious tortures which the pagan spectators eagerly watched, and the deaths were made public spectacles, burning, drowning and the wild beasts in the arena being the favorite forms of execution.[36]

Along with those who were executed, Eusebius records that a number of confessors were condemned to hard labor in the imperially-owned mines and quarries in Palestine, Egypt and Cilicia. To increase their sufferings, these victims were lamed or otherwise mutilated before being sent to the mines. Men of dignified station were sometimes sentenced to serve as keepers of camels, or to work in the government stables. The treasures of the churches were confiscated, including the liturgical silver, and the churches themselves were destroyed. Fortunately the Christian library does not seem to have been harmed.

At one point in the persecution, soldiers were stationed at the entrances to the public baths, to exact pagan sacrifices from all those who sought to enter.[37] In the Mediterranean climate, in which the daily bath was essential to health, this was a most effective way of singling out Christians.

The persecution evidently did not put an end to the religious activities of the Christians in Caesarea. Three years after the first martyrdoms, the theological school was still in operation, as we have seen, Eusebius apparently being a member of the staff.[38] Throughout the period Eusebius was able to carry on his scholarly research and literary activity, and the major portion of his *Ecclesiastical History* was composed during the persecution years.

The picture we gain of the church at Caesarea at this time shows a Christian community of marked strength and vitality. Not only did the martyrs seek death eagerly, but throughout the whole time of trial there are records of Christians coming and going, and of many connections between Caesarea and other churches in the Empire. The presence at Antioch of Romanus, a deacon and exorcist of Caesarea, at the time of the outbreak of the persecution, suggests that he may have gone from Caesarea to Antioch on business of the church, and it is possible that some at least of the other journeys Eusebius mentions were on similar errands.

The library at Caesarea had now, in spite of the persecution, become one of the great libraries of the Christian church, ranking with those of Jerusalem and Alexandria; and as a center for research and instruction it was to have an important influence on the development of Christian doctrine and literature in the future. The most learned and distinguished scholar connected with it at this time was Eusebius, and it was on the basis of his learning and scholarly prestige, as well as his personal sanctity, that Eusebius was chosen to be bishop of Caesarea, at some time between 312 and 314. Whether he succeeded Agapius, or whether there was a bishop named Agricolanus who held office between Agapius and Eusebius, is not clear; if Agricolanus was in fact bishop of Caesarea, he would have held office about 312-314.[39] Much of Eusebius' literary work was now complete, and from being a scholar and man of letters he turned to a new career as theologian and administrator.

The election of a man such as Eusebius to the see of Caesarea just at the time of the conversion of Constantine and the emancipation of the church marked an important epoch in the history of the Christian community at Caesarea. Thanks to his notable gifts, spiritual and scholarly, as well as to his personal prestige, Eusebius became the emperor's closest ecclesiastical adviser, and his influence at court brought Caesarea, with its famous library, into a position of special prominence. It was to Eusebius, with the resources of the *scriptorium* at Caesarea at his disposal, that Constantine wrote when he desired fifty copies of the Bible for the new churches that were being built at Constantinople,[40] and it was Eusebius who worked out the new political theory of the administrative position and powers of the emperor, made necessary by the change from the old pagan Empire to the new Christian Empire.[41]

Eusebius' role in the Arian controversy is well known. When Arius left

Alexandria in 321 he first sought the support of Macarius, bishop of Jerusalem; but not being favorably received, he found shelter with Eusebius of Caesarea and Paulinus, bishop of Tyre.[42] He then went to Nicomedia to seek the patronage of another Eusebius, the bishop of that city.

At the Council of Nicaea, in 325, Eusebius showed that he was more gifted for scholarship and literature than for theology, and he became an Arianizer although he evidently desired to remain orthodox. The Creed of Caesarea, which Eusebius offered for the consideration of the council, did not, as was once thought, form the basis of the Nicene Faith (with the addition of the *homoousion* and certain other phrases), but was put forward when Eusebius felt it necessary to clear himself of the taint of heresy.[43] The famous letter Eusebius wrote to his congregation in Caesarea to explain his position at the council is important as showing that he had been vindicated at the meeting.[44]

It is not necessary to trace here the remainder of Eusebius' role in the Arian controversy. It will be sufficient to recall the well-known Council of Caesarea in 334, summoned by Constantine to deal with accusations made against Athanasius by Theognis, bishop of Nicaea.[45]

In his last years Eusebius was able to return to the scholarly and literary pursuits which had been his first occupation, and he crowned his career with the *Laudes Constantini*, embodying a panegyric and a treatise presented to the emperor in 335, and finally with the *Vita Constantini*, a vivid picture of the emperor, written after Constantine's death (May 22, 337). Eusebius died a year or two after the sovereign with whom he had been closely associated over a period of nearly twenty-five years. It is fitting that it is for his literary work more than for his theological activities that he is remembered.

The great prestige enjoyed by the see of Caesarea at this time is reflected in the seventh canon of the Council of Nicaea, which declared that the bishop of Aelia or Jerusalem was to have honorary precedence after the metropolitan of Caesarea. Caesarea was the capital of the province, and so was automatically the seat of the metropolitan bishop who was the head of all the bishops in the province; but Jerusalem had a special claim to prominence as the mother-church of Christendom, and so could be given precedence over the other bishoprics of Palestine. The canon attests the importance which was attached to keeping the ecclesiastical administrative arrangements in conformity with the civil dispositions.[46]

Following Eusebius' death the tradition of scholarly bishops of Caesarea was continued with the appointment of Acacius, "the one-eyed" (340-366). Acacius brought special qualifications to the post, being a pupil of Eusebius, whose biography he wrote, as well as learned commentaries on Scripture.[47] The papyrus manuscripts in the library had begun to deteriorate from age and from use, and Acacius arranged to have them copied on parchment. In this he was assisted by Euzoius, who later became bishop of Caesarea himself.[48]

The Emperor Constantius (337-361), Constantine's son, supported the

Arians, and Bishop Acacius was in effect an Arian, though he put forward
the "Homoean" formula which declared that Christ was "like the Father,"
the word "like" being intentionally left vague.[49] Acacius was an unprincipled but versatile and able man. He engaged in a protracted controversy
with Bishop Cyril of Jerusalem, who refused to recognize the precedence of
Caesarea as established by the seventh canon of the Council of Nicaea,
because, he claimed, Jerusalem was an apostolic foundation, whereas
Caesarea was not. In 358 Acacius was able to depose Cyril. Cyril was
restored at the Council of Seleucia in the next year, but was banished again
at the Council of Constantinople in 360, and the controversy over precedence was to continue.[50]

With Stephen of Antioch, Acacius was leader of the Arianizers at the
Council of Sardica in 343, and again at the Council of Seleucia in 359.[51]
Acacius was deposed, along with others of his party, at the Council of
Seleucia, but having been restored when the Emperor Julian recalled the
exiled bishops, he was present at the Council of Antioch in 363, where he
made a formal acknowledgement of the Nicene Creed, but in terms which
were capable of interpretation in an Arian sense.[52] He was again deposed at
the Council of Lampsacus in 364.[53]

During the episcopate of Acacius we have testimony to the continuing
scholarly activities of Caesarea. Gregory of Nazianzus (ca. 330-389 or 390)
studied for a time at Caesarea under Thespesius, a sophist and professor of
rhetoric, before going on for further studies at Alexandria and Athens.
Another pupil of Thespesius was Euzoius, the future bishop of Caesarea.[54]
Hilary of Poitiers, exiled in the East from 356 to 361, very probably visited the
library at Caesarea during the travels he was allowed to make while in exile,
for he made extensive translations and adaptations of the works of Origen,[55]
and the library at Caesarea would be the natural place for such work.

For a period following the death of Acacius, not a great deal is known of
the history of the church at Caesarea. Acacius' successor was an Arian,
Philumenus, instituted by Cyril of Jerusalem. He was followed by Cyril, an
elderly man and an Arian, and Cyril was succeeded by Euzoius, likewise an
Arian.[56] The dates of all three can only be placed at some time during the
years 366-379.

Euzoius as bishop saw to it that the copying of the papyrus manuscripts
in the library on parchment was continued.[57] Jerome remarks that Euzoius
wrote a number of treatises on different subjects, but even the names of
these are no longer preserved.

In opposition to the Arian Euzoius, the orthodox Cyril of Jerusalem had
secured the consecration of his nephew Gelasius as bishop of Caesarea. At
first Euzoius managed to occupy the see, but at the accession of the orthodox
Emperor Theodosius in 379 Gelasius was able to establish himself, and as
bishop of Caesarea he attended the Councils of Constantinople in 381 and
394, being one of the leaders of Palestinian bishops at the meeting of 381.[58]
His successor John appears in office for the first time in 395.

Gelasius, described as a virtuous, learned and eloquent man, continued the tradition of scholarly bishops of Caesarea.[59] According to Photius[60] he wrote a continuation of Eusebius' *Ecclesiastical History*, but the evidence is not clear and his authorship has been disputed.[61]

Jerome was living in the East between the years from 385 to 392, and during Galasius' episcopate, he visited the library at Caesarea.[62] From Jerome's writings we learn a good deal about that library. He speaks of examining the works of Origen, including the Hexapla, and notes that this is the only copy of the Hexapla he has ever seen. He also mentions finding a copy of the *Gospel According to the Hebrews* in the library, and speaks of using the catalogue of the library prepared by Pamphilus.[63] Doubtless Jerome found the library of great value for his own literary work, for example, for the information he records in the *De viris illustribus*.

In the year 393 Caesarea figured briefly in the controversy revolving around the schism of Antioch, when Bishop Theophilus of Alexandria, in line with the efforts of Pope Siricius to resolve the schism, convened a synod at Caesarea to consider the consecration of Evagrius as successor to Paulinus, bishop of Antioch, the legality of the consecration's having been challenged by those of the opposite party in the schism. The council condemned Evagrius, and its synodical letter has been preserved.[64]

Gelasius was succeeded in 395 by John. John assisted Porphyrius, bishop of Gaza, to obtain imperial support in his campaign against paganism in Gaza, and John and Porphyrius visited Constantinople for this purpose in 400.[65]

The Fifth Century

John was succeeded by Eulogius, whose name appears in first place, as metropolitan of Caesarea, in the signatures of the synodical letter sent by Theophilus of Alexandria to the members of the Council of Jerusalem in September, 400.[66] Eulogius was one of the bishops who persecuted the adherents of John Chrysostom after Chrysostom's exile from Constantinople, though Chrysostom, apparently not knowing this, wrote to Eulogius from his exile in Cucusus, between 404 and 407.[67] Eulogius presided at the Council of Lydda-Diospolis in 415,[68] and ruled the church at Caesarea until about 417. His successor was Domninus, who was consecrated as metropolitan although he had been twice married, a circumstance which should have been an impediment to his serving as bishop.[69] He was consecrated by Praylius of Jerusalem, the bishops of Caesarea and Jerusalem having a custom of mutual consecration, apparently in an effort to keep the province of Palestine free from the influence of the bishop of Antioch, who might have claimed jurisdiction there.[70] Aside from his uncanonical matrimonial history, nothing further seems to be known about Domninus.

After this time our knowledge of the history of the church at Caesarea is less consecutive. We have one glimpse of the city in 439, when the Empress Eudocia, having made her first visit to Jerusalem, passed through Caesarea on her return journey to Constantinople; she was escorted from Jerusalem to Caesarea by the younger Melania, the noble Roman lady who was living a life of devotion in Palestine at this time.[71] The details of the empress' visit to Caesarea are not preserved, but we may be sure that as a pious lady and an accomplished author she visited the famous library.

It was at this time that the metropolitan of Caesarea was losing his precedence over the bishop of Jerusalem, which had been guaranteed by the seventh canon of the Council of Nicaea. The prelate responsible for the new ascendancy of Jerusalem was Juvenal, bishop of that city from ca. 422 to 458.[72] During his whole tenure of the episcopate Juvenal's goal was the elevation of Jerusalem from its traditional subordination to Caesarea, one of the important aims being to put the see at least on an equal footing with Antioch. The sources are so scantily preserved that we cannot follow all the steps by which Juvenal accomplished this end, and in particular we do not know what counter-measures were taken at Caesarea. In this struggle the bishops of Caesarea do not seem to have been able to leave their mark on history. The results, however, are clear. Whereas (as has been noted above) Eulogius of Caesarea (400-417) was named in documents before John of Jerusalem (386-416), by the time of the Council of Ephesus in 431 Juvenal had reached a position of predominance over the Palestinian bishops.[73] Likewise he took a leading part at the "Robber-Council" of Ephesus in 449.[74]

In all this process we hear nothing, in the preserved sources, concerning the bishops of Caesarea; but the situation is made clear in the records of the Council of Chalcedon in 451. On this occasion it is significant that Glycon, the bishop of Caesarea, did not even attend the council, but allowed himself to be represented by Bishop Zosimus of Menoïs.[75] Nothing seems to have been said at the sessions about the traditional rights of Caesarea over Jerusalem, and we can only guess at the methods by which Juvenal imposed his will upon Glycon.

But Juvenal did not enjoy unbroken success. Some monks who had attended the council returned to Palestine before him, to spread the word that he was an "apostate" and a "traitor." Juvenal had once supported Cyril of Alexandria and his successor Dioscorus in their theological warfare with Nestorius of Constantinople over the application of the term *Theotokos* to the Virgin. Cyril and Dioscorus had become theological heroes in Palestine; but the Council of Chalcedon had in effect condemned Cyril by deposing Dioscorus.

To the monks of Palestine this meant that Juvenal, having, as was well known, deserted Dioscorus during the meetings, was a deserter to the enemy. Palestine was a land of monks; and throughout the country people had reported supernatural signs and portents which foretold the "apostasy" of Juvenal. One of these omens occurred during a celebration of the Eucharist in the Church of the Apostles at Caesarea. The awesome message was conveyed as follows. A large gathering of monks had set out to meet Juvenal on his return from the council, to remonstrate with him and endeavor to persuade him to change his views; but when they came to Caesarea, where Juvenal had already arrived, the governor of the city, seeing their number and their temper, forbade them to enter the city. Instead, he persuaded them to hold a celebration of the Eucharist in the Church of the Apostles, which was outside the city. Many of those present at the service carried away the consecrated elements with them and kept them in their dwellings, and (according to the account of one of the partisans of Cyril and Dioscorus) these people later discovered that the bread and wine were changed into real flesh and blood.[76]

Juvenal, it is related, did have a conference with the monks outside Caesarea, under the protection of an imperial official who was on duty in the city. After a bitter exchange, Juvenal returned to the city and the monks had to depart.[77]

Soon after, Juvenal addressed a synodical letter to the priests, archimandrites and monks under his jurisdiction in Palestine, stressing that the fathers at Chalcedon had followed strictly the Creed of Nicaea. In this circular, Juvenal's signature, in the first place among the subscriptions, was followed by the signature of Irenaeus, bishop of Caesarea, in the second position.[78]

The protests of the monks on the return of Juvenal from Chalcedon were only the prelude to a regular insurrection among the monks and priests of Palestine who had supported the theology of Cyril of Alexandria. The disorders lasted for two years and spread over the whole of Palestine. Passions became so excited that houses were set on fire and sometimes the monks even killed their adversaries.[79] From this time on the adherents of Cyril of Alexandria, forming the Monophysite party in Syria, Palestine and Egypt, waged constant warfare against the orthodox, or, as they considered them, the representatives of the imperial government's policy of oppression. Our scanty sources tell us nothing of what happened at Caesarea during these theological-political troubles, which continued, indeed, until the rise of Islam and the loss of Palestine by the Empire.

During the reign of Zeno (474-491) there was a revolt, late in 484, of the Samaritans, who had always been on bad terms with the Christians among whom they lived. This time they proclaimed a bandit chief, Justasas, as their King, and captured the cities of Neapolis (ancient Shechem) and Caesarea. They began a bloody persecution of the Christians, and in Caesarea they burned the Church of St. Probus. The revolt was put down by Asclepiades, the *dux* or military commander in Palestine, acting with Rheges, the governor *(axiomatikos)* of Caesarea. The account of the events in Caesarea gives the name of the bishop of the city as Timothy; but nothing further is known about him.[80]

The Fifth and Sixth Centuries

We next hear of Caesarea in the reign of the Emperor Anastasius (491-518). As a result of his careful financial policy, this prudent sovereign was able to carry out a number of important public works in various parts of the Empire. Among these was a restoration of the harbor at Caesarea, which, Procopius of Gaza (ca. 465—ca. 528) says in his panegyric of the emperor, had deteriorated by the passage of time and no longer provided proper shelter for ships. But as a result of the emperor's work the harbor once more became (in Procopius' words) "youthful and virgorous," and the prosperity of the city was restored. This work is to be dated at some time after 501.[81]

It was around the turn of the century, or perhaps a little before, that Procopius of Caesarea, the famous historian of the reign of Justinian, was born.[82] After going through the basic part of his rhetorical studies in his native city, he moved to Gaza for advanced training, Gaza being at that time one of the best centers for advanced studies in literary subjects. Though our scanty sources preserve no other similar evidence, other young men of Caesarea doubtless migrated to Gaza for advanced work at this time.[83] It would be interesting to know how much of Procopius' interest in literary studies may have been due to the influence of the great library of Caesarea and of the teachers associated with it.

The accession of the orthodox Emperor Justin (518-527) brought a reversal of the religion policy of the imperial government, and the Monophysites, who had been favored by the Emperor Anastasius, now found themselves cast out of their positions of influence and persecuted.[84] Justin ordered that the orthodox bishops exiled by the Monophysites under Anastasius should be recalled and that the faith of Chalcedon should be restored everywhere. When the imperial orders reached John, the bishop of Jerusalem, he requested the saintly Sabas, one of the most distinguished and influential of the Palestinian ascetics, to take with him some others of the *higoumenoi* of the desert and go to Caesarea and Scythopolis to announce the imperial communication. When he reached Caesarea, Sabas was met by the bishop of the city, John the Chuzibite, a saintly figure much venerated among the orthodox and a supporter of the theological views of the new emperor.[85]

While nothing is said in the extant texts about the accession of John the Chuzibite to the episcopal throne of Caesarea, his adherence to the orthodox faith would hardly have allowed him to be bishop under the Monophysite regime of Anastasius, and we may assume that Justin on his accession removed the incumbent at Caesarea, presumably a Monophysite, and appointed John.[86] John had become well known for his personal sanctity as abbot of the monastery of Chuziba, which lay to the north of the road from Jerusalem to Jericho,[87] and his elevation to the see of Caesarea is typical of the contemporary practice of selecting monks for episcopal appointments because of their learning and personal holiness, in which they were reputed to surpass the clergy living in the world. There is recorded a miracle in which John healed a lady of Caesarea, wife of one of the most prominent men of the city, who had accidentally put out her eye with a weaving shuttle.[88]

Only three more bishops of Caesarea are known by name in the last century before the Moslem occupation of Palestine. Elias of Caesarea was among the signers at the Council of Jerusalem in 536;[89] nothing more seems to be known about him. Sergius of Caesarea is named in a decree of Justinian of 541 concerning the Samaritan troubles (see below).[90] Finally, John of Caesarea took part in the Ecumenical Council of 553, where he was among the bishops sent to invite Pope Vigilius to attend the meeting.[91]

During much of the reign of Justinian (527-565) the old strife between the Samaritans and their Christian neighbors continued. In the spring of 529 there was a Samaritan uprising which included an attack on Scythopolis and Caesarea. Christian churches were pillaged and burned, and Christians were slain in numbers.[92] This outbreak, it is recorded, was severely repressed by the government troops.

The Samaritans were included in Justinian's program for the suppression of paganism, though they were treated a little less harshly than the pagans properly so called. In 551 Bishop Sergius of Caesarea petitioned the emperor for some relaxation of the laws against the Samaritans, on the ground that they had become less aggressive. The petition was granted,[93] but the Samaritans were not yet ready for peaceful co-existence. There was a new outbreak in 555, in which the Samaritans joined with the Jews in an attack on the Christians in Caesarea and killed numbers of them. When the governor of the city, Stephen, sought to aid the Christians, the Samaritans and the Jews killed him outside his own praetorium and pillaged the building. The emperor ordered Amantius, the *magister militum per Orientem*, to proceed to Caesarea and punish the rebels, which he did with great severity.[94]

From the reign of Justinian we have one of our rare references to a church building at Caesarea. A Greek inscription found at Caesarea in 1895 records the transformation of the Temple of Hadrian into a Christian basilica. The text speaks of the installation of marble flooring and mosaic pavement, as well as repair of the steps.[95] This was evidently a temple built in honor of Hadrian's visit in 130, when the philhellene emperor ordered the construction of an aqueduct for the improvement of the water supply of the city.[96] It is of interest to note that this conversion of the temple into a church, like some similar undertakings of Justinian, is not recorded in Procopius of Caesarea's treatise on the emperor's building activities, the *De Aedificiis*. To some it might seem surprising that a Temple of Hadrian should have survived in Caesarea until the reign of Justinian; but the building was imperial property, and it might well have been converted to secular uses long after it ceased to serve as a temple of the deified emperor. In the inscription it is called simply "the *Hadrianeion*," which to Christians might only have seemed a historical name, not offensive to their religious sensibilities. Certainly the survival of the temple into the reign of Justinian cannot be taken to mean that public pagan worship continued in Caesarea until that period.[97]

The story of the end of Christian Caesarea is soon told, for the preserved sources are not extensive. Chosroes II of Persia, after invading Syria and Cappadocia in 611, turned south and took Damascus in 613. The Persians then proceeded to capture the cities along the Palestinian coast, including Caesarea and Lydda, in 614, and appeared before Jerusalem, which they took and pillaged.[98] While we have no details of the occupation of Caesarea, it is safe to assume that the city suffered the same experience as Jerusalem, where the city was ransacked and the inhabitants enslaved.

The Persians remained in Syria and Palestine from 611 to 629. They had hardly left when the Moslem invasion of Palestine began, in 634. This time we hear that Caesarea was able to make a vigorous resistance and that it was able to hold out against the Arabs for some time, since it could be supplied by sea and the invaders at that time had no naval forces. As the military and administrative center of Palestine, Caesarea was a stronghold of great importance to the Arab campaign, and several commanders in turn tried unsuccessfully to take it. The Romans were able to collect a fleet in the harbor of Caesarea and organize raids on the rear of the Moslem forces. Eventually, however, the imperial resources began to fail and it was no longer possible to send reinforcements from Constantinople. Finally, after a long siege (said by one source to have lasted for seven years) the city fell, through the treachery of a Jew who, hoping to save himself and his family, revealed to the besiegers a way of getting inside the walls through a subterranean aqueduct. We are told that after the city was taken the Moslems employed some of the captives as scribes and skilled craftsmen.[99]

If Caesarea, like other great cities of the Greek East, fell to the Moslems, this did not in any way mean that the city's role in history had come to an end. Caesarea's share in the shaping of the Christian faith and Christian culture had been fulfilled and its heritage in doctrine and in scholarship had been handed on to Constantinople and would be preserved for transmission to the West. Other Christian cities which shared the fate of Caesarea —Alexandria, Gaza, Antioch—had likewise realized and transmitted their special shares in the Greek Christian heritage.[100] Caesarea's history illustrates the way in which each of the ancient cities, given the individual circumstances in which it developed, was destined to work out a special achievement and a unique contribution as its own part in the building up of the Body of Christ. Here Caesarea supplied the great figures of Origen and Eusebius, seen against the setting of the matchless library. If the physical aspects of the city disappeared or were altered to something quite different, the spiritual and literary accomplishment, more enduring than bronze, could not be wholly destroyed. Caesarea had already joined with its sister cities in the shaping of the Byzantine heritage, which in turn would be transmitted to Western Europe and thence to the modern world.

Footnotes

1. On the similar situation at Antioch, and the role of the city in the development of the mission to the Gentiles, see G. Downey, *A History of Antioch in Syria,* (Princeton 1961) 272 f.
2. Eusebius, *H. E.* III 39; *cf.* III 31; V 24. See F. F. Bruce, *The Acts of the Apostles,* 2 ed. (London 1952) 387.
3. Bruce, *op. cit.* 429.
4. *Constitutiones Apostolorum,* VII 46, 3, ed. F. X. Funk, *Didascalia et Constitutiones Apostolorum* (Paderborn, 1905) I 453; "Praedestinatus," I 11 and 13 (Migne, *PL* LIII col. 591. *Cf.* M. Le Quien, *Oriens Christianus* (Paris 1740) III cols. 533-38.
5. C. H. Turner, "The Early Episcopal Lists," *JTS* 1 (1900) 181-200, 529-53; 18 (1926-1927) 103-34. Another legend associated with the early history of the Christian community at Caesarea appears in the Pseudo-Clementine romance, a novel with a didactic purpose written in the early third century. This work purports to be an account of the travels in the East of Clement, later bishop of Rome in the first century. In his travels he visits Caesarea and meets St. Peter, who gives him instruction and invites him to accompany him on his own travels (*Recognitiones,* I 12).
6. Eusebius, *H. E.* V 22. Eusebius gives Theophilus' date as the tenth year of the reign of Commodus, i.e. 189.
7. *Ibid.* 23; Le Quien, *op. cit.* III, cols. 538-41; J. D. Mansi, *Concil.* I, cols. 711-15.
8. The modern literature on Origen is so extensive that it could not be cited in detail here. Convenient accounts of his life and work based on the sources may be found in W. von Christ, *Geschichte der griechischen Litteratur,* ed. by W. Schmid and O. Stählin, 6 ed., pt. II vol. 2 (Munich 1924) 1317 f.; B. J. Kidd, *A History of the Church to A.D. 461* (Oxford 1922) I 394 f.; J. Quasten, *Patrology* (Utrecht and Antwerp, 1953) II, pp. 37ff.; *idem.,* 49 f. On his work as a theologian, consult Hugh T. Kerr, *The First Systematic Theologian, Origen of Alexandria* (Princeton 1958), and J. Daniélou, *Origen,* trans. W. Mitchell (London 1955).
9. See G. Downey, "The Christian Schools of Palestine: A Chapter in Literary History," *Harvard Library Bulletin* 12 (1958) 297-319; also by the same writer, *Gaza in the Early Sixth Century* (Norman, Oklahoma, 1963) in the *Centers of Civilization Series.*
10. Eusebius, *H. E.* VI 19, 16; Kidd, *op. cit.* I 396.
11. Eusebius, *H. E.* VI 19, 17-19.
12. *Ibid.* VI 23.
13. *Ibid.* VI 26; Kidd, *op. cit.* I 398.
14. Eusebius, *H. E.* VI 28.
15. *Ibid.* VI 27 and 30.
16. There is an English translation by W. Metcalfe, *Gregory Thaumaturgus, Address to Origen* (London 1920).
17. Kidd, *op. cit.* I 399 f.
18. Eusebius, *H. E.* VI 28.
19. *Ibid.* VI 39. On the instrument of torture applied to Origen's feet which Eusebius mentions, the *lignum* or *nervum,* see E. Le Blant, "De quelques monuments antiques relatifs à la suite des affaires criminelles," *RA* ser. 3, 13 (1889) 148 f.
20. Eusebius, *H. E.* VII 1.
21. On the work of Pamphilus, see Eusebius, *op. cit.* VI 32, 3 and 36, 3 f.; VII 32, 25 with *Martyrs of Palestine,* 11; Jerome, *De viris illustribus,* 75 and *Contra Rufinum,* I 9 (Migne, *P.L.* XXIII col. 422); Photius, *Bibliotheca,* cod. 118; Isidore of Seville, *Etymol.* VI 6. On the library as it developed in Origen's time and later, see A. Ehrhardt, "Die griechische Patriarchal-Bibliothek von Jerusalem," *Römische Quartalschrift* 5 (1891) 217-265, 329-331, 383; 6 (1892) 339-365; R. Cadiou, "La Bibliothèque de Césarée et la formation des chaînes," *RSR* 16 (1936) 474-483. For an account of ancient libraries in general, see C. Callmer, "Die antiken Bibliotheken," *Opuscula Archaeologica* 3 (1944) 145-193. Ehrhard (*op. cit.* 224-243) discusses some of the known MSS which appear to have a connection with the library at Caesarea.
22. Eusebius, *H. E.* VII 4-5; *cf.* Kidd, *op. cit.* I 446, 453.
23. Eusebius, *H. E.* VII 14.
24. *Ibid.* VII 12.
25. *Ibid.* VII 14.
26. *Ibid.* VII 15; *cf.* F. Görres, "Die Toleranzedikt des Kaisers Gallienus und ihre staatsrechtliche Geltung unter Aurelian," *JPT* 3 (1877) 620-623.

27. Eusebius, *H. E.* VII 27-30; *cf.* Downey, *History of Antioch,* 264, 310-315.

28. Eusebius, *H. E.* VII 32, 21 f.; Jerome, *De viris illustribus,* 73.

29. Eusebius, *H. E.* VII 32, 25.

30. *Ibid.* VI 32, 3 f.

31. Some autobiographical information may be obtained from the letter Eusebius wrote to his congregation in Caesarea after the Council of Nicaea, quoted by Socrates, *Hist. eccl.* I 8. On Eusebius' life and work, reference may be made to E. Schwartz, "Eusebios," no. 24, *RE* VI (1909) cols. 1370-1439; Christ-Schmid-Stählin, *op. cit.* (above, n. 8), II 2, 1359 f., and J. Quasten, *Patrology,* III (Utrecht and Westminster, Md., 1960) 309 f. On the chronology of Theotecnus and Agapius, which is not securely established, see R. Janin, "Césarée de Palestine," *DHGE* XII (1953) cols. 206-209, and S. Salaville, "Agapios," *ibid.* I (1912) col. 893.

32. Eusebius, *Vita Constantini,* I 19.

33. Eusebius, *H. E.* VII 32, 25; VIII 13, 6; *Mart. Pal.* 7 and 11; *cf.* Kidd, *op. cit.* I 523.

34. Eusebius, *Mart. Pal.* 2; Downey, *History of Antioch,* 329.

35. Eusebius, *Mart. Pal.* 4.

36. The first victim of the persecution in Caesarea was the great martyr Procopius, of whom a hitherto unknown life by Nicetas the Paphlagonian has lately been published: F. Halkin, "Le Panégyrique du martyr Procope de Palestine par Nicétas le Paphlagonien," *Analecta Bollandiana* 80 (1962) 174-193. The roster of martyrs who suffered in Caesarea, according to Eusebius' list, is as follows: Procopius, Alphaeus and Zacchaeus (*Mart. Pal* 1); Agapius, Timolaus of Pontus, Dionysius of Tripolis in Phoenicia, Romulus, a subdeacon of Diospolis in Palestine; Paesis and Alexander, both Egyptians, and another Alexander, from Gaza (*ibid.* 3); Apphianus of Pagae in Lycia (*ibid.* 4); Thecla (*ibid.* 6); Theodosia of Tyre, Domninus, Auxentius (*ibid.* 7);Valentina, Paul, and a woman of Gaza whose name is not recorded (*ibid.* 8); Antoninus, Zebinas of Eleutheropolis, Germanus, and Ennathas, a woman of Scythopolis (*ibid.* 9); Peter, also called Apselamus, an ascetic, from the village of Anea, near Eleutheropolis, with Asclepius, a bishop of the Marcionite sect. (*ibid.* 10); Pamphilus, the friend of Eusebius, with eleven others, including Valens, a deacon from Jerusalem, Paul of Jamna, Porphyry, a slave of Pamphilus; Seleucus, a soldier from Cappadocia; Theodulus, one of the governor's household; Julian of Cappadocia, Adrianus and Eubulus from Manganea (*ibid.* 11). On the death of Porphyrius, see F. J. Dölger, "Der Flammentod des Märtyrers Porphyrios in Caesarea Maritima," *Antike und Christentum* I (1929) 243-253.

37. Eusebius, *Mart. Pal.* 9.

38. *Ibid.* 4.

39. A bishop Agricolanus appears among the signers at the Council of Ancyra in 314. In some lists he is described as bishop of Caesarea in Palestine, in others his see is given as Caesarea in Cappadocia, in still others he is described simply as "of Caesarea." Eusebius speaks of Agapius as the most recent of his own predecessors (*Hist. eccl.* VII 32, 24), and this would seem to indicate that Agricolanus did not occupy the throne of Caesarea in Palestine, unless we suppose that Eusebius had some special reason for not speaking of him. See S. Salaville, "Agricolanos," *DHGE* I (1912) cols. 1027 f.

40. Eusebius, *Vita Constantini,* IV 36 f.

41. See the study of N. H. Baynes, "Eusebius and the Christian Empire," in his *Byzantine Studies and Other Essays* (London 1955) 168-172.

42. Kidd, *op. cit.* II 16.

43. See J. N. D. Kelly, *Early Christian Creeds* (London 1950) 211 f.; and; for the older view, Kidd, *op. cit.* II 19 f.

44. The letter is preserved by Socrates, *Hist. eccl.* I 8; on its significance, see Kelly, *op. cit.* 220 f.

45. Hefele-Leclercq, *Histoire des conciles,* I pt. 2, 654, f.; Kidd, *op. cit.* II 59 f.; H. I. Bell, *Jews and Christians in Egypt* (London 1924) 45-53; K. Holl, "Die Bedeutung der neuveröffentlichten melitianischen Urkunden für die Kirchengeschichte," *Sitzungsberichte der Preussischen Akademie der Wissenschaften, philosophisch-historische Klasse* (1925), 18-31.

46. Kidd, *op. cit.* II 49.

47. Jerome, *De viris illustribus,* 98; Socrates, *Hist. eccl.* II 4; Sozomen, *Hist. eccl.* III 2.

48. Jerome, *Epist.* 34; *cf.* Cadiou, *op. cit.* (above, n. 21) 477.

49. Kelly, *Early Christian Doctrines* (London, 1958) 251, with his *Early Christian Creeds* (above, n. 43) 290, 292.

50. Socrates, *op. cit.* II 40-42; Kidd, *op. cit.* II 150, n. 8, 158. On the controversy over precedence between Caesarea and Jerusalem, see E. Honigmann, "Juvenal of Jerusalem," *Dumbarton Oaks Papers* V (1950) 210-279.

51. Kidd, *op. cit.* II 83-85, 168, 170.

52. *Ibid.* II 170, 215.

53. Socrates, *op. cit.* IV 4; Kidd, *op. cit.* II 227 f.

54. Jerome, *De viris illustribus* 113; W. Stegemann, "Thespesios," no. 1, *RE* Zweite Reihe VI A (1936) col. 60.

55. Jerome, *op. cit.* 100.

56. Epiphanius, *Haereses,* LXXIII 37 (Migne, *P.G.* XLII col. 472); Jerome, *op. cit.* 113.

57. Jerome, *loc. cit.* A later copy of one of the manuscripts transcribed under the auspices of Euzoius has been preserved, cod. Vindobon, theol. gr. 29, saec. XI, containing works of Eusebius, Philo of Alexandria and Cyril of Jerusalem. The copy preserves the notation of the original, recording that Bishop Euzoius had this manuscript transcribed; cf. Ehrhardt, *op. cit.* (above, n. 21), V (1891) 223.

58. Epiphanius, *loc. cit.* (above, n. 56); Theodoret, *Hist. eccl.* V 8; Jerome, *loc. cit.* (above, n. 56); A. Jülicher, "Gelasius," no. 1, *RE* VII (1910), cols. 964 f. See the new study of the Council of 381 by N. Q. King, *The Emperor Theodosius and the Establishment of Christianity* (London and Philadelphia 1960) 32-49, 97-101.

59. Jerome, *op. cit.* 130.

60. *Bibliotheca,* cod. 89.

61. See Jülicher, *op. cit.* (above, n. 58), and Quasten, *Patrology* (above, n. 31) III 347. Photius, *Bibliotheca,* cod. 102, *cf.* 88 f., notes that he had read a treatise against the Anomoeans by a Gelasius, bishop of Caesarea, who was apparently to be distinguished from the Gelasius who was Cyril's nephew. If the work Photius read was by another Gelasius, and not by the nephew of Cyril, we have no evidence for the date at which this second Gelasius was bishop of Caesarea. Photius believed that Gelasius of Cyzicus, the well known writer who flourished about 475, might have been a bishop of Caesarea, possibly to be identified with the Gelasius who was Cyril's nephew; but it seems certain that Gelasius of Cyzicus was never bishop of Caesarea; see Jülicher, "Gelasius" no. 2, *RE* VII (1910) cols. 965 f.

62. F. Cavallera, *Saint Jérôme, sa vie et son oeuvre* (Paris 1922) I 127.

63. Jerome's allusions to the library at Caesarea are conveniently assembled by Cavallera, with valuable commentary, *op. cit.* II 8 f., 117 f., 120.

64. E. W. Brooks, *The Sixth Book of the Select Letters of Severus, Patriarch of Antioch* (London 1902-1904) Translation, II, 1, 223 f.; *cf.* L. Duchesne, *Histoire ancienne de l'église* (Paris 1910) II 608; F. Cavallera, *Le schisme d'Antioche* (Paris 1905) 285-287; Kidd, *op. cit.* II 376.

65. Mark the Deacon, in his biography of Porphyrius, the bishop of Gaza, states that John of Caesarea and Porphyrius visited the imperial court at Constantinople in 395: *Marc le Diacre, Vie de Porphyre, Évêque de Gaza,* ed. by H. Grégoire and M. A. Kugener (Paris 1930) chap. 33 f., pp. 28 f. Grégoire and Kugener in their edition of the text have thrown doubt on the historicity of John of Caesarea, but it seems to the present writer that their considerations are of such a hypothetical character that they are not sufficient to overthrow the testimony of Mark the Deacon, who was a contemporary. See Grégoire and Kugener in their introduction, pp. xxxvii-xxxix, lxxiii, n. 2; also Honigmann, *op. cit.* (above, n. 50) 216.

66. Jerome, *Epist.* 92. *cf.* Hefele-Leclercq, *Conciles,* II, 1, 122, and Honigmann, *loc. cit.*

67. Palladius, *Dialogue on the Life of St. John Chrysostom,* 73; Chrysostom, *Epist.* 87 (Migne, *P.G.* LII col. 654).

68. Augustine, *Contra Iulianum,* I 19 and 32 (Migne, *P.L.* XLIV cols. 652, 663); *cf.* Kidd, *op. cit.* III 92.

69. Theodoret, *Epist.* 110 (Migne, *P.G.,* LXXXIII, col. 1305 C). *cf.* 1. Tim. 3:2, Tit. 1:6.

70. Honigmann, *op. cit.* (above, n. 50) 217.

71. H. Delehaye, "S. Melaniae Iunioris Acta Graeca," *Analecta Bollandiana* 22 (1903) 41.

72. For a monographic study of his career, see Honigmann, *op. cit.* (above, n. 50). See also Kidd, *op. cit.* III 330-332.

73. Honigmann, *op. cit.* 222.

74. *Ibid.* 233-237.

75. *Acta Conciliorum Oecumenicorum,* ed. E. Schwartz, vol. 2, part 2 (Berlin, 1936) 69, line 32, no. 116.

76. John Rufus, *Plerophoriae,* ed. and trans. F. Nau, *Patrologia Orientalis,* VIII (1912) 24. This appears to be the only extant reference to the Church of the Apostles at Caesarea.

77. John Rufus, *op. cit.* 111-113.

78. *Acta Concil. Oec.* (above, n. 75), tome II, vol. 5 (Berlin, 1936) 9.

79. See the letter addressed by the Emperor Marcian to the archimandrites and monks of Jerusalem, *Acta Concil. Oec.,* tome II, vol. 1, pt. 3 (Berlin 1935) 125, line 2. On the insurrection, see Honigmann, *op. cit.* (above, n. 50) 247f.

80. Malalas, *Chronicle,* 382, Bonn ed., extant also in *Excerpta de insidiis,* frag. 34, p. 162 ed. De Boor. See also the translation of the Church Slavonic version of Malalas, *Chronicle of John Malalas, Books VIII-XVIII,* trans. by M. Spinka in collaboration with G. Downey (Chicago 1940) 101. Malalas' account is repeated in the *Chronicon Paschale,* 603 f. Bonn ed. In all the versions of Malalas' account it is said that at Caesarea Justasas "burned St. Procopius," the saint's name being given in the masculine accusative as though it were a martyrdom. However, in the *Chronicon Paschale,* at the same point in the narrative, it is stated that Justasas "burned the Church of St. Probus." A martyrdom of St. Procopius in these circumstances has not been accepted by modern scholars, and it seems plausible that here, as elsewhere, the *Chronicon Paschale* has preserved an earlier form of the text of Malalas, which, as is well known, was subsequently garbled in transmission. Our extant sources do not preserve any other reference to a Church of St. Probus at Caesarea. This Probus apparently would be the martyr of Anazarbus in Cilicia during the reign of Diocletian.

81. *cf. Procopii Gazaei in imperatorem Anastasium panegyricus,* ed. C. Kemper (Diss., Bonn 1918) ch. 19, p. 13. On the date of the work at Caesarea, see Kemper's introduction, xxv.

82. *cf.* B. Rubin, "Prokopios von Caesarea," *RE* XXIII (1957) col. 296.

83. See the writer's study of Gaza at this period (above, n. 9).

84. On the reign of Justin, and his religious policy, see the monograph of A. A. Vasiliev, *Justin the First* (Cambridge, Mass. 1950).

85. Cyril of Scythopolis, *Life of St. Sabas,* ed. E. Schwartz (*Texte und Untersuchungen,* 49, pt. 2, 1939) 162.

86. John was present at the Council of Jerusalem in 518; see Le Quien, *op. cit.* (above, n. 4) III col. 571.

87. John Moschus, *Pratum spirituale,* 24. f.

88. Evagrius, *Hist. eccl.* IV 7. In the same passage Evagrius records the sanctity of a monk named Zosimas, of the monastery of Sinde, near Tyre, who visited Caesarea and performed feats of extra-sensory perception, as well as taming a lion.

89. Mansi, *Concil.* VIII col. 1171. Elias signed in second place, after Peter of Jerusalem.

90. Justinian, *Novella* 129, p. 648, lines 2 f. ed. Schoell.

91. Mansi, *Concil.* IX cols. 174 B, 191 A (mission to Vigilius), 192 B, 389 E.

92. Malalas, pp. 445-447 Bonn ed., with frag. 44 in *Excerpta de insidiis,* 171, ed. De Boor; Cyril of Scythopolis, *Life of St. Sabas* (cited above, n. 85), ch. 70, pp. 171-173, ed. Schwartz. See E. Stein, *Histoire de Bas-Empire* (Brussels 1949-1959) II 287 f., and Irfan Kawar, "Arethas, Son of Jabalah," *JAOS* 75 (1955) 207 f.

93. *Novella* 129, cited above, n. 90

94. Malalas, pp. 487 f., with frag. 48, *Excerpta de insidiis,* 173. See Stein, *op. cit.* II 373 f.

95. *PEFQS* 28 (1896) 87; W. J. Moulton, "A Caesarean Inscription," *AASOR* (1919-1920) 86-90; F. M. Abel, *Histoire de la Palestine* (Paris 1952) II 81 f.

96. Abel, *loc. cit.;* Z. Vilnay, "A New inscription from the Neighborhood of Caesarea," *PEFQS* 60 (1928) 45-47.

97. *cf.* Moulton, *op. cit.* 89. On survivals of paganism in parts of Syria and Egypt at this period, see Downey, *History of Antioch,* 483 f., 491 f., 558 f., 563 f. One more text, which has been taken to refer to a church in Caesarea, may be discussed here. This is a Greek inscription of Caesarea, first published in 1892 by P. Germer-Durand, "Épitaphes du sixième siècle trouvées à Gaza et sur la côte de Palestine," *RB* 1 (1892) 246 f. The inscription reads Μημά ριον διαφέρων (i.e. διαφίρου) Μαρίας καὶ Λαζάρου. P. Germer-Durand took this to be a Jewish epitaph, but H. Gelzer, "Inschrift von Kaisareia," *ZDPV* 17 (1894) 180-182, suggested that it might belong to a martyrium housing relics of Mary of Bethany and her brother Lazarus which had been brought to Caesarea. The facsimile of the inscription, as published by P. Germer-Durand (which Gelzer had not seen, not having access to the *Revue Biblique*), is appropriate for an epitaph but hardly seems suitable as the titular inscription of a martyrium.

98. Michael the Syrian, *Chronicle,* IX 1 (vol. II, p. 401, transl. Chabot); Abel, *op. cit.* (above, n. 95) II 389; H. Vincent and F. M. Abel, *Jérusalem* (Paris 1912-1926) II pt. 4, 927.

99. The Arabic sources, which are often at variance as to details, are collected and studied by L. Caetani, *Annali dell'Islam* (Milan, 1905-1926), IV, 31 f., 156-163. See also M. J. De Goeje, *Mémoire sur la conquête de la Syrie,* 2 ed. (Leyden 1900) 166-169. Some details are supplied by Theophanes, *Chronicle, anno* 6124, p. 336, lines 16 ff. ed. De Boor.

100. See the present writer's studies *Constantinople in the Age of Justinian* (1960), and *Antioch in the Age of Theodosius the Great* (1962), published by the University of Oklahoma Press in the *Centers of Civilization Series.* See also the author's *Gaza in the Early Sixth Century* (Norman, Okla., 1963). The writer is planning a volume on Caesarea in the time of Eusebius for the same series.

CAESAREA AND THE JEWS

Irving M. Levey

The following account of the Jews of Caesarea Maritima is neither exhaustively complete as regards substance nor rigidly continuous as regards chronology. The sources pertaining to this subject, from which our knowledge must be gleaned, are very vast and far-flung, and almost invariably without definitive identification as regards time. This is true, and virtually without exception, for the entire rabbinic literature. And although Josephus possessed a far better sense of history than the Rabbis did, this is also applicable in a very large measure to nearly all of his works. As a rule, therefore, we are usually compelled to determine our chronology by whatever media we have at our disposal, both inside and outside of the sources, or, whenever this procedure is not possible, to forget time altogether and concentrate upon the evaluation of the event or situation or utterance per se.

Hence this study does not aim to present an historical sketch as such, but rather an analytical and interpretive synopsis of the material selected for study.

When we first read about the Jews in their Caesarean setting, we discover that they are already a well established community with synagogues[1] and elders[2] and wealth[3] and organized strength.[4] They are not a segregated group living in a ghetto of their own, as was the custom in Egypt and Cyrene.[5] In Caesarea they are thoroughly integrated among their Syrian neighbors.[6] Even their synagogue is located amidst buildings owned by a Greek.[7] And they constitute a fairly large segment of the city's population, possibly as much as one half of it, in view of their having an equal voice with all the other citizens in the affairs of government.[8]

It is important as well as interesting to note that Josephus's description of the Jews of Caesarea not only is fragmentary but reveals primarily their economic and sociological situation. They are prosperous materially, and, on this account, they despise their less prosperous Syrian neighbors.[9] They are strongly group conscious, and this leads them to provocative words and actions against their Syrian neighbors.[10] Insofar as their religion is concerned, we are informed only that they worship in their synagogues on the Sabbath.[11] Everything else about their religious life we are left to supply by inference. We must assume that they practice the tenets of their religion, mostly Biblical to be sure, just as their brethren do throughout Palestine and the Diaspora.[12] And we must also take for granted that the tenets of their religion are certainly taught and transmitted to the children, in all likelihood by the parents themselves.[13] The Jews of Caesarea probably make the pilgrimage to Jerusalem for the three appearance festivals, Maẓot, Shavuot,

and Sukkot.[14] And, like Jews throughout the inhabited world, they undoubtedly support the Temple at Jerusalem with their gifts.[15] When the
ensigns bearing the effigies of the Emperor are removed from Jerusalem by
Pontius Pilate, owing to the persistent protests and petitions of the Jews of
that city, and are returned to Caesarea,[16] the seat of the Roman Procurators[17]
and the headquarters of the Roman auxiliary garrison,[18] the Caesarean Jews
raise no objections.[19]

This, then, is the outline of Jewish Caesarea at this earliest period of our
acquaintance with it. It is comparatively brief, and, with very rare exceptions, extremely barren of details. Above all else, it lacks clear and definitive
traces as to the possible existence of a religiously creative or intellectually
vibrant Jewish life at Caesarea at this stage of its history, even as it wants
direct and trustworthy testimony which might shed light on the problem as
to when and how the Jewish settlement at Caesarea came into being.

With few exceptions, the sources are completely silent with respect to
the origin of the Jewish community at Caesarea.[20] It is also an historic fact
that creative or intensive Jewish life at Caesarea, in its religious and intellectual dimensions, begins very much later than the period outlined above and
extends for only a relatively short span of time, factually, for about three
centuries more or less.

The *terminus a quo* of this Golden Age of Caesarea, as it might well be
designated, may be set during the patriarchate of Yehudah Ha-Nasi, called
Rabbi, during the latter quarter of the 2nd century A.D., when he and his
court released Caesarea from the condition of impurity decreed earlier upon
the land of the Gentiles,[21] and declared it to be levitically clean.[22] Thereafter,
it may be assumed, Jews settled there in large numbers.[23] The *terminus ad
quem* coincides with the completion of the Palestinian Talmud, called the
Yerushalmi,[24] some time during the 5th century A.D.[25] Between these two
termini, Caesarea takes her place with Tiberias and Sepphoris as a pulsating
center of Rabbinic learning: hereditary learning in terms of transmitting
traditions of the past, and creative learning in terms of innovating traditions
of her own, on the eternal theme of Torah. Caesarea attains this status
essentially through the work of the Amoraim, the speakers, those towering
personalities who there established their yeshivot, the Rabbinical
academies, wherein they taught the imperishable lore and wherein, through
their inspiring teaching, they fulfilled a fundamental precept of their pre-
Tannaic forebears to "raise up many disciples."[26]

Caesarea could rightfully boast of many illustrious teachers and very
many dedicated disciples, every one of whom contributed in some measure
to her lasting fame. All of them have been immortalized in the literature of
Rabbinic Judaism. A considerable number of their contributions will enter
into the discussions that ensue. And, for special study, three names have
been chosen from the brilliant constellation of Caesarean Rabbis because of
their particular interest and relevance to our theme: (1) Bar Kappara, (2)
Hoshaiah Rabbah, and (3) Abbahu.[27] All three had their schools at Caesarea.

Their teachings and influences, examined in the chronological frame of reference in which they lived and flourished, will help to illuminate in depth this very significant epoch of Jewish history, in both of its manifestations, temporal and spiritual.[28]

In his *Antiquities of the Jews,* Josephus relates that during the quarrels between Syrians[29] and Jews at Caesarea "concerning their equal right to the privileges belonging to citizens," the ἰσοπολιτεῖς, which soon led to physical strife and to armed conflict, and finally to the Jewish rebellion against Rome,[30] the Syrians contended, in support of their demand for the right to pre-eminence, "that Caesarea was formerly called Strato's Tower, and that then there was not one Jewish inhabitant (in it)."[31]

In the parallel passage in his *Wars of the Jews,* Josephus does not mention the use of this argument by the Syrians. Instead, they maintain that Caesarea "was a Grecian city; for that he who set up statues and temples in it could not design it for the Jews."[32]

Neither of these arguments of the Syrians is contested or refuted by the Jews of Caesarea. Ignoring the contentions of the Syrians, they claim Caesarea to be theirs by virtue of the fact that "Herod their king was the builder of Caesarea, and because he was by birth a Jew."[33] Josephus himself, although not infrequently injecting his own personal opinions into a situation, is here, also, altogether silent, acting as the recorder, not the evaluator, of history, and consequently making no effort to uphold either side in the controversy.

Since the assertion of the Syrians regarding the absence of Jewish inhabitants at Strato's Tower was not disproved, it might be accepted as an historic fact that the Jewish settlement at Caesarea dates from the time of the founding of that city by Herod the Great during the last decade of the 1st century B.C. There is no valid reason for assuming that the Syrians invented their argument as a matter of expediency, in order to accomplish their primary purpose, to get rid of the Jews in the government of Caesarea. Such an invention, it seems certain, would not have been permitted to pass unchallenged.

Some support for the viewpoint that the Jewish settlement at Caesarea was not in existence during the pre-Herodian period may perhaps be implicit in some of the Rabbinic traditions. Thus it is recorded that, on her eastern side, Caesarea was surrounded by graves,[34] presumably pagan. It is also apparent that the Jews of Caesarea, once the community had been established, carried their dead elsewhere for burial,[35] from which procedure it is to be inferred that there was no Jewish cemetery in the vicinity of the city. Eliezer ben Hyrcanus and Aciba ben Yoseph, older and younger contemporaries of the second generation of Tannaim, both died at Caesarea but were removed from there for burial, the former to Lydda,[36] and the latter to Antipatris.[37] The existence of a Jewish necropolis at or near the site on which Caesarea was later built would have indicated the existence of a Jewish settlement at that place. Archaeology has unearthed very little mate-

rial which can be used in the solution of this problem for this period of
pre-Caesarean or early Caesarean history insofar as it relates to the Jews.

Nevertheless, notwithstanding the claim of the Syrians chronicled by
Josephus in the *Antiquities of the Jews,* or the inferences which can be drawn
from the Talmudic statements cited above, another, rather early, tradition of
the Rabbis was current to the effect that Jews had been settled on the site
which later became Caesarea during the height of the Hasmonean conquests
of the Palestinian territories occupied by the Greeks, in other words, around
a century before that city was built by Herod the Great.

Megillat Taanit,[38] the misnamed Scroll of Fasts, consisting of a calendar
of days on which it is forbidden to fast or to mourn, commemorates the
following event: "On the fourteenth of Sivan occurred the annexation of the
Tower of Zur."[39]

The Scholiast, writing sometime during the early Gemara epoch,[40] in
commenting upon this passage, states that Zur "is Caesarea, daughter of
Edom,[41] situated among the dunes. She was an imbedded wedge to Israel in
the days of the Greeks. . . But when the Hasmoneans got the upper hand,
they conquered her, deported her inhabitants, and populated her with
Israelites."[42] Unless it is assumed that this explanation is a figment of the
Scholiast's imagination, there seems to be no sound reason to doubt its
authenticity as an ancient tradition during Talmudic times.[43] As a matter of
historic possibility, this assertion of the Scholiast may be intimately related
to the report by Josephus that Alexander Jannaeus, the Hasmonean, captured Strato's Tower, among the numerous conquests of his career.[44] It
certainly is strengthened by it, even as it is strengthened by a similar report in Rabbinic literature concerning the military exploits of Alexander
Jannaeus, which, however, does not mention Strato's Tower by name.[45]

Although it is not likely that the Jewish conqueror emptied the place[46]
completely of its original inhabitants, it is equally unlikely that he left it
altogether as he found it, in the hands of the Greeks. The most logical
conclusion is that he did people it with some Jews and that he left a Jewish
garrison in control. Josephus confirms this hypothesis by a further report
that, together with other cities taken by Alexander Jannaeus, Strato's Tower
was "left in a state of freedom"[47] and "restored to their own citizens"[48] by
Pompey, when he brought the "Pax Romana" to Palestine.

Yet another Rabbinic tradition makes the fantastic claim that the
Caesarean site was in the possession of Jews from the time of the conquest of
Canaan under Joshua.[49] According to this tradition, it would be possible to
assume that the site of Strato's Tower was already occupied when Joshua
conquered Dor.[50] This may perhaps be implied in the singular expression,
"the territory (?) of Dor",[51] which is employed by the writer in the description of the conquest.

The foregoing analysis of our sources of information, interesting and
instructive as they may have been, has not advanced our knowledge of the
beginnings of the Jewish community at Caesarea Maritima very far. How-

ever, whether this community originated in the days of Alexander Jannaeus, the Hasmonean, or in the days of Herod the Great, the Idumean, it had reached considerable proportions when at last the rebellion against Rome broke forth in all of its fury.

Part II

During the 192nd Olympiad (12-8 B.C.), in the year 10-9 B.C., which was the 28th year of his reign, Herod the Great, builder of many cities, dedicated Caesarea Maritima to his master and benefactor, Caesar Augustus, amidst extraordinary festivities and a grand display of pagan pomp.[52] He had received the site on which the city was erected, Strato's Tower, as a gift from the Emperor to whom he dedicated it.[53] The city itself was "built of fine materials, and was of a fine structure;"[54] its edifices, "all along the circular haven," were "made of the most polished stone;"[55] its harbor, also, was unique in its construction, being "always free from the waves of the sea," and, in size, "not less than the Pyreum (at Athens)."[56] More than a decade had been consumed in building it.[57] Externally, Caesarea Maritima was magnificent in its panoply of heathen adornment.

Internally, however, Caesarea was seething with bitterness and discord and hostility and malevolence and the lust for blood. Throughout the land, the Syrians nourished an "innate enmity against the Jewish nation,"[58] and the Syrians of Caesarea "had always a quarrel against those (Jews) that lived among them."[59] The Jews, for their part, reciprocated the ill-will and hatred shown by the Syrians,[60] and, at times, even started the provocations which led to violence.[61] This intolerable condition reached its tragic climax in the year A.D. 66, when, on one day, and "in one hour's time about twenty thousand Jews were killed, and all Caesarea was emptied of its Jewish inhabitants; for Florus caught such as ran away, and sent them in bonds to the galleys."[62]

The causes and reasons for the strained, and ultimately desperate, situation at Caesarea are many, and, when brought together from the various parts of the record where they are dispersed, they tell a tale of inevitable disaster. Some are applicable to all places inhabited by both Syrians and Jews; others are relevant to Caesarea alone. A few, in this latter category, have already been alluded to in passing earlier in this study, but must be restated here in somewhat expanded form in order to round out the picture of the Caesarean setting. Some are remote; others are immediate. Some are manifest; others are hidden. Some are historical; still others are psychological. All, in some measure, are traceable in the Caesarean catastrophe.

(1) Prior to the conflict between Syrian and Jew everywhere in Palestine, there looms the revolt of the Maccabees against the Syrian tyrant, Antiochus

IV, Epiphanes, who set out to annihilate the Jew spiritually through the eradication of Judaism, his religion.[63] The aftereffects of this revolt permeate the relationship of Jew and Syrian at every point of contact. The deep-seated animosities engendered then did not disappear with the passage of time, but, on the contrary, increased in intensity. It is even quite conceivable that among the Syrians and Jews of Caesarea there could be found direct descendants of soldiers who fought one another to the death in that earlier struggle. Jewish observance of the eight-day festival of Ḥanukkah, with its ceremony of the lights and its special prayers, instituted then and there, was a vivid annual reminder and commemorative of that historic and far-reaching struggle.[64] Tradition (and later, Rabbinic law) prescribed that these Ḥanukkah lights must be kindled on the outside of the house, beside the entrance, clearly visible to all passers-by.[65] To the Jew who lit them, or saw them, the lights were a joyful reminder of the Jewish victory over the hated heathen oppressor. To the Syrian who beheld them, however, the lights were a sorrowful reminder of the Syrian defeat at the hands of the hated Jewish minority. The fires of hatred, already smoldering in the breasts of Syrian and Jew, were thus excited to an even greater intensity.

(2) The military enterprises and accomplishments of Alexander Jannaeus constitute a continued and vital phase of the Maccabean impact upon Caesarea, even long before it was built by Herod the Great. It has already been noted, on the authority of Josephus,[66] with some supporting evidence from the Talmud,[67] that Alexander Jannaeus took Strato's Tower, the site on which Caesarea was later built, by force, wrested the government from the Gentile population, and turned it over to the Jews whom he settled there. His distrust of the Syrians was so deeply rooted, as a result of their fanatical animosity toward the Jews, that he never admitted them among his mercenary troops.[68] The withdrawal of power from the vanquished, and the vesting of power with the victors, was, of course, (and still is today) standard military procedure. And although Pompey later restored freedom and self-government to the Gentile citizens of Strato's Tower,[69] he did not, with this act, liberate them from the bondage of resentment and enmity which they nourished against the Jews, their former conquerors. There can be little doubt that this feeling of rancor was handed down from generation to generation of Syrians, and became the heritage of the Gentiles of Caesarea.

(3) Like Hyrcanus I[70] before him, and like Agrippa I[71] after him, Alexander Jannaeus imposed forceful conversion to Judaism, with the rite of circumcision, upon many of his subjugated peoples.[72] And while it is not clear from the record whether this practice of his was restricted to the non-Semites in the population, such as Syrians and Greeks; or whether it also included non-Jewish Semites of the western coastal region in the population; and, furthermore, whether it was imposed at all upon the inhabitants of Strato's Tower, there is, nevertheless, no room for speculation regarding the deep feeling of resentment and hatred that this Judaising tendency induced in the non-Jewish inhabitants of the conquered cities.

(4) The contemptuous attitude of the Jews of Caesarea toward the Syrians and Greeks among whom they lived, and in whose midst they even had their synagogues,[73] would tend only to intensify the sense of hostility which these people already felt toward them. Whether this spirit of scorn was inspired by Jewish superiority in wealth, or in physical prowess, or both, as the record indicates,[74] it succeeded in calling forth from the Gentile population a counter-spirit of reproach and enmity, fortified by the sure knowledge that the Roman military garrison, comprised chiefly of Caesareans and Sebastians, was always ready to take up arms against the Jews in any major conflict.[75] The superior riches of the Jews would surely evoke Gentile jealousy in addition to the existing hatred, and the superior physical strength of the Jews, which usually brought them victory over the Gentiles in the daily brawls in the streets of Caesarea, would surely evoke memories of the humiliating defeat of their ancestors by the despised Maccabean patriots.

(5) Although it was customary in the ancient world for the conquerors to transplant populations, and possible therefore that the Jews of Caesarea could conceivably have originated through such a process of transplantation when the pre-Caesarean site, Strato's Tower, was taken by Alexander Jannaeus,[76] or even if, as some historians maintain,[77] the Jews settled there by a natural process of immigration after Caesarea was built by Herod the Great because it possessed commercial and maritime and other qualities that attracted them, the Gentiles of Caesarea, nevertheless, stubbornly refused to recognise and accept the situation as an accomplished fact. They insisted that Caesarea belonged to them, and to them alone. For, although he was a Jew by birth, Herod the Great favored them, the pagans, rather than the Jews.[78] In his long and unique role as a master-builder of cities, and temples,[79] he had never built a single synagogue for Jews.[80] And Caesarea, lying in Phoenicia, outside of the territory of Judaea,[81] he had built expressly for pagans, not for Jews. For in addition to other public buildings of a pagan character, such as the amphitheater and the hippodrome, he had adorned Sebastos, Caesarea's excellent harbor, with giant colossi, and Caesarea herself with a magnificent pagan temple in which he had placed statues of the Emperor Augustus and of the city of Rome.[82] Consequently, in view of all this vast manifestation of paganism, the Jews were alien intruders. They did not belong in Caesarea. And their very presence was deeply resented by the Gentile population. This resentment must have been deepened even more by the unusual fact that in Caesarea, the city of pagans and of paganism, the Jewish inhabitants were not segregated and ghettoized, as in other Gentile communities, but were thoroughly interspersed among the rest of the population.[83]

(6) And even as they abhorred the mere physical presence of Jews at Caesarea, the Gentiles took strong umbrage to Jewish participation in the governmental affairs of the city. For the Jews had an equal voice with the Gentiles in all matters affecting the common public life.[84] This right of

equality must have been conferred upon them by Herod the Great, from the beginning of Caesarea's history, as the Gentiles, perennial enemies of the Jews, never would have granted it to them. It is known, also, from the chronicle of Josephus, that Pompey (in c. 63 B.C.) restored full autonomy to the Gentiles of Strato's Tower, which later became Caesarea, after Alexander Jannaeus (in c.100 B.C.) had deprived them of it.[85]

In such a setting of almost interminable stress and strain and animosity, the early history of the Jews of Caesarea begins, and unfolds, and ends.

Part III

According to Josephus, two catastrophic events were directly responsible for the outbreak of the Jewish war against Rome. Both of these occurrences originated at Caesarea, and were rooted in the reciprocal hatreds of the Syrians and the Jews. Still another incident, listed by Josephus, belongs to this category, although it took place nearly a quarter of a century earlier. Together they represent the denouement of the initial phase of the epic of the Jews of Caesarea.

(1) *The defamation of the memory of Agrippa I by the Gentiles of Caesarea.*[86]

After he had reigned for three years over all Judaea, Agrippa I established his residence at Caesarea (c.A.D. 41).[87] But his life here was of short duration, for in less than four years he died a violent death, in all probability having been poisoned by the Gentiles in the very theater built by his grandfather, Herod the Great, on the very day in which he was celebrating a grand festival in honor of the Emperor Claudius. During these same festivities, the Gentiles had declared Agrippa to be their god.[88] But upon his death, the hatred which they nurtured for him deep in their hearts welled up in all of its vileness and virulence. Josephus reports what transpired in the following words:

"But when it was known that Agrippa was departed this life, the inhabitants of Caesarea and of Sebaste forgot the kindnesses he had bestowed on them, and acted the part of the bitterest enemies; for they cast such reproaches upon the deceased as were not fit to be spoken of; and so many of them as were then soldiers, which were a great number, went to his house, and hastily carried off the statues of this king's daughters, and all at once carried them into the brothel houses, and, when they had set them on the tops of those houses, they abused them to the utmost of their power, and did such things to them as are too indecent to be related. They also laid themselves down in public places, and celebrated general feastings, with garlands on their heads, and with ointments and libations to Charon, and drinking to one another for joy that the king was expired. Nay, they were not only unmindful of Agrippa, who had extended his liberality to them in abundance, but of his grandfather Herod also, who had himself rebuilt their cities, and had raised them havens and temples at vast expenses."[89]

Such was the prevailing attitude of Gentile toward Jew at Caesarea around the middle of the first century A.D.

(2) *Nero's edict depriving the Jews of Caesarea of their citizenship rights.*[90]

After the death of Agrippa I (in c. A.D. 44) the situation at Caesarea worsened. The relations between Jews and Gentiles deteriorated steadily under the rule of the Roman procurators (c. A.D. 44-66), who, with almost no exceptions, were wicked men, brutally exploiting their positions of authority for personal aggrandizement. One of these procurators, Felix (c. A.D. 52-60), was in power when the first of the two calamitous disturbances, designated by Josephus as immediate causes of the Jewish rebellion against Rome, occurred at Caesarea. As already noted elsewhere,[91] this conflict was over the question of citizenship rights which both Gentiles and Jews were enjoying on the basis of equality, and which they were trying desperately to wrest from each other on the grounds of priority claims to the city. The outcome of this struggle, decided by Nero at Rome, was disastrous for the Jews of Caesarea, and, subsequently, for the entire Jewish nation. The ensuing paragraphs contain Josephus's description of the succession of events which preceded Nero's edict depriving the Caesarean Jews of the rights of citizenship and their reaction when news of the edict reached them at Caesarea:

"And now it was that a great sedition arose between the Jews that inhabited Caesarea, and the Syrians who dwelt there also, concerning their equal right to the privileges belonging to citizens, for the Jews claimed the pre-eminence, because Herod their king was the builder of Caesarea, and because he was by birth a Jew. Now, the Syrians did not deny what was alleged about Herod; but they said, that Caesarea was formerly called Strato's Tower, and that then there was not one Jewish inhabitant. When the presidents of that country heard of these disorders, they caught the authors of them on both sides, and tormented them with stripes, and by that means put a stop to the disturbance for a time. But the Jewish citizens, depending on their wealth, and on that account despising the Syrians, reproached them again, and hoped to provoke them by such reproaches. However, the Syrians, though they were inferior in wealth, yet valuing themselves highly on this account, that the greatest part of the Roman soldiers that were there, were either of Caesarea or Sebaste, they also for some time used reproachful language to the Jews also; and thus it was, till at length they came to throwing stones at one another, and several were wounded, and fell on both sides, though still the Jews were the conquerors. But when Felix saw that this quarrel was become a kind of war, he came upon them on the sudden, and desired the Jews to desist, and when they refused so to do, he armed his soldiers, and sent them out upon them, and slew many of them, and took more of them alive, and permitted his soldiers to plunder some of the houses of the citizens, which were full of riches."[92] "And as the sedition still continued, he chose out the most eminent men on both sides as ambassadors to Nero to argue about their several privileges."[93]

"Now, when Porcius Festus was sent as successor to Felix by Nero, the principal of the Jewish inhabitants of Caesarea went up to Rome to accuse Felix; and he had certainly been brought to punishment, for his misdeeds towards the Jews, unless Nero had yielded to the importunate solicitations of his brother Pallas, who was at that time had in the greatest honor by him. Two of the principal Syrians in Caesarea persuaded Burrhus, who was Nero's tutor, and secretary for his Greek epistles, by giving him a great sum of money, to disannul that equality of the Jewish privileges of citizens which they hitherto enjoyed. So Burrhus, by his solicitations, obtained leave of the emperor that an epistle should be written to that purpose. This epistle became the occasion of the following miseries that befell our nation; for, when the Jews of Caesarea were informed of the contents of this epistle to the Syrians, they were more disorderly than before, till a war was kindled."[94]

Such is the irony of history. Insult had now been joined to injury. In the city of Herod the Jew, Jews had been stripped of the civic symbol of their humanity.

(3) *The desecration of the Jewish religion by the Gentiles of Caesarea.*[95]

"The combustible materials which had been gathering for years had now grown into a vast heap. It needed only a spark, and an explosion would follow of fearful and most destructive force."[96]

That spark which set off the explosion that devastated the land and destroyed the Jewish nation was ignited at Caesarea during the rule of Florus (c. A.D. 64-66), the last and one of the very worst of the Roman procurators. This greedy and abusive and cruel tyrant, in order to "conceal his enormities" and prevent the Jews from becoming "his accusers before Caesar, . . . did every day augment their calamities, in order to induce them to a rebellion."[97]

Florus was aided and abetted in his evil intent by the Gentiles of Caesarea. For now that the Jews of that city had been divested of their rights as citizens, the Gentiles felt completely free to vent their hatred upon them in the fullest measure. Like their persecuting ancestors before them during the days of the Maccabees, they struck at the Jew through his religion, in the deliberate and certain knowledge that such an attack would produce the desired result, namely, a revolution against Rome which must inevitably lead to a war of destruction. In this respect, they succeeded in their evil intentions even far better then they had anticipated.

As a target for the attack, they selected a synagogue[98] located in a courtyard and among buildings owned by a Greek. As the time for the attack, they chose the hour of worship on the Sabbath day. The drama of pathos and humiliation is pictured by Josephus in the following vivid manner:

"Now at this time it happened, that the Grecians at Caesarea had been too hard for the Jews, and had obtained of Nero the government of the city, and had brought the judicial determination; at the same time began the war, in the twelfth year of the reign of Nero and the seventeenth of the reign of Agrippa, in the month of Artemisius (Iyar). Now the occasion of this war was by no means proportionable to those heavy calamities which it brought upon us. For the Jews that dwelt at Caesarea had a synagogue near the place, whose owner was a certain Caesarean Greek; the Jews had endeavored frequently to have purchased the possession of the place, and had offered many times it value for its price; but as the owner overlooked their offers, so did he raise other buildings upon the place, in way of affront to them, and made working shops of them, and left them but a narrow passage, and such as was very troublesome for them to go along to their synagogue. Whereupon the warmer part of the Jewish youth went hastily to the workmen, and forbade them to build there: but as Florus would not permit them to use force, the great men of the Jews, with John the publican, being in the utmost distress what to do, persuaded Florus, with the offer of eight talents, to hinder the work. He then, being intent upon nothing but getting money, promised he would do for them all they desired of him, and then went away from Caesarea to Sebaste, and left the sedition to take its full course, as if he had sold a license to the Jews to fight it out.

"Now on the next day, which was the seventh day of the week, when the Jews were crowding apace to their synagogue, a certain man of Caesarea, of a seditious temper, got an earthen vessel, and set it with the bottom upward at the entrance of that synagogue, and sacrificed birds. [99] This thing provoked the Jews to an incurable degree, because their laws were affronted, and the place was polluted. Whereupon the sober and moderate part of the Jews thought it proper to have recourse to their governors again; while the seditious part, and such as were in the fervor of their youth, were vehemently inflamed to fight. The seditious also among the (Gentiles of) Caesarea stood ready for the same purpose; (for they had by agreement, sent the man to sacrifice beforehand, as ready to support him); so that it soon came to blows. Hereupon Jacundus, the master of the house, who was ordered to prevent the fight, came thither and took away the earthen vessel, and endeavored to put a stop to the sedition; but when he was overcome by the violence of the people of Caesarea, the Jews caught up their books of the law, and retired to Narbata, which was a place belonging to them, distant from Caesarea sixty furlongs. But John, and twelve of the principal men with him, went to Florus, to Sebaste, and made a lamentable complaint of their case, and besought him to help them; and with all possible decency put him in mind of the eight talents they had given him: but he had the men seized upon, and put in prison, and accused them for carrying the books of the law out of Caesarea." [100]

Not long thereafter, the Gentiles of Caesarea, with the help of the procurator Florus, wiped out the Jews of that city, slaughtering 20,000 in one hour and enslaving those who were caught after running away. [101] On hearing the news of the "stroke that the Jews received at Caesarea, the whole nation was greatly enraged; so they divided themselves into several parties, and laid waste the villages of the Syrians, and the neighboring cities . . ." [102]

The rebellion, incited by Florus and the Gentiles of Caesarea, was on in full swing. It was followed almost immediately by the war of national destruction. After the long and bloody contest, to celebrate the victory of Rome over Judaea—and his brother Domitian's birthday—Titus brought 2,500 Jewish prisoners in chains from Jerusalem to Caesarea, and in one day destroyed them all by having them thrown to the wild beasts, or burned at the stake, or killed in the gladiatorial games, to the hysterical joy of the jeering Gentiles, in the very stadium built by Herod the Jew.[103]

Part IV

   Notwithstanding the massacre of its Jewish population by the Gentiles at the beginning of the rebellion against Rome, Jews gradually returned to Caesarea after the cessation of hostilities.[104] In due course of time, considerably after the revolt of Bar-Kokhba, they are living there in sufficiently large numbers so as to compel the attention of the Rabbis respecting the religious status of the city. When this question has been favorably resolved,[105] Caesarea becomes a fit place for the ultra-observant among the laity and even for the Rabbis. Jews are attracted to Caesarea after the war by the same forces that drew them there when the city was founded by Herod the Great. Caesarea, it is obvious, afforded a multitude of opportunities for earning a good livelihood, even for becoming rich.[106] Her renowned port, Sebastos, which is mentioned in the Talmud,[107] must have been the center of commerce and trade from all over the inhabited world. The provisions for the public expression of art and sport, although these were not particularly attractive to the Jews who lived by the Torah, must nonetheless have constituted a very powerful allurement. Caesarea's surrounding territory, also, was unusually rich in agricultural potential and produce. In Rabbinic literature, Caesarea and her environs are designated "lands of the living" (Ps. 116.9), having a cheap market, wanting for nothing, and possessing everything to satiety.[108] The Talmud, in passing, makes mention of Caesarea's replete market.[109] Even her bakers and her chefs are so skilled that it requires many years of apprenticeship to learn their trade.[110] Some of the fruits of her fields and some of the wares of her artisans bear her name.[111] The Rabbis of Caesarea, like their peers everywhere, earned their livelihood by the labor of their hands.[112] In addition to all of its material advantages, Caesarea was considered a good place in which to live, owing to its topographical situation and its excellent climate.[113] There is some evidence, however, that in the newly established community, the Jews lived in a ghetto of their own, in contrast to their massacred brethren who had lived well integrated among the Gentile population of Caesarea.[114]

   But although a Jewish community had been reestablished at Caesarea after the war with Rome, very little is known about this community, particularly its internal religious and cultural constitution, before the end of the

Tannaic period. The record indicates that there was a time during the Tannaic period when questions of ritual law had to be taken elsewhere, out of Caesarea, for determination.[115] The inference to be drawn is that there were no Rabbis or other qualified teachers living in Caesarea at that time. Indeed, very few Tannaim made their home in Caesarea. Two may be mentioned as in all probability having lived there. One of these two was Jose Berabi, who was visited by Shimon ben Gamliel II at Caesarea during a certain Sukkot festival,[116] the latter receiving from him at his home in Sepphoris, on another occasion, a Caesarean Etrog.[117] The other one was Yehudah Ha-Nahtom, a teacher and legislator,[118] who earned his livelihood in Caesarea as a baker, and who testified that the eastern columnated section of Caesarea, from the Tetrapylon to the Press-House, was levitically pure, whereas the remainder of Caesarea was levitically impure, falling under the decree of impurity issued against the land of the Gentiles.[119] It may very well be, that, in consequence of this condition of levitical impurity, which was not removed until the very close of the Tannaic period,[120] no Tannaic academy was established at Caesarea, such as could be found at Jamnia, or Usha, or Bene Beraq, or Bekiin, or Beror Hayil, or Bet Shearim, or elsewhere.

a

The first school for the study of Torah, ישיבה, מתיבתא, at Caesarea, was opened by Bar Qappara[121] around the end of the second century or the beginning of the third century, A.D.[122] Bar Qappara belongs to the generation of intermediate teachers, the last generation of the Tannaim and the first generation of the Amoraim. He was a renowned pupil of Yehudah Ha-Nasi, whose school was at Sepphoris, and possibly may have been a member of his court, בית דין, which liberated Caesarea from the status of impurity decreed upon the land of the Gentiles.[123] A state of tension existed between master and pupil,[124] which may have prompted the pupil to remove to Caesarea, where his school, owing to its supreme excellence, soon became a serious rival to that of the master at Sepphoris.[125] After the passing of Yehudah Ha-Nasi, Caesarea assumed the academic leadership over all of the Rabbinical schools in Palestine; a supremacy which she retained unchallenged throughout the Amoraic period.

Bar Qappara revised and added to the Mishniyot of Yehudah Ha-Nasi, compiler and codifier of the authoritative Mishnah.[126] But he also is reputed to have been the author of a Mishnah collection of his own,[127] designated as "the great Mishniyot" in the tradition.[128] Many apocryphal halakhot, called baraitot, are cited in his name in the Talmud,[129] thereby indicating that he was considered to be a Tanna from this aspect of authorship.

He was eminent not only as a teacher, but also as a preacher.[130] He was fond of poetizing,[131] and he delivered a eulogy in the form of a poem at the funeral of his master, Yehudah Ha-Nasi, at Sepphoris.[132] He possessed a cutting wit,[133] which probably contributed to the strained relations between himself and his master. He was also a prolific creator of fables.[134] He was distinguished as an astronomer, and was able to calculate the cycles of the seasons and the planets.[135] He opposed idle metaphysical speculation.[136] And he carried on some polemics with Christians.[137]

Yehudah Ha-Nasi had favored Greek, above Syriac, together with Hebrew, as the vernacular languages for the Land of Israel.[138] Bar Qappara, his disciple, leaped far beyond him. He advocated the use of the Greek language even in the synagogues and the schools, and bolstered up his view with a quotation from the Torah.[139]

Bar Qappara was held in high regard by the Roman authority at Caesarea.[140] An anecdote depicting his relations with the proconsul is of many-sided interest. It is related that once, while Bar Qappara was strolling back and forth along the rocky strand of the sea at Caesarea, he beheld a ship that had been wrecked in the Mediterranean, from which a naked person was emerging. On recognizing that it was the Roman proconsul, he went up to him, and greeted him, and gave him two sla'im. Then he brought him to his home, gave him food and drink, and an additional three sla'im, saying to him, "A great person like you will need to spend the three extra sla'im." After some days, some Jews were caught in a riot. When the question came up as to who could go and appease the government on their behalf, they all decided on Bar Qappara, "for he is esteemed by the government." To his remark, "Have you known this government to do anything for nothing?" they replied that they had five hundred dinari which he could take and go and carry out the appeasement. So he took the five hundred dinari, and went to the government. When the Roman proconsul saw him, he arose and greeted him. "Rabbi, why did you take the trouble to come here?" he asked. Bar Qappara answered, "My request of you is that you be merciful to these Jews." "Have you known this government to do anything for nothing?" he asked further. To which Bar Qappara said, "I have five hundred dinari with me. Take them and pacify the government for us." The proconsul then answered, "These dinari are pledged to you in lieu of the five sla'im which you gave to me, and your nation is spared in lieu of the food and drink which I ate and drank in your home. And as for you, go in peace and in great honor."[141]

Some of the outstanding teachers of the intermediate period between the Tannaim and the Amoraim were among Bar Qappara's peers. These include Hiyyah Rabbah,[142] identified with the work of editing the baraitot;[143] Hama bar Bisa,[144] father of Hoshaiah Rabbah; and Shim'on bar Rabbi,[145] youngest son of Yehudah Ha-Nasi.

Nearly all of the renowned Amoraim of the first generation were among his disciples. These include Hoshaiah Rabbah;[146] Shim'on ben Laqish;[147] and Yehoshua ben Levi,[148] transmitter of his haggadic teachings.

Bar Qappara's entire life was governed by one principle: "In all of thy ways know Him, and He will make straight thy paths" (Prov.3.6). "This is a small section," he used to say, "but all of the essential parts of the Torah depend on it."[149]

b

Caesarea's fame as a center for the propagation and the dissemination of Torah initiated by Bar Qappara was advanced by his disciple, Hoshaiah Rabbah.[150] The pupil established a school at Caesarea, which achieved great distinction, during the lifetime of his master.[151]

Hoshaiah Rabbah's most illustrious pupil, Yohanan bar Nappaha, erroneously credited with the compilation of the Palestinian Talmud,[152] compared him to Meir, the Tanna, whose intellect was "so profound that none of his companions in his generation was able to fathom it."[153] His mind was as wide open as the entrance to the Temple hall.[154] So illustrious was he as a teacher, that Yohanan, together with other Amoraim, "were in the habit of going to Hoshaiah Rabbah to Caesarea to study Torah."[155] On one occasion, when he was in doubt about a certain question of law, Yohanan made a special trip to Caesarea in order to obtain the expert opinion of his master.[156] These pilgrimages to Caesarea were made by Yohanan while he was teaching in the Babylonian synagogue at Sepphoris,[157] and also after he had become head of the celebrated school at Tiberias.[158] Notwithstanding the facts that he no longer required tutorial assistance and that he had become famous on his own account, Yohanan spent thirteen extra years in study with Hoshaiah Rabbah, so overpowering was the esteem of the pupil for the master.[159] Yohanan reports that the students sat crowded, four to the span, at the discourses of Hoshaiah Rabbah.[160] Yohanan further relates that Hoshaiah Rabbah had twelve disciples who were especially brilliant.[161] Elazar ben Pedat[162] and Shim'on ben Laqish,[163] Yohanan's brother-in-law, were among the many disciples who transmitted Hoshaiah Rabbah's teachings.

In addition to the titles of honor which were conferred on him by his contemporaries, Hoshaiah Rabbah was called, "Father of the Mishnah,"[164] not with the implication that he either composed or compiled the Mishnah, but rather that he expounded and interpreted it. "Thus R. Hoshaiah, father of the Mishnah, explained it."[165] He and Hiyyah Rabbah, a contemporary of his teacher, Bar Qappara, were recognized as the authorities par excellence on the baraitot, to the extent that "any Baraita which was not edited by R. Hiyyah or R. Oshaiah is erroneous."[166] Hoshaiah Rabbah's collection of baraitot, which is no longer extant,[167] was sometimes also designated as "great Mishniyot," like the collections of Aqiba, Bar Qappara, and Hiyyah.[168] His authority as a legislator was so great that he was able to prevent Gamliel III, son of Yehudah Ha-Nasi, from instituting the observance of "demai"[169] in Syria.[170] He also held the view that standards of weights and measures are not Sinaitic in their origin and therefore rigid, but that they fluctuate, and must therefore be fixed by each generation of scholars.[171] His attitude toward Gentile witnesses, even in such strict areas as that of the "agunah,"[172] was moderate and humane, notwithstanding the opposite position maintained by the Mishnah.[173] He introduced the radical principle that "custom nullifies law."[174] And when he came to a strange place, he always would apologize for his ignorance of its customs, and then he would greet the people genially.[175] His sensitiveness for the feelings of others is illustrated by his extraordinarily considerate treatment of his son's blind tutor, whom, on certain occasions, he spared from embarrassment.[176] He was on very friendly relations with Yehudah II Nesiah, the grandson of Yehudah Ha-Nasi,[177] and even took the liberty, on one Purim festival, to chide him on the niggardliness of his Purim present.[178]

Hoshaiah Rabbah's method of Biblical exegesis parallels, in some instances, the method of Philo of Alexandria.[179] His haggadic utterances abound in Rabbinic literature, particularly in the Midrash on Genesis which has been attributed to him mistakenly because it opens with a homily by him on the manner of creation.

Theological discussions and disputations between Jews and Christians at Caesarea were, without doubt, frequent. Origen established and headed a school for the study of Christianity even as Hoshaiah Rabbah established and headed a school for the study of Judaism. In his *Contra Celsum*, Origen states in a number of instances that he consulted Jews who were supposed to be wise—meaning Rabbis—regarding the meaning of passages of the Hebrew Scriptures and on various points of Jewish tradition.[180] In one instance, he mentions the Jew whom he consulted by name; he was Hillel, the brother of Yehudah II Nesiah.[181] The Hexapla, in all likelihood, was inspired by Origen's conversations with Jews.[182] He generally speaks about the Jews with kindness and friendliness,[183] in contrast to Eusebius who, in spite of his intense zeal for their conversion, seems never to miss an opportunity to vilify them, characterising them as "our enemies, the Jews."[184] That Origen had discussions with Hoshaiah Rabbah seems to be a reasonable assumption,[185] although it is difficult to understand the absence of any mention of Hoshaiah Rabbah by name in Origen's writings, in view of his great renown as teacher, legislator, and exegete.

Hoshaiah Rabbah's polemical method in his disputations with Christians is illustrated in the following instances, one involving circumcision, abrogated by Christianity, and the other involving the incarnation, the central dogma of Christianity:

A certain philosopher[186] asked Hoshaiah Rabbah why circumcision, if it were so beloved by God, was not given to Adam. "Why do you trim the hair of your head but not the hair of your beard?" Hoshaiah Rabbah asked in reply. "Because the hair of my head developed during my infancy, when I was foolish," the philosopher answered. "If that is so," Hoshaiah Rabbah questioned, "then you should blind your eyes, cut off your hands, and break your legs, for these also developed during your infancy, when you were foolish." "Is this what our words have led us to?" the philosopher asked, "I am amazed." "Since it is impossible to change your mind," Hoshaiah Rabbah responded, "I can say to you only that we hold that everything created during the six days of creation requires completion: mustard and lupines need to be sweetened; wheat needs to be ground; even man needs to be perfected."[187]

On Genesis 1.26, "Then God said: Let us make man in our image, after our likeness;" Hoshaiah Rabbah comments: "When the Holy One, blessed be He, created man, the ministering angels erred concerning him, and sought to recite the doxology before him (as though he were God). What did God do? He cast a deep sleep upon him, and everyone then knew that he was a man; as it is written: "Cease ye from man, in whose nostrils is a breath, for of what account is he?" The relation between God and man may be likened to that of a king and a prefect who were riding in a carriage. The populace desired to say "domine"[188] but did not know which one was the king. What did the king do? He nudged the prefect, and removed him from the carriage. Then everyone knew that he was only the prefect.[189]

With respect to Israel's dispersion among the peoples of the earth, concerning which Christianity had formulated its special theological doctrine, Hoshaiah Rabbah maintained that it was an act of philanthropy on God's part; otherwise the Jews would have been totally annihilated by the Gentiles.[190]

It may be assumed with confidence that Hoshaiah Rabbah, like his master Bar Qappara, was familiar with the Greek language, and that he represented the Jews of Caesarea, whenever the occasion warranted it, with the Roman authorities. The record, however, does not contain any explicit evidence about these matters.

c

Caesarea as the Metropolis of Torah par excellence of the Palestinian Amoraic epoch is the handiwork of Abbahu.[191] Abbahu settled in Caesarea after he had completed his studies in Tiberias, at the school of Yoḥanan bar Nappaḥa,[192] the disciple of Hoshaiah Rabbah. It may have been Yoḥanan, Abbahu's master, who urged him to go to Caesarea to take up the burden of teaching the Torah after the passing of Hoshaiah Rabbah. And it also may have been Yoḥanan who requested his own brother-in-law, Shimón ben Laqish, to accompany Abbahu when the latter left Tiberias in order to settle in Caesarea.[193] Yoḥanan loved Abbahu like a son.[194] Abbahu's generation was respected on his account.[195]

Unlike his predecessors, Bar Qappara and Hoshaiah Rabbah, who established their schools in buildings of their own which were called by their names, the School of Bar Qappara and the School of Hoshaiah Rabbah,[196] Abbahu established his school and taught in the "Synagogue of the Rebellion at Caesarea,"[197] where the uprising against Rome first began.[198] However, he declined the honor of being elected head of the school,[199] and, in his own stead, recommended Abba of Acco, whom he esteemed highly for his learning and humility, and who, in addition, was deeply in debt.[200] In this synagogue Abbahu sat as solitary judge.[201]

Abbahu's love of Torah showed on his face. On one occasion, when he went to Tiberias to visit his master Yohanan, the students saw that his face was beaming, and informed Yohanan that Abbahu had found a treasure because his face was flushed. Yohanan, however, replied that it was due more likely to his having heard a new teaching. When Abbahu entered, Yohanan asked him what new teaching he had heard; to which question Abbahu answered that it was, on the contrary, an old Tosefta that he had learned. Yohanan then applied to him the Scriptural verse, "A man's wisdom maketh his face to shine (Eccl. 8.1)."[202]

Abbahu was very elegant in appearance,[203] like Yohanan,[204] and very strong physically,[205] like Yohanan.[206]

He was greatly respected by the Roman authorities,[207] which fact elicited additional respect for him from his own rabbinical peers,[208] and, undoubtedly, from Jews everywhere. On coming to the home of the proconsul from the school, Abbahu would be met by the maidens with these words of welcome: "Thou, master of his people, spokesman for his nation, radiant light, may your coming in peace be blessed."[209]

In keeping with the Rabbinic tradition that "Torah is good when combined with a mundane occupation,"[210] Abbahu dealt in women's veils,[211] from which business he became very wealthy. On the Sabbath, he would sit in a chair of ivory,[212] and at the close of the Sabbath, a three-year old calf would be slaughtered for him, from which he would eat only the kidneys.[213] He kept his treasures locked in a chest, and would hold the key in his hand during his discourses, even on the festivals.[214]

Although his own school at Caesarea enjoyed an unrivaled reputation, his son, Hanina, he sent away to Tiberias, to study at the school where he himself had studied as a youth. But, instead of applying himself to his studies, Hanina spent his time doing good deeds, specifically, burying the dead. When Abbahu was informed what his son was doing, he sent him a very cryptic message, playing wittily upon a popular Scriptural passage: "Are there no graves in Caesarea, that I had to send you to Tiberias?"[215]

Abbahu excelled in his knowledge of the Scriptures, in his ability as expounder and interpreter, and in his quality as haggadist and preacher.[216] His pre-eminence as a preacher was widespread, far beyond the confines of Caesarea. It is related that once he and another Caesarean Rabbi, Hiyyah II bar Abba, were visiting Tiberias, where Abbahu was to deliver a discourse on Haggadah at the same time that Hiyyah was to deliver a discourse on Halakhah. To Hiyyah's profound embarrassment, his audience forsook him in favor of Abbahu. To comfort Hiyyah, Abbahu invented a fable-proverb which illustrates his genius for Haggadah. "You and I are like two merchants," he said to Hiyyah, "one is selling precious stones, while the other is selling baubles. The masses will, of course, flock to buy the baubles. I am the purveyor of the baubles, but you are selling the precious stones." Out of respect for Abbahu, it had been customary for Ḥiyyah to accompany him every day to his inn, but on this particular day, Abbahu accompanied Ḥiyyah to his inn.[217]

This incident with Ḥiyyah, and many others like it, serve as an index to Abbahu's character, revealing his innate humility and his profound respect for his fellowmen. The one, all-inclusive, purpose of his life, it appears, was the glorification of God. Whether this purpose was accomplished directly through his own efforts, or indirectly through the efforts of others in which he was involved, did not matter, so long as the objective was achieved. Therefore Abbahu never became upset, as did his wife, when the interpreter in the synagogue ignored his ideas and presented the listeners with novel notions of his own.[218]

Abbahu was renowned as a halakhist, even as he was famous as an haggadist.[219] His halakhic utterances abound in the Talmud, especially the Palestinian Talmud, and include not only the opinions of his teachers, but also his own decisions. He was called upon, not infrequently, to render decisions in controversial instances.[220]

Abbahu's energy and talents were not spent in the interests of the Jews of Caesarea alone. It has already been noted that he was a very popular preacher in Tiberias.[221] But the range of his travels extends considerably beyond the confines of these two cities. The record indicates that he visited Lydda,[222] Usha,[223] Arbel,[224] Boẓrah,[225] Tarsus,[226] Alexandria,[227] and in other, unidentified places.[228] He may have traveled to all of these places not alone as teacher and preacher and judge and legislator in matters pertaining to things religious, but also as spokesman for the Roman government in matters pertaining to things political.[229] Always, on his visits to strange communities, Abbahu abided by the religious customs of the particular place he was visiting, even though that custom of the community may have been contrary to his personal point of view.[230] This practice of Abbahu's is a further illustration of his conciliatory nature, an attitude of mildness which he also expressed in all areas which involved the public well being and in all situations which were fraught with danger.[231] The wide-spread variations in religious practices bear testimony to the non-monolithic structure of the Jewish community of Palestine of that day. However, whenever and wherever the occasion demanded strictness, Abbahu could be very severe, particularly when he had to deal with persons of small spiritual stature who happened to be in authority.[232]

Although Rabbinic literature points to the existence of a constant controversy regarding the permissibility and place of Greek in Jewish life,[233] the entire question appears to be essentially academic in nature and scope insofar as the mere learning and using of the vernacular are concerned. The Jewish community of Caesarea was Hellenised to such an extent, at least from the point of view of its knowledge of Greek, (and its ignorance of Hebrew), that an Amora, Levi bar Ḥaitah, heard the "Shema" being recited in Greek in one of the Caesarean synagogues.[234] The Jews, by dint of their environmental circumstances, simply had to learn Greek. It was the language-medium of communication between Gentile and Jew in their manifold daily relationships, cultural as well as material. And mention has already been made of the very important fact that Greek was the language of mediation between the Jewish leaders and the Roman authorities resident at Caesarea.[235]

In addition to his many other accomplishments, Abbahu was also pre-eminent in his knowledge of the Greek language.[236] His familiarity with it was so thorough, that at times he actually played with it as with a toy.[237] Once he created a truly embarrassing situation when he cited a decision in the name of Yoḥanan, his teacher, to the effect that "it is permissible for a person to teach his daughter Greek because it is an orna-ment for her." He was accused by a colleague of using Yoḥanan's name improperly in order to support this idea which he had innovated himself. But Abbahu swore that he had really heard the decision from Yoḥanan.[238] Without doubt, however, Abbahu put his knowledge of Greek to its most effective and important use in his work of intercession with the Roman government on behalf of his people throughout Palestine.[239]

His reputation as scholar and preacher and Bible interpreter, and his position as Jewish leader, brought Abbahu into direct and frequent contact with Christians, both Gentile and Jewish, at Caesarea, who, by this time, had become numerous and politically powerful. As in the days of Hoshaiah Rabbah, so now in the days of Abbahu, the Christians of Caesarea looked to the Rabbis for explanations and interpretations of the Hebrew Scriptures. In most instances, the questions were serious and stemmed from an earnest desire to understand the Biblical text or the theological doctrine under consideration. On the other hand, some of the questions were purely polemical in design, and, at times, even contained the elements of derision and deprecation. The discussions covered a variety of theological and doctrinal subjects, including sin, baptism, immortality, heaven and hell, the composition of the Hebrew Scriptures, and God.[240]

Not all Rabbis qualified as interpreters of the Scriptures or as polemi-cists. It is related that Abbahu once recommended a certain Rabbi Safra, who had come to Caesarea from Babylon, for tax exemption, which power was then already in the hands of the Christians, on the grounds that this Rabbi was a great scholar. One day, these Christians asked this Rabbi to expound for them the verse in Amos 3.2: "You only have I known of all the families of the earth; therefore I will visit upon you all your iniquities." "Is it possible," they asked Rabbi Safra, "that a person who becomes angry will pour out his wrath upon someone he loves?" Rabbi Safra was unable to give them an answer, so they twisted a scarf around his neck and tortured him. Abbahu came upon the scene and asked them why they were annoying the Rabbi. "But did you not tell us that he was a great scholar? Yet he cannot even explain this verse to us!" "When I said that he was a great scholar," Abbahu answered, "I meant a great scholar in Rabbinics, not a great scholar in the Scriptures." "But how does it come about that you (Palestinians) know the answers?" they asked further. "We who live among you (Christians) make it our responsibility to probe the Scriptures for this very purpose; but they (in Babylon, where there are no Christians) have no need for this sort of Scriptural study." Then, at their request, Abbahu explained the verse for them.[241]

Abbahu was also a very powerful polemicist. He utilized his extraordinary talent as an exegete to refute fundamental Christian doctrines. The following examples illustrate his method of interpreting the Scriptures toward this end:

(1) *Against the doctrines of the divinity of Jesus, the Son of Man, and the ascension.* Numbers 23.19: "God is not a man, that He should lie; neither the son of man, that he should repent: When He hath said, will He not do it? or when He hath spoken, will He not make it good?" If a man says to you, "I am God", he lies. If he says to you, "I am the Son of Man", he will regret it in the end. And if he says to you, "I am going to ascend to heaven", he may say it, but he will not fulfill it.[242]

(2) *Against the doctrine of the Trinity.* Exodus, 20.2: "I am the Lord thy God", and Isaiah, 44.6: "I am the first, and I am the last, and beside Me there is no God." A king of flesh and blood may reign even though he has a father or a son or a brother. God said: "I am not like this mortal king. I am the first, for I had no father; and I am the last, for I had no son; and beside Me there is no God, for I had no brother."[243] Apropos this core principle of Judaism, the unity of God, Abbahu asserted that "Jerusalem was destroyed only because they abrogated the recitation of the 'Shema' morning and evening."[244] Through the abrogation of the "Shema," the Jews ceased to witness to God's unity.

The "Shema" was always recited audibly at prayer, and it was regulatory to follow it up immediately with the benediction, "Blessed be the name of his glorious kingdom forever and ever," the "Barukh Shem," which was always said inaudibly. But the Christians accused the Jews of slandering Christianity in this silent prayer, after having proclaimed the confession of their own Jewish faith with the recitation of the "Shema." Therefore, Abbahu instituted a reform in the service; henceforth, "Barukh Shem" benediction was to be recited out loud just like the "Shema."[245]

Whether or not Abbahu equated Christianity with idolatry is a moot question.[246] However, notwithstanding his personal conviction that the basic doctrines of Christianity are negated by the Hebrew Scriptures, his attitude toward Christianity was not hostile. This is evident from his indecision touching the legal problem of whether or not the "sifre d'bé Abidan"[247] might be saved from a conflagration on the Sabbath,[248] and would be in conformity with the general mildness of his nature.

But although Abbahu established friendly relations with most of the Christians with whom he had contact in one way or another, and although he was held in very high regard by them, he, nevertheless, did incur the intense hatred of some of them; in all probability, the Jewish Christians among them. Thus it was reported that a certain Jacob the Christian,[249] an expert doctor, tried to kill Abbahu by rubbing poison into a wound of his. Ami and Asi, two older contemporaries of Abbahu's, detected the plot, and saved his life by sucking the poison from the wound.[250] This Christian's hatred of Abbahu must have been very strong, for he not only risked his own life through this homicidal attempt, but, owing to Abbahu's position of esteem with the Roman government, he also endangered the entire Christian community.[251]

Abbahu's relations with the Samaritans of Caesarea resulted in the final and permanent break between them and the Jews during the reign of Diocletian (A.D. 284-305). When this emperor decreed that he should be worshipped as a god by all of his subjects with the exception of the Jews, the Samaritans joined up with the worshippers and poured libations of wine in an act of worship. On the testimony of Ḥiyyah and Asi and Ami, Abbahu thereupon issued a decree against the use of the wine of the Samaritans, which signalized their peremptory separation from the Jews in all matters of religion. When the Samaritans of Caesarea complained, saying, "Your fathers ate of our food, why don't you eat?" Abbahu answered them, saying, "Your fathers did not corrupt their deeds, but you have corrupted your deeds."[252]

Besides the decree against the Samaritans and the reform in the recitation of the "Shema," Abbahu ordained that no one may be appointed interpreter for the synagogue who is under fifty years of age.[253] He also instituted certain regulations relative to business transactions with the intent to improve them.[254] And still further in the area of synagogue worship, he introduced a reform in the manner of sounding the shofar on Rosh Ha-Shanah which is still in use to this day and which is designated, ever since he introduced it, as the "Reform of Rabbi Abbahu."[255]

The trying and fearsome conditions under which the Jews were living at that time are reflected in the principle by which Abbahu directed his life,—"Always be among the persecuted, not the persecutors,"[256] and by the prayer which was ever on his lips,—"May it be the will before Thee, O Lord our God and God of our fathers, that Thou wilt rescue us from the irresistable, hard, and evil times that have gone forth and are being felt to come upon the world."[257]

Abbahu lived till ripe old age.[258] The legend of a miracle clung to him during his lifetime, namely, that when he sat and discoursed, a fire glowed round about him.[259] And legends of miracles clung to him at the time of his death. As his life was ebbing, they (the angels) passed before him thirteen rivers of perfumed balsam. "For whom are all of these destined?" he asked. "They are for you," they replied. "All of these for me! 'I had thought, I labored in vain, and spent my strength for nought and vanity; but my case is with the Lord, and my accomplishment is with my God' (Isaiah 49:4)." And when Abbahu died, the pillars of Caesarea wept.[260]

With Abbahu's passing, the school at Caesarea ceased to have a leader. Henceforth, authority was vested in a Collegium of Rabbis designated as the "Rabbis of Caesarea," רבנו דקיסריו,[261] whose opinions and decisions are cited more than one hundred times in the Palestinian Talmud. Among the numerous interesting utterances of this Collegium, one is a clarification of, and a commentary upon, the controversy which had been raging among the Rabbis since early Tannaic times whether "study," תלמוד, takes precedence over "deed," מעשה, or vice versa.[262] Although individually Rabbis maintained either one of these two opinions, the decision of the consensus of Rabbis, when a vote was taken, ruled in favor of study over deed.[263] But the "Rabbis of Caesarea" made the important observation that the majority decision is valid only in those instances when the deed can be performed by someone else; otherwise, deed always takes precedence over study.[264]

The office of judge, which Abbahu occupied by himself, except on those occasions when he would invite other peers to adjudicate with him, was now, after his death, also taken over by another Collegium of Rabbis designated as the "Judges of Caesarea," דייני דקיסרי.[265] Both of these Collegia of Rabbis continued to function through the post-Abbahu period of the Amoraim.[266] The "Talmud of Caesarea," as it has been called,[267] consisting of the three treatises, Baba Qamma, Baba Mezia, and Baba Batra, of the Order of Neziqin, of the Palestinian Talmud, may, perhaps, have been compiled by the Caesarean Rabbis who comprised these Collegia. Essentially, however, they are the transmitters of earlier Rabbinic traditions, not the inventors of Rabbinic novellae of their own.

With the end of this epoch, creative Jewish life at Caesarea Maritima, insofar as it is traceable, comes to a permanent end.[268]

Part V

The attitude toward Caesarea expressed in Rabbinic literature is predominantly unfavorable, and, at times, even bitterly hostile. It is true that Jews prospered there materially and flourished there spiritually; and that, for this first perspective, Caesarea is, therefore, one of the "lands of the living." (Ps. 116.9).[269] But it is also true that Jews were denigrated there together with their religion and their way of life;[270] they were persecuted[271] and martyred there.[272] From this second perspective, Caesarea is, therefore, the "daughter of Edom." (Lam. 4.21).[273]

Caesarea—idolatrous, cruel, and immoral—represented everything which was abominated by the spirit of the Jew. Even the spot on which the city stood was encrusted with disturbing memories. Troubling traditions harked back all the way to the days of the Hasmoneans, when Caesarea was not yet Caesarea, when it was still a Graeco-Phoenician fortress named Strato's Tower. But already then it was a peg wedged into Israel, a thorn in the flesh of the Jew, not alone because of the prostitution cult of Astarte which was practiced there in all probability, but also because incursions into the neighboring villages and towns of Judaea must have been made from there. And although Alexander Jannaeus conquered the fort, and perhaps even settled some Jews there together with his garrison, it is most unlikely that its heathen character was changed very much. At all events, whatever Alexander Jannaeus may have accomplished actually to change its character, was undone shortly thereafter by Pompey when he restored it to its former status. The very soil on which Caesarea was yet to be built was already polluted.

But Caesarea was also the "daughter of Edom." In Rabbinic literature, this description—daughter of Edom—carries with it every conceivable connotation which is base and odious.[274]

As the daughter of Edom, Caesarea personified Herod the Idumean, her conceiver and builder, who descended from Edom, which became a very early enemy of Israel. To the pious Jewish masses, to the zealous Jewish patriots, and to the dedicated Jewish sages, that is, to all Jews who were aware of their Jewish identity in one way or another, Herod was not a Jew. He was an alien Edomite and a heathen. And although the Temple he rebuilt at Jerusalem was praised for its beauty, this praise has all of the earmarks of a begrudged concession.[275] Herod was hated thoroughly and he was despised thoroughly. He was hated by all of his subjects, Jew and Gentile alike, for his brutalities.[276] And he was despised by the Jews for his arrogant indifference to their religious sensitivities, and for his flagrant violations of the Jewish way of life.[277] To his multitudinous crimes of murder, which included the consummate eradication of the Hasmonean dynasty, Rabbinic literature adds the sin of immorality in its most loathsome form.[278] Caesarea served as a perpetual reminder to the Jews that Herod had preferred the Gentiles and heathenism to the Jews and Judaism.[279] When he built Caesarea, Herod had erected a temple with statues for the pagans, but he had built no synagogue for the Jews.[280] Herod had also built the theater at Caesarea where Jews and Judaism were ridiculed and sullied at the performances.[281] And Herod, furthermore, had built the amphitheater and the hippodrome at Caesarea where Jews, by the thousands, were slaughtered in gladiatorial games, or thrown to the wild beasts, or burned alive at the stake, or crucified—all to the joy and delight of the Gentiles.[282] Herod the Idumean had immortalized himself at Caesarea. Caesarea, as a memorial of Herod, conjured up only bad dreams.

And also as the daughter of Edom, Caesarea was the embodiment of Rome,[283] Herod's mistress, whom he served throughout his life as a loyal lackey, but whom he exploited, nevertheless, as his incontrovertible alibi for his interminable trampling over Jewish law and life.[284] Rome, for the Jew, was the enemy of enemies. Rome was the foreign invader who imposed the yoke of slavery and persecution and death upon the life-loving and freedom-loving Jewish people. And this yoke of slavery and persecution and death was not always only political, but very frequently it was also spiritual.[285] And his religion was even more precious to the Jew than life. Rome's government was "the evil government of Edom;"[286] Vespasian was "the adversary;"[287] and Titus, son of Vespasian, was the evil one, son of the evil one.[288] Rome invaded the Land of Israel, laid it waste, decimated its people, brought an end to the national life, and destroyed the Sanctuary. And in all of these manifestations of evil, Rome was symbolized by Caesarea. For Caesarea was "Little Rome."[289]

The anti-Jewish decrees originating at Rome were disseminated and, in all likelihood, enforced at Caesarea. For Caesarea was the "metropolis of rulers,"[290] the seat of the procurators and governors and proconsuls,[291] and headquarters of the military garrison.[292] The mockery and greed and ruthlessness of nearly all of these Roman rulers, and the rapaciousness of the Roman troops—encouraged and frequently inspired by these rulers[293]—burned a deep scar into the soul of the Jews. And even if they could forget the pains of minor skirmishes with the local Gentile population, they could never erase from their memories the humiliating insult to their religion[294] and the coldly calculated butchery of 20,000 of their brethren——men, women, and children—in one hour at Caesarea.[295]

The unjust courts of justice and the dungeons of infamous fame were also located at Caesarea.[296] Malefactors and all who were considered to be enemies of the state were brought to Caesarea for trial and punishment. Paul the Apostle languished here for two years in prison.[297] Here, too, the aged sage, Aqiba ben Yoseph, was imprisoned for teaching the Torah in violation of the Roman decree; here he was tried and condemned; and here he died a martyr's death—one of the "Ten Royal Martyrs"—his flesh being torn from his bones with iron combs, his life expiring with the "Shema."[298] Yehudah Ha-Naḥtom, a Caesarean Tanna, who seemed to have some knowledge of the Jewish religious history of that city,[299] probably was martyred there also.[300] And the extent of the Jewish martyrs executed at Caesarea during the periods of Roman persecution is, without doubt, innumerable, in spite of the fact that only a handful of names of those who gave their lives for the "santification of the name" has come down to posterity, and that of these names only a few can be associated definitely with those places where they met their deaths as martyrs. That Caesarea was a very popular Roman center for the production of martyrologies has been attested to, with voluminous evidence, by Eusebius, the father of church history, who personally witnessed the heart-rending spectacles over a period of many years while he served as bishop of that city.[301] Like Herod her slave, Rome the mistress also had immortalized herself at Caesarea. Caesarea, as a memorial of Rome, conjured up only nightmares.

And Caesarea was the antithesis of Jerusalem. In the Rabbinic mind, the two cities could not even exist simultaneously, let alone prosper side by side.[302] "Until Jerusalem was destroyed, no city had any true rank; but since the destruction of Jerusalem, Caesarea has become a metropolis."[303] But "a ruler shall arise from the house of Jacob, and he shall capture and destroy the insurrectious city of Caesarea."[304]

But the Rabbis did not close their eyes to the evils which were corroding Jewish life from within all the while that they were condemning the outrages of Roman occupation which were crushing Jewish life from without. And although the record in Rabbinic literature dealing with this phase of Caesarean Jewish history is scanty by comparison with the other, inferences may, nevertheless, be drawn from some of the given utterances which will reveal the forces of deterioration that were at work.

Thus while Abbahu speaks of Gentile Caesarea as "Ekron" which "shall be rooted up" (Zeph. 2.4),[305] he describes Jewish Caesarea as "a city of blasphemers and revilers."[306] It is true that Shim'on ben Laqish, who was with him, objected strenuously to this statement of Abbahu's, and even put sand into the latter's mouth in token of his protest, saying to him that "God takes no delight in that person who levels such accusations against Israel;"[306a] but the charge remained unanswered. It is possible that Jewish Caesarea was far too over-Hellenized for the Rabbis as was evidenced by the use of Greek in the synagogue service.[307] It has also been noted that according to Abbahu the Jews of Jerusalem had ceased to pray mornings and evenings.[308] A similar situation could have prevailed at Caesarea. Even in the days of the Temple, the High Priest offered a special prayer on the Day of Atonement on behalf of "our brethren at Caesarea, that they may not assume authority over one another."[309]

Another mark of deterioration was the practice of buying positions of honor and authority in the synagogue for a price from the Nasi by men of inferior stature as regards both learning and personality, while at the same time there were men like "Rabbi Yizhaq berabbi Elazar in the synagogue of the uprising at Caesarea" about whom it could be said, "God is in His holy Temple" (Hab. 2.20).[310] There were, however, men of courage who criticized the Nasi for carrying on this practice, and who even proposed penalties if the practice were not stopped.[311] Insofar as the appointees themselves were concerned, it was ruled that one was not to stand up in their presence nor address them as "Rabbi," "for his prayer-shawl fits him like the pack saddle on an ass." With reference to them, Immi used to say, "gods of silver, or gods of gold, ye shall not make unto you" (Ex. 20.20).[312]

An older contemporary of Abbahu's, also a disciple of Yohanan, probably also a Caesarean, did not entertain the pessimistic views and the visions of certain doom regarding Caesarea. His, on the contrary, was a vision of hope and regeneration such as shall surpass all earlier glory. Yose bar Hanina said: "What is the meaning of that which is written, (Zech. 9.7) 'And I will take away his blood out of his mouth, and his detestable things from between his teeth, and he also shall be a remnant for our God, and he shall be a chief unto Judah, and Ekron as a Jebusite;' 'And I will take away his blood out of his mouth,'—this refers to their houses of revelation; 'and his detestable things from between his teeth,'—this refers to their houses of oracles; 'and he also shall be a remnant for our God,'—this refers to the synagogues and academies which are in Edom (Caesarea); 'and he shall be a chief unto Judah, and Ekron as a Jebusite,'—this refers to the theaters and circuses which are in Edom (Caesarea), in which the princes of Judah are yet destined to teach the Torah in public."[313]

Footnotes

(All citations from Rabbinic literature refer to the various tractates of the Babylonian (B) and the Palestinian (Y) Talmuds, or the commentaries thereto, and the Halakhic and Midrashic works of the Rabbis. Abbreviations of the various works of the Talmud are based generally on the system outlined in H. L. Strack's *Einleitung in Talmud und Midras* (München 1921) p. IX. Translations of Josephus are adapted from *The Works of Flavius Josephus,* trans. William Whiston. (Philadelphia, n.d.)

1. *JW* II, 14, 4.
2. *JW* II, 13, 7. Cf. *JA* XX, 8, 7.
3. *JW* II, 13, 7. *JA* XX, 8, 7.
4. *JW* II, 13, 7.
5. *JA* XIV, 7, 2.
6. *JW* II, 13, 7. This non-segregated condition did not prevail in later times, when the Jews resettled in Caesarea, after the War. Cf. *Tos. Ahilot,* XVIII, 13, where the existence of a Jewish Quarter on the eastern side of Caesarea is implied.
7. *JW* II, 14, 4.
8. *JA* XX, 8, 7. *JW* II, 18, 1 states that a massacre of 20,000 Jews took place in one hour which emptied Caesarea of its entire Jewish population.
9. *JA* XX, 8, 7.
10. *Ibid.*
11. *JW* II, 14, 5.
12. Schürer, *HJP* II, II, 281-291.
13. *JAA* I, 12; II, 18. Philo Judaeus, *Legatio ad Cajum,* 31. Schürer, *op. cit.,* 47-48. Organized elementary schools are of later origin. Some scholars accept the tradition that Simeon b. Shataḥ is associated with their establishment.
14. Schürer, *op. cit.,* 51 and 288-290. Of particular interest is the statement of Josephus that the seditions usually started at the gatherings which took place during the festivals. *JW* I, 4, 3.
15. *JA* XIV, 7, 2.
16. *JA* XVIII, 3, 1. *JW* II, 9, 2.
17. *JA* XVIII, 3, 1; XX 5, 4. *JW* II, 9, 2; II, 14, 4; II, 15, 6; II, 17, 1. Acts 23: 23-33; 25: 1-13.
18. *JA* XVIII, 3, 1; XIX, 9, 1; XX, 6, 1; XX, 8, 7. *JW* II, 12, 5; III, 4, 2.
19. Cf. *JA* XVIII, 3, 1, and *JW* II, 9, 2.
20. See below, Section I.
21. B. *Shab.,* 14b and 15a-b. התיר and טהר are two distinct technical terms. The former means to legitimatize in a general way; the latter means to declare to be ceremonially or levitically clean or pure.
22. Ohalot, 18, 9, according to Büchler's emendation in "Der Patriarch R. Jehuda I und die Griechisch-Römischen Städte Palästinas", *JQR* 13 (1901) 683-740. Cf. also the controversy in *Tos. Ahilot,* 18, 13.
23. *Tos. Ahilot,* 18, 17.
24. On the name 'Yerushalmi' see Strack, *op. cit.,* 64ff.
25. Strack, *loc. cit.*
26. *Abot,* 1, 1.
27. See below, Section IV.
28. For further reference, see Schürer, *op. cit.;* Avi-Yonah, M., *In the Days of Rome and Byzantium* (Jerusalem 1962 [Hebrew]); Allon, G., *Studies in Jewish History,* 2 vols. (Tel-Aviv 1957-1958 [Hebrew]).
29. It is never quite clear exactly what people Josephus has in mind when he uses the term "Syrians".
30. *JW* II, 14, 4. This incident together with the one recorded and described in the very next paragraph, *JW* II, 14, 5.
31. *JA* XX, 8, 7.
32. *JW* II, 13, 7.
33. *JA* XX, 8, 7. Cf. *JW* II, 13, 7.
34. Ohalot, 18, 9. It may have been cleared of human remains later. Cf. *Tos. Ahilot,* 18, 13, the testimony of Jehudah Ha-Nahtoin.
35. *Y. Moed Katan,* 82c, according to the reading of Rabenu Asher. Cf. *Tosefot B. Moed Katan,* 22a. Cf. also, Frankel, Z., *Introductio in Talmud Hierosolymitanum* (Vratislaviae 1870 [Hebrew]), 5.

36. *B. Sanh.*, 68a. *Abot d'R. Natan*, chap. 25.

37. *Masekhet Semahot*, chap. 8. *Yalkut Proverbs*, 944. *Midrash Proverbs*, 9, 6.

38. Mentioned in *Ta'anit*, 2, 8, and elsewhere in *Bavli (Babylonian Talmud)* and in *Yerushalmi (Jerusalem or Palestinian Talmud)*.

39. *Megillat Ta'anit*, III. See also, Hildesheimer, H., *Beiträge zur Geographie Palästinas*, (Berlin 1886) 4-10. Schürer, *op. cit.*, II, I, 84-87. Graetz, H., *Geschichte der Juden* (Leipzig, 1897-1911) III, 2, 565. Zeitlin, S., *Megillat Ta'anit* (Philadelphia 1922) 91. Strato's Tower has come down into the Rabbinic literature under a variety of names. That all of the designations identify Strato's Tower, and that it, in turn, is identified with Caesarea, a passage in the Tosefta makes incontrovertibly clear. In this passage, where the borders of the Land of Israel are discussed, "the wall of the Sharshon Tower of Caesarea" (חומת מגרל שרשז דקיסרי)(*Tos. Shevi'it*, 4, 11) is given as one of the landmarks.

40. Weiss, I. H., *Dor Dor V'dorshav*, 5 vols. (Berlin-New York, 1923-1924 [Hebrew]) II, chap. 25.

41. Built by Herod, the Edomite. Rome, when not referred to by its own name, is always referred to as *"Edom"* in Rabbinic literature. *Exodus R.* 35, and frequently. See also below, Section V.

42. *Megillat Ta'anit, loc. cit.*

43. Graetz, Zeitlin, and others, have each gone his own way in emending the text of *Megillat Ta'anit* in order to make it fit his special theory, respectively. The historical value, or possible authenticity, of the interpretation of the Scholiast has also been denied, it seems, without adequate proof or reason.

44. *JA* XIII, 12, 4; XIII, 15,4.

45. *Cf. B. Kid.* 66a, on the exploits of Alexander Jannaeus.

46. Josephus speaks of Strato's Tower as though it were a city, *JA* XIII, 15, 4.

47. *JA* XIV, 4, 4.

48. *JW* I, 7, 7.

49. *Tos. Ahilot*, 18, 17, according to the interpretation of the Rash.

50. Joshua 12:23.

51. לנמה דור.

52. *JA* XVI, 5, 1. *JW* I, 21, 8. But see Foerster, "History," p. 4, and n. 12.

53. *JA* XV, 7, 3. *JW* I, 20, 3.

54. *JA* XV, 9, 6.

55. *Ibid.*

56. *Ibid.*, XVI, 5, 1. *JW* I, 21, 5-8.

57. *JA* XV, 9, 6. *Cf. JA* XVI, 5, 1, where the period is given as 10 years.

58. *JW* I, 4, 3; II, 18, 2.

59. *JW* VII, 8, 7.

60. Acts 10:28.

61. *JA* XX, 8, 7.

62. *JW* II, 18, 1.

63. Schürer, *op. cit.*, I, I, 202-233.

64. Megillat Ta'anit, IX. I Macc. 4: 36-59. II Macc. 10: 1-8. *JA* XII, 7, 6-7.

65. *B. Shab.*, 21b f.

66. See above, p. 9. *JA* XIII, 12, 4; XIII, 15, 4.

67. *Ibid.* There can be no doubt whatsoever that the בולחית mentioned in the Rabbinic record is identical with the Valley of the Celices mentioned in *JA* XIII, 15, 4.

68. *JW* I, 4, 3.

69. *JW* I, 7, 7.

70. *JA* XIII, 9, 1.

71. Schürer, *op. cit.*, II, I, 86, and elsewhere (and all historians who simply copied him, including Haefeli, L., *Caesarea am Meer*, (Münster 1923) 38, as also the author of this study!) emphasizes the Judaising tendencies and practices of Agrippa I, and makes reference to *JA* XIX, 9, 1, where, however, no mention is made by Josephus to any such preoccupations. In point of fact, Schürer is altogether inconsistent in taking this stand about Agrippa's Jewish interests, accusing him at one and the same time of indulging in Judaising and of actually having no devotion to Judaism whatsoever. *Cf. op. cit.*, I, II, 160.

72. *JA* XIII, 15, 4.

73. See above, p. 1. *Cf.* also *JW* II, 13, 7, and *JW* II, 14, 4.

74. See above, p. 1, and *cf. JA* XX, 8, 7, and *JW* II, 13, 7.

75. *JA* XX, 8, 7. *JW* II, 13, 7.

76. See above, p. 9.
77. Graetz, *loc. cit.*
78. *JA* XIX, 7, 3.
79. See Schürer, *op. cit.*, I, I, 432-438.
80. *JA* XIX, 7, 3.
81. *JA* XV, 9, 6.
82. *JA* XIX, 9, 1. *JW* I, 21, 7; II, 13, 7.
83. See above, p. 1.
84. See above, p. 2.
85. See above, p. 9.
86. Schürer, *op. cit.*, I, II, 150 f. *JA* XIX, 8, 2. Acts 12: 19-23.
87. Agrippa I struck coins at Caesarea. Kadman, L., *CC*, 20. B. *Avoda Zara*, 6b, mentions a Caesarean dinar.
88. *JA* XIX, 8, 2.
89. *JA* XIX, 9, 1.
90. *JA* XX, 8, 7, 9. *JW* II, 13, 7; II, 14, 4.
91. See above, p. 6.
92. *JA* XX, 8, 7.
93. *JW* II, 13, 7.
94. *JA* XX, 8, 9.
95. *JW* II, 14, 4-5.
96. Schürer, *op. cit.*, I, II, 191.
97. *JW* II, 14, 3.
98. This Caesarean Synagogue, which Josephus (*JW* II, 14, 4-5.) places at the very hub of the Jewish rebellion against Rome, occurs in Rabbinic literature under the following variety of forms: כנישתא מרזדתא דקיסרין (*Mid. Sam.*, 7.); כנישתא מרדתא דקיסרין (*Y. Nazir*, 56a.); כנישתא מדרתה דקיסרין (*Y. Ber.*, כנישתא מרדתא דקיסדיו (*Y. Bikd.*, 65a.; *Y. San.*, 18a.); כנישתא מדוכתא דקסרי (*Lam. R.*, 1, 30.); כנישתא מדוכתא דקסרין (*Num. R.*, 12, 3.); 6a.); כנישתא מדרשא דקיסרין (*Y. Bikd.*, 3, 3., ed. Horev.)
Graetz (*op. cit.*, IV, 286), on the basis of the initial forms, which indeed are translatable as ''Synagogue of the Rebellion'', has ingeniously identified the Caesarean Synagogue mentioned by Josephus with this Caesarean Synagogue of the Rabbinic tradition. He is followed by S. Krauss (*Synagogale Altertümer* [Berlin-Wien 1922] 204, and *JE* III, 488), and by J. M. Jost (*Geschichte des Judenthums und seiner Secten* [Leipzig 1857-1859] II, 162). However, A. Rosenzweig (*Jerusalem und Caesarea* (Berlin 1890) 13) maintains the correct reading to be כנישתא מרדתא דקסרי, indicating merely that the Synagogue was situated on an incline.
In recent years, M. Schwabe, (in *Sepher Ha-Yovel lezekher Alexsander Marx* (New York 1950 [Hebrew] 433-449,) endeavored to identify this Synagogue further on the strength of an analysis of inscriptions on pieces of tile which were found in the remains of the old walled city of Roman Caesarea. (For the inscriptions, see below, pp. 000) Schwabe claims to have satisfactorily deciphered the very name of this Synagogue on the pieces of tile as being the same as that which is mentioned in Rabbinic literature, the Synagogue which was the seat of R. Abbahu's academy and court at Caesarea, and which was described as the ''Temple of the Lord'' when R. Yizhaq bar Lezer discoursed in it (*Y. Bikd.* 65d.). The event of the uprising against Rome was undeniably of very momentous importance to the Jews of Caesarea, even as it was to the Jews of Palestine at Jerusalem and every other city and town and village. That this event should have been memorialized by naming the Synagogue in which it occurred, the ''Synagogue of the Rebellion'', appears to be both plausible and appropriate. See, however, Frankel (*op. cit.* 5), who leaves the problem as being in need of further study.
99. To insinuate that the Jews were lepers, of which affliction the Jews were stigmatised by Manetho, as Josephus (*JAA* I, 26) reports, for which reason also they were driven out of Egypt by the Egyptians. The killing of the bird and the use of the earthen vessel by the Gentile was in mockery of the Scriptural commandment (Lev. 14: 1 f.), which prescribes the sacrificing of a clean bird in an earthen vessel on the day of the cleansing of the leper.
100. *JW* II, 14, 4-5.
101. *JW* II, 18, 1.
102. *Ibid.*
103. *JW* VII, 3, 1.
104. *JW* III, 9, 1. *Cf,* Haefeli, *op. cit.* 30. *Tos. Hullin*, 2, 13.
105. See above, p. 3.

106. See above, p. 1.
107. *Y. Gittin*, 43b.
108. *Y. Ket.* 45b. *Y. Kil.* 32c.
109. *Tos. Ahilot*, 18. 16.
110. *Eccl. R.* 1. 23.
111. *Tos. Makh.* 3. 10., *Y. Ber.* 6a., *Y. Ned.* 40c., *Y. Moed Katan*, 83c., *Y. Kil.* 32a., *Y. Shab.* 4c., *Tos. Demai*, 3. 14, 4. 23, and others.
112. The Caesarean Tanna, Yehudah Ha-Naḥtom, as his name implies, was probably a baker. R. Abbahu, the most renowned of all Caesarean Amoraim, dealt in women's veils. Such instances in Rabbinic literature are very numerous.
113. *Cf. JW* III, 9, 1. Also, Hyman, A., *Toldoth Tannaim Ve'Amoraim* (London 1910) I 174b.
114. *Tos. Ahilot*, 18. 13.
115. *Tos. Hullin*, 2. 13.
116. *Tos. Suk.*, 2. 2.
117. *Tos. Demai*, 3, 14.
118. *Tos. Men.*, 1. 15.
119. *Tos. Ahilot*, 18. 13. See above, p.
120. See above, p.
121. Regarding his name, see Bacher, W., *Die Agada der Tannaiten* (Strassburg 1884-1890). II. 503 f. Hyman, *op. cit.* I 288a f. Frankel, *op. cit.* 71.
122. The exact date is uncertain, depending, to some extent, on the date of the death of Yehudah Ha-Nasi, about which date historians disagree. See Strack, *op. cit.* 118.
123. Maimonides, in his introduction to the *Mishneh Torah*.
124. *Y. Moed Katan*, 81c. *B. Ned.* 50b.
125. See, article in *JE.* II 503, by L. Ginzberg.
126. See discussion in Strack, *op. cit.* 18-25.
127. *Y. Hur.* 48c. *B. Avoda Zara*, 31a. *Mid. Ps.* 1. 17.
128. *Eccl. R.* 6. 1.
129. *B. Ber.* 13a, *B. Shab.* 68a, 141b, *B. Eruvin*, 2b, *B. Pes.* 39b, *B. Beza*, 32b, *B. Moed Katan*, 9b, 27a, *B. Yev.* 109a, *B. Ket.* 5a, *B. Bab. Bat.* 39b. 158b, *B. Avoda Zara* 75b, *B. Mak.* 21a, *B. Zev.* 31a, 87a, *B. Hullin* 27b., *Y. Yoma* 41d; and very many others.
130. *B. San.* 7b, 93a-b, 94a, *B. Ber.* 63a, *B. Kid.* 40b, 82a, *B. Meg.* 27a, 29a, *B. Ket.* 5a.
131. *Y. Ber.* 3a. *Y. Moed Katan*, 81c.
132. *Y. Kil.* 32b, *Y. Ket.* 35a, *B. Ket.* 104a, *Eccl. R.* 7. 11.
133. *B. Ned.* 50b, *Y. Moed Katan*, 81c.
134. *Lev. R.* 28. 2.
135. *B. Shab.* 75a.
136. *Gen. R.* 1. 13.
137. *Y. Shab.* 6a, *Y. Beza*, 61c.
138. *B. Sota*, 49b.
139. *Gen. R.* 36. 12. *Cf. Y. Meg.* 71b.
140. *Eccl. R.* 11. 1.
141. *Ibid.*
142. *B. Yev.* 32a.
143. *B. Hullin*, 141a.
144. *B. Moed Katan*, 22a, *Y. Nid.* 50c.
145. *B. Kid.*, 33a.
146. *B. Moed Katan*, 24a, *B. Ket.* 8a.
147. *B. Pes.* 15a, *B. Hag.* 23b, *B. Ta'anit*, 8a.
148. *B. Ber.* 34a, *B. Shab.* 40a.
149. *B. Ber.* 63a.
150. See Bacher, W., *Die Agada der Palästinenischer Amoraer* (Strassburg 1892-1899). I 89-108. Hyman., *op. cit.* I 110-117. Strack, *op. cit.* 120. In *Bab. T.* nearly always, Oshaiah.
151. *Y. Shab.* 8a and *Y. San.* 28a indicate that the schools of Bar Qappara and Hoshaiah Rabbah were in existence at Caesarea at the same time.
152. Maimonides, in his introduction to the *Mishneh Torah. Cf.* Frankel, *op. cit.* 47b-48a.
153. *B. Eruvin*, 53a.
154. *Ibid.*
155. *Y. Ter.* 47a.
156. *Y. Halla*, 58a.

157. *Y. Ber.* 9a.
158. *Y. Shev.* 38c, *Y. Beza,* 60a.
159. *Y. Eruvin,* 22b, *Y. San.* 30b.
160. *B. Eruvin,* 53a.
161. *Ibid.*
162. *B. Ber.* 32b, *B. Shab.* 28b.
163. *B. Pes.* 34b, *B. Kid.* 80a, *B. Nid.* 25a.
164. *Y. Yev.* 4d, *Y. Ket.* 32d, *Y. Kid.* 60a, *Y. Bab Kam.* 4c.
165. *Ibid.*
166. *B. Hullin,* 141b, *B. Shab.* 21a, *B. Ta'anit,* 21a.
167. The collection of Hoshaiah's baraitot was evidently lost, and should not be confused with the Tosefta which is extant, as the two are not identical, and as those baraitot cited in his name in the Talmud are overwhelmingly not to be found in our Tosefta. On this subject, see, Weiss, I. H., *Dor, Dor, Ve'Dorshav* (Berlin-New York 1923-1924). II chap. 23, p. 217 f., III. chap. 5, p. 56 f.
168. *Eccl. R.* 6.1.
169. *"Demai"* are fruits, usually acquired from an *"am ha-arez",* about which there is a suspicion whether or not the tithes therefrom were properly taken.
170. *Y. Halla,* 60a.
171. *Y. Hag.* 76b.
172. *"Agunah"* is a woman who is tied to an absent husband, for whatever reason or reasons, and therefore is prevented from marrying.
173. *Y. Yev.* 15d, *B. Yev.* 121b.
174. *Y. Bab. Mez.* 11b.
175. *Y. Ber.* 5d, *Y. Moed Katan,* 82d.
176. *Y. Peah,* 21b.
177. *Y. Yev.* 9b, *Y. Beza,* 60d, *Y. Kid.* 65d.
178. *Y. Meg.* 70d.
179. See Bacher, *op. cit.* (see n. 150). *Cf.* further, Bacher, *Aggadoth Amora'e Erez Ysráel* (Tel Aviv 1925-28) Vol. I., p. 108, n 2.
180. Origen, *Contra Celsum,* trans. H. Chadwick. [Cambridge 1953] 1. 44, 1. 55, 2. 31.
181. *Selection to Ps.* 11, 352.
182. Moore, G. F., *Judaism* (Harvard 1927). I 165 n. I. Graetz, H., "Hille, der Patriarchen-sohn", *MGWJ.* 30 (1881) 437 f.
183. Throughout the cited work.
184. *History of the Martyrs in Palestine,* trans. W. Cureton. (London-Paris, 1861) p. 30.
185. See, "The Church Father, Origen and Rabbi Hoshaya," *JQR* 3 (1891) 357-360, by Wilhelm Bacher on this subject.
186. Bacher, *loc. cit.,* (see n. 150) maintains that this "philosopher" is Origen. In his discussion on circumcision in *Contra Celsum,* however, Origen does not oppose it on this ground. On the use of the term "philosopher" in the early writings of the church fathers, *cf.* Eusebius, *Ecclesiastical History,* 6. 3., p. 208 (London 1879). The term "philosopher" is very frequently used in Midrashic and Talmudic literature in a very broad sense.
187. *Gen. R.* 11.7.
188. *In Yalkut Isaiah,* sect. 394, the reading is "hymnon."
189. *Gen. R.* 8. 9.
190. *B. Pes.* 87b.
191. See Bacher, *op. cit.* II 88-142.
192. *B. Gittin,* 44b.
193. *Cant. R.* 1. 39.
194. *Y. Ber.* 4b. Yohanan lost all his 10 sons in childhood. *B. Ber.* 5b.
195. *B. Hag.* 14a. *Yalkut Isaiah,* sect. 394.
196. *Y. Shab.* 8a, *Y. San.* 28a.
197. *Mid. Sam.* 7. *Y. Nazir,* 56a.
198. *JW* II, 14, 4-5.
199. S. Lieberman (*Greek in Jewish Palestine* [New York 1942] 21) is in error when he calls Abbahu head of the school at Caesarea. So are all the others who maintain this view. Abbahu taught in the school but never became head of it. The report in *B. Sota,* 40a of Abbahu's declining in favor of Abba of Acco refers without doubt to the office as head of the school and not to any other communal office, such as "parnes."

200. *B. Sota,* 40a.
201. *Y. San.* 18a.
202. *Y. Shab.* 11a., *Y. Shek.* 11c.
203. *B. Baba Mezia,* 84a, *B. Baba Batra,* 58a.
204. *B. Baba Mezia,* 84a.
205. *B. Ber.* 60a, *B. Ket.* 62a.
206. *Ibid.*
207. *B. Hag.* 14a, *B. Yoma,* 73a, *B. Yev.* 65b, *B. Sota,* 40a. In contrast with this respectful attitude toward Abbahu, the Jew, the humiliating and even insulting attitudes of the consular staffs generally toward the Jews, even toward great and renowned Jewish scholars and teachers, are reflected in incidents like the following: When Yehoshua ben Levi, a teacher of Abbahu's, and Hanina entered the office of the proconsul, and he stood up to greet them, his assistants would say to him: "You rise in the presence of these Jews?" To which derogating question the proconsul replied. "I saw their faces in a dream, and they looked to me like angels." This incident occurred at Caesarea. Still on another occasion, at Antioch, Yonah and Yose went to see Ursicinus, and he also rose in their presence, and received the same sort of insulting query from his associates. His answer is worth noting, as it reminds one of the legend of the cross which Constantine saw in his dream which inspired the nationalization of Christianity. Ursicinus replied: "Their faces I beheld in a dream, and was victorious in battle." (*Y. Ber.* 9a.)
208. Sometimes Abbahu cited traditions and opinions in the name of Yohanan, his teacher, which were very vigorously denied by his colleagues, but who, out of respect for his high position with the Roman authorities, would not dispute with him face to face, but instead would turn their face to one side in order to indicate their disagreement. (*B. Yoma,*73a, *B. Yev,* 65b).
209. *B. Ket.* 17a.
210. *Abot,* 2. 2.
211. *Y. Baba Mezia,* 9d.
212. *B. Shab.* 119a.
213. *Ibid.*
214. *Y. Beza,* 60c.
215. *Y. Pes,* 30b, *Y. Hag.* 76c.
216. *Eccl. R.* 7. 35.
217. *B. Sota,* 40a.
218. *Ibid.*
219. Bacher, *op. cit.* II 88 f., has made too little of Abbahu as halakhist.
220. *Y. Yev.* 2d.
221. See above, p. *B. Sota,* 40a.
222. *Lev. R.* 35. 9.
223. *B. Ket.* 50a.
224. *Y. Shevi'it,* 36d.
225. *Lam. R.* 3. 17.
226. *Pesikta d'Rav Kahana,* 15.
227. *Y. Eruvin,* 21c.
228. *Y. Ber.* 12a, *B. Eruvin,* 53b.
229. See Bacher, *loc. cit.*
230. *Y. Ber.* 12a, *Y. Eruvin,* 21c, *Y. Beza,* 60d, *B. Shab.* 46a.
231. *Y. Shab.* 16b, *Y. Moed Katan,* 80b, *B. Shab.* 134b.
232. *Y. Avoda Zara,* 39b.
233. For a discussion of this subject in greater fullness, see Lieberman, *op. cit.*
234. *Y. Sota,* 21b.
235. Schürer, *op. cit.* II. I 47-50. See also Lieberman, *op. cit.*
236. See Lieberman, *op. cit.* for Talmudic citations illustrating this point.
237. *Ibid.*
238. *Y. Shab.* 7d, *Y. Sota,* 24c, *Y. Peah,* 15c, *B. Sota,* 49b.
239. *Y. Meg.* 74a. Cf. also Lieberman, *op. cit.*
240. *Yalkut Gen.* s. 47, *B. Suk.* 48b, *B. Shab.* 152b, *Gen. R.* 25. 1, *B. San.* 39a, *B. Ber.* 10a.
241. *B. Avoda Zara,* 4a. Abbahu did not mean to imply that Safra did not know the Hebrew Scriptures, but merely that he did not know how to use them effectively in polemics with Christians. His questioners were trying to tell him that God must hate Israel if He visits punishment upon them.

242. *Y. Ta'anit,* 65b.

243. *Ex. R.* 29. 4. The sequence in Abbahu's utterance is according to the reading of Etz Yoseph commentary, which is logical and gives added intensity to the saying, although the meaning is the same without the rearrangement of the order.

This utterance of Abahu's, interpreting the Hebrew Scriptures in order to refute Christian doctrine, reflects the influence of Shim'on ben Laqish with whose mode of polemical thinking he may have become acquainted while still at school in Tiberias, since the latter was one of his teachers as well as a friend. Shim'on ben Laqish draws upon Jer. 10: 10 for his polemic against the Christian doctrines of the incarnation and trinity. Instead of accepting the meaning of the verse in Jeremiah to be, "The Lord God is the true God," Resh Laqish conceives the meaning to be, "The Lord God is truth," playing upon the word אמת ;the א being the first letter of the Hebrew alphabet, implies that God is the first; the מ being the middle letter of the Hebrew alphabet, implies that God has no partners with whom to share his divinity; and the ת being the last letter of the Hebrew alphabet, implies that God has no offspring to whom to leave his divinity. (*Y. San.* 18a.). (For the purposes of polemics, it seemed of no consequence to Resh Laqish that the Hebrew letter מ was not exactly the middle letter of the alphabet).

244. *B. Shab.* 119b.

245. *B. Pes.* 56a.

246. Rosenzweig, *op. cit.* 24.

247. A sect, without doubt, like the "bé niz̤rafi" mentioned in the same context. They may both have been Christian or gnostic sectaries, but until further light has been shed on the problem, speculation is not productive of results. They were problem sects, this is certain, and Samuel would not enter the meeting or study house of one of them, the "bé niz̤rafi". The suggested emendations make very little sense and solve no problems.

248. *B. Shab.* 116a.

249. His full name was Jacob of Kefar Naboriah, (*Eccl. R.* 7. 47). Issi of Caesarea, who may be the Asi who, together with Ami, saved Abbahu's life, not only identifies him in this passage as a Christian, but sets him down as a sinner. In *Y. Bik.* 65d, and in *Mid. Sam.* 7, this same Jacob of Kefar Naboriah was praised by the Rabbis for giving an interpretation of a Scriptural passage that they liked. This may have been before he became a Christian.

250. *B. Avoda Zara,* 28a.

251. *Ibid.*

252. *Y. Avoda Zara,* 44d.

253. *B. Hag.* 14a, *Yalkut Gen.* sect. 394.

254. *Y. Demai,* 23a.

255. *B. Rosh Hash.* 34a.

256. *B. Baba Kamma,* 93a.

257. *Y. Ber.* 8d.

258. On date of Abbahu's death, see Lieberman, S., "The Martyrs of Caesarea," (*Annuaire de L'Institut de Philologie et d'Histoire Orientales et Slaves* VII 1939-1944) 395-446.

259. *Cant. R.* 1. 52.

260. *Y. Avoda Zara,* 42c.

261. See Frankel, *op. cit.* 123a-b; Bacher, W., "Die Gelehrten von Caesarea," *MGWJ* 45 (1901) 298-310.

262. *Y. Hag.* 76c, *B. Kid.* 40b, *B. Baba Kamma,* 17a, *B. Meg.* 27a.

263. *Ibid.*

264. *Y. Pes.* 30b.

265. *B. Suk.* 8a, *B. Eruvin,* 76b.

266. See Frankel, *op. cit.* 123b.

267. Liebermann, S., *The Talmud of Caesarea, Tarbiz* (Supplement; Jerusalem 1931 [Hebrew] II 4).

268. This does not mean to imply that Caesarean Jewish history comes to an end at this time. Sporadic references indicate that Jewish life continued at Caesarea for many centuries, and that during certain given periods, the Jewish community was comparatively large.

Vespasian (A.D. 69-79) had made Caesarea into a Roman colony, thereby severing completely all political ties of the city with its Jewish past. He named it, "Colonia Prima Flavia Augusta Caesarea." Alexander Severus (A.D. 222-235) extended the title to, "Metropolis Provinciae Syriae Palaestinae," to which title, undoubtedly, the Talmudic reference in *B. Meg.* 6a, points. Later, under Decius and Gallus, Caesarea's full title becomes, "Colonia Prima Flavia Augusta Caesarea Felix Concordia Metropolis Provinciae Syriae Palaestiniae." Justinian

(527-565) declared Caesarea to be the capital of "Palaestina Prima," and prohibited the Jews from erecting any new synagogues in it.

There was a good-sized Jewish community at Caesarea during the Middle Ages (Megillat Eviatar, in Schechter's *Saadiana*, [Cambridge, 1903] 91), which dwindled away very considerably after the onslaughts of the Crusades. Arab history has it that a Jew by the name of Joseph aided in the Moslem conquest of the city by leading the invading armies through the underground tunnels built by Herod the Great. (Weil, G., *Geschichte der Chalifen* (Mannheim 1846-1851) App. I, p. 2)

The thoroughgoing work of the Crusaders in destroying the Jewish community of Caesarea is attested to by Benjamin of Tudela, the most renowned of the Jewish itinerarians, in his "Massaot Binyamin." When he visited Caesarea in 1170-1171, he found there no more than 10 Jews (Asher, A., ed. and trans., *The Itinerary of Rabbi Benjamin of Tudela* [London and Berlin 1840-1841] 65). Earlier estimates of the Jewish population are extremely exaggerated, ranging from 80,000 to 220,000 but would nevertheless indicate that during the Arab occupation of Caesarea, from 640 to 1107, the Jewish community was not a small one. At the beginning of the 17th century, seven or eight Jewish families dwelt in Caesarea. Today, a kibbutz, Sedot-Yam (Fields of the Sea) occupies the southern portion of the site which was once Caesarea Maritima.

269. See above, p.

270. See note 207. Jews and Judaism were subjects of derision in the theaters and circuses of Caesarea. Abbahu gives some interesting examples of these expressions of Caesarea's art in his day, in an exposition of Psalm 69:13, "They that sit in the gate talk of me, and I am the song of the drunkards."

"They that sit in the gate talk of me," refers to the heathen who sit in the theaters and circuses;" and I am the song of the drunkards" refers to their eating, to gluttony and drinking, to intoxication and ridiculing the Jews because they eat dry carobs during the entire week and save their money to buy good food for the Sabbath. In another skit, one says to the other, "How long would you like to live?" And the other replies, "I would like to live as long as the tunic which the Jew wears on the Sabbath will last!" (On the presumption that since the Jew wears this tunic only once a week it will last a very long time.) Again, they bring a camel covered with a sackcloth onto the stage, and one says to the other, "Why is this camel in mourning?" And the other says, "These Jews observe the Sabbatical year, and, since they have no vegetables to eat, they eat the thorns that belong to the camel, and he is mourning for them." (that is, for the thorns.) Or, one asks the other, "Why has the price of oil gone up?" And the other answers, "These Jews keep the Sabbath, and everything for which they labor during the week, they eat up on the Sabbath. Because they have no wood with which to cook, they break up their beds to use for firewood. They then must sleep in the dirt on the ground, after which they rub themselves with oil. And that is why the price of oil is at a premium." (*Introduction to Lam. R.* sect. 17).

Scenes and skits like the ones described above (and there are still more) could not possibly be the products of the Jewish imagination, since they involve the profanation of institutions sacred to the Jew, such as the Sabbath and the Sabbatical year. They must consequently be accepted as the actual productions in the theaters and circuses of Caesarea in the days of Abbahu.

271. During the various periods of persecution, the Jews of Caesarea were without doubt subjected to the same degradations and deprivations as were the Jews throughout Palestine. Although it was not a crime as such against the state or the emperor to admit that one was a Jew as it was a crime for one to admit that he was a Christian during the persecutions of the Christians, nevertheless, nearly every Jewish practice which made Jewish identification meaningful was prohibited. These prohibitions included (1) Teaching of the Torah (*B. Ta'anit*, 18a); (2) Circumcision *(ibid.)*; (3) Observance of the Sabbath *(ibid.)*; (4) Recitation of the "Shema" (*Tos. Ber.* 2. 14); (5) Eating mazah on the Passover (*Lev. R.* 32. 1); (6) Building a sukkah or sitting in one (*Tos. Suk.* 1. 7., *Lev. R.* 32. 1.); (7) Taking of the lulav and etrog on Sukkot (*Lev. R.* 32. 1); (8) Reading the Scroll of Esther on Purim (*Tos. Meg.* 2.4); (9) Lighting candles on Hanukkah (*B. Shab.* 21b); (10) Wearing tefillin, or (11) zizit (*Lev. R.* 32. 1; *B. Shab.* 49a); (12) Mezuzah (*Tos. Meg.* 4. 29); (15) Observance of the tithes (*M. Maaser Sheni*, 4. 11); (14) Observing mourning customs (*Semahot*, 9); (15) Divorce (*M. Ket.* 9. 9); (16) Marriages on Wednesday (*Tos. Ket.* 1. 1.); (17) Separation during the menstrual period (*B. Meilah*, 17a); (18) Convening in assemblies (*B. Ber.* 61b; *B. Avoda Zara*, 17a); (19) Ordaining of Rabbis (*B. San.* 14a).

Violations of the prohibitions, according to the Rabbinic record, were punishable by fixed and specified penalties (*Lev. R.* 32. 1. and elsewhere). For observing the rite of circumcision, the penalty was beheading or stoning to death (*Lev. R.* 32. 1.); for preoccupation with the Torah, or for observing the Sabbath, the penalty was burning alive at the stake *(ibid)*; for eating mazah on the Passover, the penalty was crucifixion or beheading *(ibid. Yalkut Ex.* 292); for wearing the tefillin, the penalty was cracking the skull (*B. Shab.* 49a); for building the sukkah, taking the lulav (and etrog), or wearing the zizit, the penalty was being scourged or pierced with a lance (*Lev. R.* 32. 1; *Mekh. Bahodesh, Yalkut Zach.* sect. 581, *Yalkut Ex.* sect. 292); for the recitation of the "Shema," which was considered a denial of the belief in the divinity of the emperor, the penalty was having the flesh torn from the bones with combs of iron (*B. Ber.* 61b). (Eusebius [*op. cit.*] throughout the work) describes this form of torture as being the most popular with the Romans during the persecutions.)

A summary of the conditions at Caesarea during the persecutions is given in Rabbinic literature through the exposition of Deuteronomy 28:66, "Thy life shall hang in doubt before thee; and thou shalt be afraid night and day; and thou shalt have no assurance of thy life." "Thy life shall hang in doubt before thee"—this refers to him who has been put into the diaeta of Caesarea; "and thou shalt be afraid day and night"—this refers to him who goes forth to be judged; "and thou shalt have no assurance of thy life"—this refers to him who goes forth to be crucified (*Esther R.* 1. 1.). The rulers were corrupt and immoral and practicers of witchcraft (*Yalkut Ps.* sect. 830). Strangers were not safe in the streets (*Yalkut Ps.* sect. 702).

272. See below, pages 53 and 54, and notes.
273. See below, for implications of this designation.
274. *Ex. R.* 35. 5 f. *Bet Hamidrash,* 6, 22.
275. *B. Baba Batra,* 4a.
276. *JA* XVI, 5, 4.
277. *JA* XV, 8, 1; XV, 9, 5. Jews did not believe his alibi that all of this pagan construction was done under pressure from or by Rome.
278. *B. Baba Batra,* 3b.
279. See above, p. *JA* XVI, 5, 4; XIX, 7, 3.
280. *JA* XIX, 7, 3.
281. See above, n. 270.
282. See above, n. 103.
283. *Bet Hamidrash,* 6, 22.
284. *JA* XV, 8, 1; XV, 9, 5.
285. See above, n. 271.
286. *Eccl. R.* II, 9 f; *Mid. Ps.* 9, 13; *Mid. Prov.* 9.
287. *Lam. R.* 1, 32.
288. *Eccl. R.* 5, 9.
289. *Yuhasin,* 38b. *Seder Hadorot,* 215a.
290. *B. Meg.* 6a.
291. See Schürer, *op. cit.* I, II, 48, n. 32 and references.
292. *Ibid.* 51-54.
293. See above, p. and references.
294. *Ibid.*
295. *Ibid.*
296. See above, n. 271.
297. Acts 23-24.
298. See above, n. 37.
299. *Tos. Ahilot,* 18, 13.
300. See Bacher, n. 261 above.
301. See above, n. 184 for Eusebius's work.
302. *B. Meg.,* 6a.
303. *Lam. R.* 1. 32.
304. *Targum Pseud. Jonathan,* to Numbers 24:19.
305. *B. Meg.* 6a.
306. *Cant. R.* 1.39.
306a. *Ibid.*
307. See above, p. 41 and references.
308. See above, p. 45 and references.
309. *Tanhuma, Ahre,* 3.
310. *Mid. Sam.* 7.
311. *Y. Bik.* 65d; *Y. Hur.* 47a; *Mid. Sam.* 7.
312. *Y. Bik.* 65d; *Y. Hur.* 47a.
313. *B. Meg.* 6a.

CAESAREA AND THE CRUSADES

Harry W. Hazard

1. The history of the city of Caesarea from 640 to 1291

Between the Arab conquest of Caesarea in 640 and the arrival of the crusaders in 1099, little of moment occurred there. With the rest of Palestine, it changed rulers several times,[1] but the chroniclers record no sieges, no assaults, no sacks. For four and a half centuries, in fact, it seems to have qualified as a happy place, having no history worth recording, with but a single exception.

In the year 975 the Byzantine emperor John I Tzimisces led a military expedition southward through Syria, taking Caesarea and other towns with little difficulty but failing to capture Jerusalem.[2] After a brief campaign he returned home, leaving no garrison at Caesarea, which promptly and peacefully reverted to Fāṭimid rule.

The paucity of other references in the chronicles does not stem from any drastic reduction in the importance of Caesarea, though it did not have nearly the political prominence it had enjoyed in Roman times, nor the strategic significance it was to have under the Franks. Our information on these centuries of Saracen rule is derived from a series of Moslem geographers and travelers, whose brief references are of interest.

Ibn-Khurdādhbih, in 844, lists Caesarea between Tyre and Acre to the north and Arsuf and Jaffa to the south, as one of the ports of Palestine.[3] Al-Ya'qūbī, who died in 897, calls it "a city on the shore of the sea, one of the most impregnable cities of Palestine, and the last of that land's cities to be captured; it was taken by Mu'āwiyah ibn-abī-Sufyān in the caliphate of 'Umar ibn-al-Khaṭṭāb."[4] Several tenth-century geographers mention it among the cities of Palestine.[5]

In 985 al-Maqdisī gives us our first real description: Caesarea is situated "on the coast of the Greek sea: there is no city more beautiful, nor any better filled with good things: plenty has its well-spring here, and useful products are on every hand. Its lands are excellent, and its fruits delicious; the town also is famous for its buffalo-milk and its white bread. To guard the city there is an impregnable fortress, and without lies the well-populated suburb which the fort protects. The drinking-water of the inhabitants is drawn from wells and cisterns. Its Great Mosque is very beautiful."[6] Apparently both Roman aqueducts were then inoperative, clogged with sand.

In 1047 the Persian traveler Nāṣir-i-Khusrau visited Caesarea and recorded his impressions: "a fine city, with running waters and palm-gardens, and orange and citron trees. Its walls are strong, and it has an iron gate. There are springs that gush out within the city; . . ."[7] for water was of paramount importance to any city in that arid land. Comparing these two descriptions, Reifenberg deduces that the low-level aqueduct was cleared of sand and vaulted between 985 and 1047; it remained in service throughout the crusading period.[8]

Meanwhile Christian pilgrims were visiting Palestine in steadily increasing numbers, culminating in the great German pilgrimage of 1064-1065,[9] with perhaps seven thousand participants. This horde definitely passed through Caesarea, as did many others, whether arriving overland or by sea, so information on the city's location, its amenities, and the strength of its fortifications was available to the Frankish commanders in 1099.

Before the oncoming crusaders extricated themselves from Antioch and marched southward along the Syrian valleys, the Fāṭimid armies retook Jerusalem from its Artukid Turkoman rulers. They garrisoned and provisioned the coastal towns, which they had recaptured in 1089, and then withdrew, leaving them to their fate, though their fleet cruised offshore. Caesarea, like its sister ports, was under the rule of an emir and the spiritual guidance of a qadi; it awaited the impending invasion, complacent in its wealth and the strength of its fortifications.

"When the crusade approached Tripoli," according to Runciman, "the emir hastened to release some three hundred Christian captives . . . and he provided pack-animals and provender for the whole army. . . . His prompt action saved the rich suburbs of Tripoli from spoliation. The crusaders left Tripoli on . . . May 14 . . . . On May 19 they crossed the Dog river, just north of Beirut, and entered Fāṭimid territory." Similar arrangements were made at Beirut and at Acre. "After pausing for the night the crusaders moved on past Haifa and around Mount Carmel, and reached the outskirts of Caesarea on May 26."[10]

This date in 1099 marks the start of Caesarea's crusading period, though the day passed peacefully enough. The army split, with the forces under Godfrey of Bouillon and Robert of Flanders camping by a spring at the foot of a hill east of the city, and those led by Raymond of Toulouse and Robert of Normandy stopping beside a marsh to the north.[11] As it was Whitsuntide, the crusaders stayed there four days, ignored by the garrison.

Two significant episodes occurred during this brief rest. A hawk killed a pigeon which proved to be carrying a message, accounts of which differ slightly. Raymond of Aguilers[12] says it was from the "king" of Acre to the "duke" of Caesarea, warning him against the "foolish, quarrelsome, undisciplined" crusaders, which sounds superfluous and belated, but possible. Baldric of Dol[13] names the sender as the "king" of Tripoli, ordering the emir of Jerusalem to collect the garrisons of Ascalon, Jaffa, Caesarea, Acre, Tyre, and Sidon to oppose the Franks, which—besides reversing the agreed strategy—is much less credible as Tripoli was independent and its ruler powerless to command Fāṭimid governors. As Raymond was present and Baldric was not, the balance of probability tips decisively toward the former.

The second event was the arrival of representatives of Jerusalem's

Christian community, presumably all adherents of Eastern rites. The anonymous crusader from Lorraine[14] reports that they supplied information on the holy city and its inhabitants; doubtless its defenses were also discussed.

On May 30 the Franks resumed their march, by way of Arsuf and Ramla, to Jerusalem, which fell to their assault on July 15. A week later Godfrey was chosen ruler, with the modest title Advocate of the Holy Sepulcher.

Early in August Tancred, prince of Galilee, and Godfrey's brother Eustace returned to Caesarea to reconnoiter a rumored Egyptian offensive based on Ascalon.[15] They confirmed it and summoned the Franks to the battle of August 12, which "ensured the crusaders' possession of Palestine."[16] Baldric asserts that the pair camped just outside town, planning to attack and despoil all who approached or left, and adds that the citizens agreed to surrender if the crusaders defeated the Egyptian army.[17] This story, too, is unacceptable, as no such surrender occurred or was demanded, while the time was hardly ripe for private freebooting. He is more plausible when he states that later in 1099 Tancred passed Caesarea on his way to attack Haifa, whose inhabitants fled to Caesarea and Acre.[18]

The final event of the crowded year 1099 was the arrival at Caesarea in mid-December of Godfrey's brother Baldwin, count of Edessa, and Tancred's uncle Bohemond, prince of Antioch, on a pilgrimage to Jerusalem in belated fulfillment of their crusading vows.[19] The only places where they could purchase provisions on their trip through hostile territory were Tripoli and Caesarea, which sold them bread and cheese at exorbitant prices.

Early in 1100 Godfrey received delegations from Ascalon, Caesarea, and Acre bringing Arab horses and other gifts, and bearing letters from their respective emirs offering a monthly tribute of 5000 gold bezants in return for immunity from attack. He accepted, and executed treaties embodying these terms.[20] He subsequently toured his domains and tributaries, being honored by the emir of Caesarea at a sumptuous banquet.[21] When he fell acutely ill, the usual medieval suspicions of poison proliferated; his death in July 1100 induced a certain coolness between the infuriated Franks and the emir.

Baldwin I and his retinue passed through Caesarea in November on their way to Jerusalem and Bethlehem, where on Christmas he was crowned king, accepting the royal title his brother Godfrey had scrupulously refused.[22] In March or April of 1101 Baldwin renewed Godfrey's treaties with the tributary emirs, but merely to mask his true intentions, which were predatory and retaliatory.[23]

The king, whose sole port was Jaffa (Haifa was held by his enemy Tancred), negotiated an agreement with the Genoese for them to assist in the capture of additional ports, and to receive as compensation a third of the booty and a street in each city for a market.[24] Then, late in April, the Genoese fleet of 26 galleys and 6 other ships blockaded Arsuf while the Frankish army took up siege positions. After three days the little port surrendered without a struggle;[25] Baldwin refrained from sacking it or massacring the inhabitants, probably because of their bloodless capitulation. He left a small garrison, and prepared to move against Caesarea.

Before he left Arsuf, however, a delegation from Caesarea arrived to protest against his proposed treaty-breaking, and possibly to attempt to buy him off, but without success; his mind was made up. He sent cardinal Maurice of Porto and the patriarch Daimbert to negotiate another bloodless surrender, but received a brusque refusal. Consequently, on May 2 the army and fleet moved north and took up siege positions around reputedly "impregnable" Caesarea.[26]

Baldwin's first move was to order the construction of stone-throwing catapults and a wooden tower to command the walls, which were twenty to thirty feet high.[27] He shortsightedly ordered the destruction of the splendid orchards outside the walls,[28] thus facilitating troop movement at the cost of transforming Caesarea's park-like and productive environs into semi-desert.

A second Saracen delegation now attempted to dissuade him on theological grounds, but the patriarch dismissed their plea against bloodshed, retorting that they had no legitimate title to the once-Christian city, and that Baldwin could do as he pleased if they continued to reject his surrender demands. The qadi wished to capitulate, but the emir steadfastly refused.[29]

When the siege had dragged on for fifteen days, the soldiery declined to wait any longer for the catapults. On May 17 a full-scale attack was launched, by sea and land. The Genoese consul, William Embriaco, called "Caputmallii," led a frontal assault on the wall by ladder-climbing Italians and Franks, which forced the defenders back to their second line of fortifications, a medial wall. This in turn was quickly overrun,[30] and the citizens, described as "soft and effeminate through long-continued leisure and peace,"[31] retired to the great mosque and pled for mercy. The fighting had lasted less than nine hours.

The emir and qadi, and some of the richer merchants, were spared for later ransoming, but Baldwin made no effort to save the other inhabitants from the avarice and blood-lust of the Franks and their Genoese allies, and the chroniclers vie in lurid accounts of the ensuing slaughter and sack.

Fulcher says the Saracens tried to flee and hide, but were soon found; the Franks killed the men and burned their corpses to recover swallowed gold, and enslaved the women for mill-labor or sold them "whether beautiful or ugly."[32] Albert includes the emir's harem among those sold, and says 500 "Ethiopian" soldiers were beheaded.[33] Caffaro puts the number of merchants spared at the improbably high figure of 1000.[34] William of Malmesbury, following Fulcher [35] and Guibert of Nogent,[36] gloats: "The scene was enough to excite laughter in a by-stander, to see a Turk disgorging bezants, when struck on the neck by the fist of a Christian. The wretched males . . . had hid money in their mouths; the females in parts not to be particularized. . . ."[37]

The booty in gold, silver, jewels, cloth, and spices, as well as in captives, was immense. Baldwin retained two thirds for himself and the Franks, as agreed, and the leaders of the Italians got large shares from the remaining third, but each of 8000 Genoese sailors received 48 Poitevin shillings and two pounds of pepper,[38] while each Frank received so much that "the poor became rich."[39] The Genoese share included a hexagonal green chalice believed to be the Grail, of solid emerald; this was triumphantly conveyed to Genoa and enshrined in the cathedral of St. Lawrence, where "though now broken and recognized as glass," it "is still highly prized."[40]

Baldwin found himself in possession of a city virtually emptied of inhabitants, but with its fortifications almost intact and possessing "great advantages in the way of running streams and well-watered gardens,"[41] though its port was hardly usable. He gave the Genoese their agreed third, not only of Caesarea itself but of the land for a league in every direction; an 1104 charter confirmed this grant and others covering Arsuf and Acre.[42]

The papal legate, cardinal-bishop Maurice of Porto, led the Frankish clergy through the ritual purification of the basilica, which had been converted into the great mosque and hence was now ceremonially reconsecrated as the cathedral of Saint Peter; the smaller church after similar rites was rededicated to Saint Lawrence, patron saint of the Genoese.[43] A Frankish abbot named Baldwin was elected archbishop,[44] a small garrison was left under the command of Harpin of Bourges,[45] and king Baldwin moved his army to Ramla and then to Jaffa, while the Genoese fleet sailed home.

The safety of the newly won city was greatly increased by Baldwin's victory at Ascalon in September, in which the garrisons of Caesarea and other Frankish strongholds of necessity participated; a defeat would have left them at the mercy of the Saracens, as did that of Hattin in 1187. But even after the victory at Ascalon, the countryside beyond the walls was repeatedly ravaged by Moslem raiders; twice in 1104 Baldwin himself had to come to drive them off.[46] It was many years before the peasants were as safe as the townspeople.

As the kingdom gradually expanded and consolidated its strength under the skillful rule of Baldwin I, Caesarea slowly acquired a small Christian population and regained some of its normal prosperity. All the Moslems who had not been killed or enslaved in 1101 had fled to Acre or Tyre,[47] and there is no record of any substantial Moslem community in Caesarea thereafter, though individual craftsmen and merchants probably trickled in to settle there after the initial antagonism had been modified by time and mutual dependence.

There were a few Jewish and Samaritan families in Caesarea,[48] and probably a substantial number of Christians of the various Eastern rites, but the bulk of the inhabitants must have been Europeans, whether Genoese and Pisans or French and Flemish.[49] The Italian colony consisted mainly of merchants and their households and employees; throughout the twelfth century Italians remained relatively rare in other walks of life.

Of the various groups of French who predominated in the First

Crusade, the contingent from what is now Belgium and northeastern France—then the counties of Flanders, Artois, and Hainault and adjacent areas—dominated Caesarea to the virtual exclusion of the southerners and the Normans. In Jerusalem Godfrey of Bouillon and his brother Baldwin had outmaneuvered Raymond of Toulouse and Tancred for political control, while Arnulf of Chocques outlasted Daimbert of Pisa and Gibelin of Arles for the Patriarchate; in Caesarea their compatriots Baldwin and then Evremar of Chocques were elected archbishop in turn, while by 1110 Eustace Granier[50] was granted the hereditary lordship of the city and the surrounding district.

The fief was not large or particularly rich, and its lord, though perhaps foremost among the secondary peers of the kingdom, did not rank quite as high as the counts. From Destroit, about 15 miles north of the city, where it adjoined the county of Haifa, to the border of the fief of Arsuf nearly 20 miles south of the city, and extending inland about 15 miles, it comprised nearly 500 square miles, about five for each of its hundred villages.[51] The peasants were mainly Palestinian Arabs, whose payments in cash and produce supported both the archbishopric and the ruling Frankish fighters.[52]

The seigneury was responsible for supplying 25 knights, while the city and the archbishopric each owed fifty mounted sergeants.[53] As Prawer points out, these figures were determined by the relative monetary value rather than the size of a fief. Some of the knights, under a "viscount," were stationed in the fort of Caco (Qāqūn), about 10 miles southeast of Caesarea on the road to Nablus, but most of them garrisoned Caesarea itself or followed its lord wherever his duties called him. In his absence the city and garrison were under the command of a second "viscount," and the fief had its own chamberlain, seneschal, and other officials.[54]

Much of the arable land-found its way into ecclesiastical hands, whether of the archbishopric, or the church of the Holy Sepulcher, or the abbey of St. Mary at Jehoshaphat, or the monastery of St. Lazarus, or—increasingly as the twelfth century gave way to the troubled thirteenth—the great military orders of the Hospital, the Temple, and the Teutonic Knights, all of which also owned property inside the city itself.

Solomon draws an instructive and valid parallel:[55] "In many respects the problems which the crusader colonists successfully encountered are similar to those which face colonists in Palestine today [1911] . . . peoples drawn from all parts of Europe, connected by a common religion, but speaking different languages and accustomed to different usages, settled side by side amid the Arabs." He goes on to point out that in both cases the original religious motivations gradually gave way to secular considerations, that both groups had to restore the dwindling fertility of the ancient land, and that both had to establish strongholds to protect agriculturalists against beduin raids. The need for alert defense of the fief's villages slackened with the construction between 1136 and 1142 of the fortresses of Ibelin, Blanche Garde, and Beth Gibelin along the southwestern frontier,[56] followed by the capture of Ascalon in 1153.

Caesarea was valued by the Franks as a fortified city, but not particularly as a port. Al-Idrīsī, who died in 1166, exaggerated in calling it "a very large town, having also a populous suburb; its fortifications are impregnable,"[57] as well as in dismissing its port as holding only one boat at a time,[58] but Abel is justified in describing this as not worth the cost of restoring it to its ancient splendor, and therefore useful only as a secondary landing-place and a shelter for small ships.[59]

Even as the Moslem al-Idrīsī overestimated Christian Caesarea, so a contemporary Frank overpraised its previous phase: "In the time of the Saracens, Caesarea flourished so greatly that . . . it grew like their paradise; and there the nobles and the powerful were buried. In the circuit of the city, among gardens, were various small caves, constructed of sawn stones, in which spices and aromatics were mingled in the fire, so that the whole city was redolent of the combining wafted odours, to the shutting out of all bad smells and the exhilaration of the countenances of citizens. But now all this has come to nothing."[60] In 1130, the approximate date of this passage, Caesarea was much more than "nothing," even as a port, but in 1177 the Byzantine John Phocas was certainly too generous in calling it "a large and populous city, built on the shore of the sea. In it is a truly wonderful harbour, made by human skill."[61] The truth lies midway between these extremes: Caesarea was a thriving city with strong walls and citadel but a mediocre port, and an area of only thirty acres.[62]

Few events are known to have affected Caesarea during its heyday, between 1101 and 1187. Its garrison continued to participate in military activities, notably in repelling an attack on Jerusalem in August 1110[63] and at the battle of Ibelin in May 1123,[64] when Eustace Granier—as baillie during the captivity of Baldwin II—commanded the army of the kingdom and presumably received the injuries which caused his death in June. Alfonso Jordan, heir to Tripoli, died at Caesarea in 1148, amid the usual charges of poison.[65] In December 1182 a council was held there to discuss plans for thwarting Saladin,[66] and in March 1186 pope Urban III ordered arbitration of the Genoese claim to their third of Caesarea, Arsuf, and Acre, from which the Franks had ejected them.[67]

In June of 1187 the garrison of Caesarea, under the command of its lord Walter II, joined the combined forces of the kingdom in an effort to bring Saladin to battle. The sultan's overwhelming victory at Hattin on July 4 left the towns defenseless, and while he besieged Jerusalem, he sent detachments under trusted emirs to take over the lesser strongholds.[68] These emirs tended to be more avaricious and less magnanimous than their chivalrous master; Badr-ad-Dīn Dulderim and Gharas-ad-Dīn Kīlīj took Caesarea without effort in mid-July,[69] looted it, ruined the cathedral, and killed most of the Franks or led them off into captivity,[70] leaving the city empty and desolate. Walter had escaped to Tyre, where he helped Conrad of Montferrat to salvage the remnants of the kingdom and hold on until the arrival of the Third Crusade. He died during the siege of Acre, leaving no male heirs.[71]

The fall of Acre in July 1191 led Saladin to raze and abandon Caesarea and other Palestinian towns which he felt unable to garrison adequately.[72] The Frankish army under Richard Coeur-de-Lion entered Caesarea on August 31,[73] and received supplies from the fleet, by barge. Ambroise says "the foe . . . had laid the city low, and fiercely battered it . . . while they pillaged, spoiled, and plundered" before they "fled incontinent."[74] Richard of London is more matter-of-fact: "The Turks had . . . broken down part of the towers and walls, and had destroyed the city as much as possible; but on the approach of our army they fled."[75] After a day's rest, the Franks marched south toward Arsuf and their victory of September 7. Richard then refortified Jaffa and two outlying forts,[76] while Saladin demolished Ascalon. During the desultory fighting and negotiating of the next few months, Caesarea remained empty and shattered. The Franks passed through it often during the skirmishing of 1192,[77] but apparently never sought to garrison and hold it, or to repair its fortifications.

Caesarea was included among the lands allotted to the Franks by the truce between Saladin and Richard, concluded late in August of 1192, but accounts differ sharply on details. One group of chroniclers[78] says that the crusaders and local barons on July 28, 1191, had granted Caesarea and Jaffa to Geoffrey of Lusignan, and that after refortifying them in September 1192 Richard delivered them to Geoffrey. This definitely errs in coupling Caesarea rather than Ascalon with Jaffa, probably because Ascalon was never recaptured; it is certain that Caesarea was neither refortified by Richard nor delivered to Geoffrey.

A second group of manuscripts[79] asserts that Saladin, after concluding peace, sympathized with certain landless nobles, including the lord of Caesarea, and generously restored their former fiefs to them. This tale is equally suspect, even aside from the odd behavior ascribed to the sultan in thus tossing away strongholds essential to his lifelong counter-Crusade. For one thing, Walter II's heir was not a "lord," but the lady Juliana, his sister;[80] for another, a fief cannot be "restored" to one who never ruled it. But the principal flaw is the fact that Caesarea and the other cities in question —Haifa, Arsuf, and Jaffa—were, though battered, actually in Frankish hands, a situation which the treaty merely confirmed, and thus were not Saladin's to bestow.

The third group,[81] though undramatic, is accurate; they simply state that Caesarea and the other cities held by the Franks were covered by the truce.

Juliana now presumably took over her fief, and archbishop Aymar "the monk" recovered his cathedral, but there is no evidence that he purified and reconsecrated it, or that she and her husband restored the walls, or even that any of them—or any other Franks—took up residence in the shattered, defenseless town. Its history is a blank between the Third Crusade's end in 1192 and the preliminaries to the Fifth Crusade a quarter-century later; until then it lay empty and abandoned.

In December 1217, while awaiting the main body of crusaders, John of Brienne, king of Jerusalem, with duke Leopold of Austria and the Knights Hospitaller, began refortifying Caesarea, while the Templars and Teutonic Knights build a fortress at Athlit, by Destroit at the northern edge of the fief. "At Caesarea the work of reconstruction was quickly completed with little interference from the Moslems, although their approach was several times reported. On February 2, 1218, the patriarch of Jerusalem, assisted by six bishops, celebrated mass in the church of St. Peter within the newly fortified city."[82] One of the bishops, Otto of Münster, died at Caesarea a few weeks later.[83] The crusaders returned to Acre at Easter, leaving garrisons at Caesarea and the new Templar stronghold of Château Pèlerin; in May they sailed to Egypt and laid siege to Damietta.

The fall of Damietta on November 5, 1219, prompted the Aiyūbid ruler of Syria, Al-Mu'azzam, brother of the Egyptian sultan al-Kāmil, to withdraw from the Delta to his own province, where he unexpectedly attacked the newly fortified but lightly garrisoned Caesarea.[84] Allegedly king John had refused to deliver the city to its lord, Walter III, until he was reimbursed for his outlay on its fortifications, but Walter was with the crusaders at Damietta and unable to repay his miserly sovereign or to defend his heritage. His Genoese friends offered to garrison and defend Caesarea if king John ceded it to them, which the baillie Warner the German agreed to on behalf of the absent king; they moved in with ample supplies and arms, sending away the royal garrison. After four days of repulsing the besieging Saracens, however, the Genoese under cover of night slipped away by sea to Acre, and Al-Mu'azzam occupied the city unopposed, razed its new walls, and left it as desolate as his uncle Saladin had, a generation earlier.[85]

The geographer Yāqūt describes Caesarea in 1225: "It used to be one of the chief cities, very superior, with good soil, abounding in goods and in inhabitants. But now, it is no longer thus; it appears more like a village than a city."[86]

Late in 1227 a new group of crusaders, Germans under duke Henry of Limburg, decided that the most useful way of occupying themselves while awaiting emperor Frederick II would be to refortify Caesarea and Jaffa, to protect the beleaguered remnant of the kingdom against attacks from Aiyūbid Egypt. Work began at Caesarea in May 1228, and was still in progress when Frederick arrived at Acre in September.[87] By the Treaty of Jaffa, ratified by Frederick and sultan al-Kāmil on February 18, 1229, the latter recognized Frankish possession of several cities, including Caesarea, and even conceded that it might be refortified without violating the truce.[88] Walter III thus finally acquired peaceful possession of his fief, only to die four months later at Nicosia fighting Frederick's venial baillies.[89]

For forty-odd years, from July 1187 to May 1228, Caesarea had been either under attack, or in Moslem hands, or abandoned. Its resurrection as a Frankish stronghold led to a second period of peace and prosperity, less durable and less brilliant than the 1101-1187 phase, but by no means negligible. Neither the "young lord" John nor the old archbishop Peter limited his energies to local affairs, but death soon ended their stormy careers, and their successors were content to try to strengthen Caesarea militarily and financially. The Knights Hospitaller, like the other military orders, increased their holdings in both the city and the surrounding fief, and even enrolled lady Margaret and her husband, John l'Aleman, among their lay adherents.

In 1250 king Louis IX of France arrived in Palestine to salvage what he could from his wrecked Crusade. After restoring Acre he spent a full year strengthening the fortifications of Caesarea, moving on to Jaffa in the spring of 1252; it is thus his final work on the citadel, walls, and sixteen towers of which remnants still survive.[90] All those who shared the labor received a papal pardon; Louis worked on the walls in person to earn this reward.[91]

The increased danger to the kingdom which inspired this burst of activity stemmed from the overthrow in 1250 of the relatively passive Aiyūbids by the aggressive Mamluks. For a few years their internal power struggle blunted the threat, and then they had to contend with invading Mongols, but their decisive victory at 'Ain Jālūt in September 1260 freed them to deal with the Franks. Baybars murdered his predecessor Kutuz and seized the throne in October 1260, determined to punish the Franks for having aided the Mongols.[92]

During the summer of 1264 Mamluk raiders "plundered, killed, and took prisoners" in the territory around Caesarea and Château Pèlerin, and Baybars threatened outright war unless the Franks returned spoils which he asserted were captured during a truce. When they sent the "vizier" (viscount?) of Caesarea to negotiate, he was seized as a hostage, and released only after the disputed goods were delivered to the Mamluk emir.[93] It was now clearly only a matter of-time, and the sultan did not keep the Franks in suspense long.

On February 27, 1265,[94] Baybars appeared before the walls of Caesarea in command of the main Mamluk army, with full siege equipment secretly prepared while he ostensibly hunted near Arsuf. The garrison manned the walls, but the Mamluks brought up mangonels, cleared portions of the walls and swarmed over them, burned the gates, and forced an entrance; the defenders retired to the "impregnable" citadel, situated on a rocky promontory cut off from the mainland by a deep cleft, and constructed of Roman columns laid crosswise to prevent mining. For six days, while the sultan directed operations from the cathedral tower, the garrison sustained powerful attacks by siege engines, Greek fire, and infantry, but on March 5 offered to surrender in return for their lives. Baybars accepted these terms, and permitted the Franks to leave Caesarea for what proved to be the last time; most of them went by sea to Acre. Then the sultan personally joined his men in demolishing the fortifications for two weeks, during which a detachment took and destroyed Haifa; on March 19 he left for Arsuf, which fell late in April after a determined resistance.

For twenty-six years Baybars and his successors chipped away at the remaining Frankish territories. At Caesarea on May 22, 1272, Baybars and the Franks, urged on by Edward of England, signed a truce for ten-odd years.[95] In June 1283 another truce identified the town of Caesarea as Moslem property, though the Hospitallers retained portions of the surrounding fief.[96] But about 1280 Burchard of Mount Sion had said of it, "Caesarea, the metropolis of Palestine, which once was an archbishop's see . . . has a strong position, but at this day is altogether ruined."[97]

The ruin was completed in 1291 by sultan al-Ashraf Khalīl, who, after taking Acre on May 18 and the rest of the Frankish strongholds by August 14, "ordered the systematic destruction of every castle on the coast, so that the Franks might never again establish a foothold in Outremer."[98] Abū-l-Fidā' in 1321,[99] Ludolph of Sudheim about 1350,[100] and John Poloner about 1422[101] testify to the completeness of this destruction at Caesarea.

2. The Latin archbishops of Caesarea 1101-1265

1101	— 1108	Baldwin (I)	
1108	— 1129	Evremar of Chocques	(patriarch 1102-1107)
1129	— 1141/2	Gaudens	
1141/2	— 1156/7	Baldwin (II)	
1157	— 1175	Hernes	
1175	— 1180	Heraclius	(patriarch 1180-1191)
1180	— 1194	Aymar dei Corbizzi	(patriarch 1194-1202)
1194/5	— 1198/9	Bartholomew (?)	
1199	— 1237	Peter of Limoges	
1237	— 1243/4	Bertrand	
1244	— 1255/6	Joscelin	
1255/6	— 1265	Lociaumes	(titular 1265-1267)

One of the first acts of the Franks and their Genoese allies, after capturing and sacking Caesarea in May 1101, was to restore its ecclesiastical status as a metropolitan see. After the ritual purification and reconsecration of the cathedral of Saint Peter and the church of Saint Lawrence, the Frankish and Genoese clergy present convened to elect an archbishop.[102]

For the first Latin archbishop of Caesarea, the allies' choice fell upon Baldwin, abbot of the monastery of St. Mary in the valley of Jehoshaphat. According to Guibert of Nogent,[103] Baldwin had accompanied Godfrey of Bouillon on the First Crusade, highly venerated for his piety and for a cross-shaped brand on his forehead, which he attributed to an angel seen in a vision. During the desperate crisis at Antioch, however, the papal legate had ordered a fast and a general confession by all crusaders, at which Baldwin's conscience had forced him to admit that his claim was fraudulent and his brand self-inflicted. While this had naturally lowered the esteem of the pious for the erring priest, apparently his repentance and efforts as abbot redeemed his reputation; his elevation to the archbishopric was presumably based on merit and general regard.

Baldwin's archiepiscopate has left few documentary traces, compared to his successors'. He participated—as both accuser and judge—in the council which in October 1102 wisely removed Daimbert from the patriarchate and elected Evremar of Chocques to replace him.[104] His last appearance is early in 1108, as witness to a grant by king Baldwin I to the abbey at Jehoshaphat;[105] he must have died very shortly thereafter, as the see was definitely vacant that spring.[106]

Evremar of Chocques, who had succeeded Daimbert as patriarch of Jerusalem in October 1102, was himself removed from this post in December 1107 by pope Paschal II.[107] He spent several weeks trying to regain the patriarchate, but upon the election of Gibelin of Sabran, papal legate and archbishop of Arles, Evremar accepted the vacant see of Caesarea, and served there loyally for over twenty years. He is described by contemporary chroniclers[108] as a pious and worthy man, simple and straightforward. He was certainly remarkable for his bravery: as patriarch he had carried the True Cross at the battle of Ramla in August 1105,[109] as archbishop he carried it at the battle of Danith in August 1119, unarmed, wearing vestments, and cursing the "infidels" from the midst of the fray.[110] He was also a man of peace: it was he who calmed king Baldwin I's righteous but murderous fury at the Genoese and Pisans when, at the fall of Acre in May 1104, they violated the surrender terms by slaying the departing garrison and stealing their belongings.[111] Evremar's name appears on a considerable number of documents from both his patriarchate[112] and his lengthy archiepiscopate,[113] through to 1129, the year of his death.

Relatively little is known of his successor, Gaudens. He is named, as archbishop-elect, on a document of October 1129,[114] while another document of that year[115] terms an unnamed archbishop-elect "formerly chancellor," so it appears that Gaudens, like some of his successors, rose to the archiepiscopate through the ecclesiastical bureaucracy. As archbishop, he appears as a witness on several documents dated between 1130 and 1138,[116] while William of Tyre names him as a participant in a synod held at Antioch late in 1139.[117] He presumably died in 1141 or 1142, as his successor appears in the latter year.

The archbishop elected in 1141 or 1142 was the second to bear the name Baldwin, and the second to be raised from the patriarchal chancellorship. His personality and accomplishments remain as obscure as those of Gaudens, but he participated in more stirring events, including both the great council at Acre in June 1148 and the siege of Ascalon in January 1153.[118] In the spring of 1155 he traveled with other prelates to Rome in a dispute with the Hospitallers;[119] his death, in Palestine, probably occurred early in 1157, though 1156 is also possible.[120]

The third successive elevation of a patriarchal chancellor to the archbishopric of Caesarea occurred in 1157 with the election of Hernes, nephew of the late patriarch William of Messines (1130-1147).[121] He first appears in his new capacity after the death in November 1157 of patriarch Fulcher of Angoulême, when he joined bishop Ralph of Bethlehem in unsuccessfully opposing the election of Amalric of Nesle.[122] After pope Hadrian IV confirmed Amalric as patriarch, however, Hernes seems to have served under him amicably. Documents bearing his name as archbishop date only from 1160 to about 1171,[123] but he lived until June or July of 1175.[124]

In 1165 king Amalric sent Hernes and Odo of St. Amand to Constantinople to obtain a Byzantine princess as his bride; two years later they brought Maria Comnena to Tyre, where the king married her in August 1167.[125] Again in 1169 Hernes was chosen to accompany patriarch Amalric and bishop William of Acre on a tour of the European courts to urge a new crusading effort, but their ship was so battered by storms that they were thankful to regain the Syrian coast alive, and archbishop Frederick of Tyre was sent in their place.[126]

At Hernes' death in 1175, the vacant see was filled, under strong pressure from queen Agnes,[127] with the handsome, unprincipled archdeacon of Jerusalem, Heraclius. His last appearance as archdeacon was in August,[128] so his elevation probably occurred in the autumn. Heraclius' further elevation to the patriarchate—in competition with the historian archbishop William of Tyre, with the queen-mother's influence again preponderant—took place in October 1180,[129] so his tenure at Caesarea lasted just five years, interrupted by a trip to Rome in October 1178[130] for the third Lateran Council (March 1179), but otherwise uneventful.[131] His subsequent misdeeds as patriarch need not concern us; he died in 1191 during the siege of Acre.

To fill the vacancy caused by Heraclius' elevation in October 1180, still another patriarchal chancellor was elected archbishop of Caesarea, a Florentine named Aymar dei Corbizzi, known as "the monk" (Monachus).[132] He is termed "electus" by William of Tyre[133] in 1181, but must have been confirmed shortly thereafter. During his archiepiscopacy Saladin overran Palestine, capturing and destroying Caesarea, among other Frankish cities. Aymar survived this catastrophe, joining Conrad of Montferrat and the remaining handful of leaders at Tyre and actively helping to salvage what was left of the shattered kingdom. Caesarea was regained during the Third Crusade, but no evidence remains as to whether he returned to his see and repurified his desecrated cathedral. He was elected patriarch of Jerusalem (now *in partibus infidelium*) in April 1194, over the violent protests of the ruler, Henry of Champagne,[134] and died in October 1202.

There is room for doubt concerning the name and dates of Aymar's successor at Caesarea. It is reasonable to assume that Peter's lengthy tenure commenced late in 1199, but it is unlikely that the see was left vacant long after 1194; indeed, there is specific mention of an unnamed archbishop of Caesarea in an August 1196 letter of pope Celestine III[135] and in a list of those present at the ceremonial foundation of the military order of the Teutonic Knights in March 1198.[136] In Röhricht's note to this document he gives the archbishop's name as "Bartholomaeus," without indicating his source; in view of his customary reliability we may tentatively designate this archbishop as "Bartholomew (?) 1194/5-1198/9."

We are back on firmly documented ground with Peter of Limoges.

Though we do not know his previous rank, he does not seem to have been either a patriarchal chancellor or an archdeacon of Jerusalem. He appears as archbishop in 1199,[137] but his "vidimus" on other documents of the same year[138] indicates that his elevation did not occur until September or later. In April 1200 he was ordered by pope Innocent III to settle a quarrel between the clergy of Tyre and the Venetians,[139] and early in 1204 he joined other clerics in reporting to the pope on the war between Antioch and Armenia.[140]

In May 1205 Peter wrote[141] (to the archbishop of Rouen?) advising the French of king Aimery's death and the sad state of the shrunken kingdom; in October 1210 he attended the coronation of John of Brienne at Acre.[142] In January 1213 pope Innocent III instructed Peter to supervise a Cypriot election,[143] and in February 1215 advised him how to handle a marriage problem.[144] The next pope, Honorius III, wrote Peter and his colleagues in August 1216 concerning Venetian holdings in Tyre.[145]

In October 1217 Peter participated in the council at Acre[146] which preceded the Fifth Crusade. During that campaign Caesarea was again lost and sacked, an occurrence which doubtless led him to join in an appeal for assistance, written at Acre in October 1220;[147] a few months later Peter was with the crusaders at Damietta,[148] though we do not know whether he was among those captured with the king.

After the Crusade had collapsed and he had returned to his devastated see, Peter in January 1222 was among those ordered by pope Honorius III to compel subjection of the Greek and Eastern churches to Latin authority.[149] Four years later the same pope ordered him to help enforce the excommunication of Bohemond IV, prince of Antioch and count of Tripoli.[150] In October 1227 Peter joined in a letter to pope Gregory IX on the problems of Outremer.[151] Thus for nearly thirty years he had actively served three popes against Saracens, Greek schismatics, Eastern separated churches, and Frankish excommunicates, but the apex of his militant career lay just ahead.

In September 1228 Peter was among the leaders who met the excommunicated emperor Frederick II on his arrival at Acre;[152] in March 1229, on the orders of the patriarch Gerald of Lausanne, he hastened to newly recovered Jerusalem and, finding himself one day too late to prevent Frederick's coronation, placed the holy city under interdict.[153] After the repercussions of this act, which led Frederick to quit Syria without refortifying Jerusalem, Peter became less active in politics, appearing principally as a witness, an arbiter, or a benefactor on documents from 1229 through 1235.[154]

When he did take an active part, as he did in 1232 when a group of neutral leaders tried to make peace between the Ibelin faction and the imperial agent Richard Filanger, it was always as the loyal supporter of the patriarch Gerald. It is not surprising, therefore, that when in 1235 the egregious papal legate, archbishop Theodoric of Ravenna, bungled his peacemaking and compounded his errors by placing the staunchly Guelf commune of Acre under interdict, Peter should have been excommunicated in company with Gerald. Our sole information on this harsh punishment of so venerable and loyal a churchman comes from the hasty absolution extended by pope Gregory IX in April 1236 to an unnamed archbishop of Caesarea.[155] It is clear that Peter rather than his successor was the victim of Theodoric's choler, for he appears once more, as a witness,[156] before his death, which must have occurred early in 1237.[157]

In contrast to the omnipresent and controversial Peter of Limoges, his successor Bertrand had a relatively brief and uneventful archiepiscopacy. He figures in several papal letters of 1237 and 1238,[158] but unimportantly and anonymously. His name appears only once, as a witness in 1239;[159] the chroniclers do not even mention him, unless it was he, rather than Peter, who, some time between 1229 and 1244, as a good friend of the Templars, advised them on a delicate problem of simony.[160] He may be presumed to have died in 1243 or 1244, when his successor first appears as archbishop-elect.

This archbishop is almost as obscure as Bertrand, though not quite as inactive. His name was Joscelin, but his origin and previous rank are unknown. He appears to have been elected in 1244,[161] but not immediately confirmed, as papal correspondence in 1246 and 1247 still refers to him, anonymously as usual, as "electus."[162] In papal letters of 1253 he is no longer "electus," though still anonymous;[163] it is not until 1254 that he appears by name among the signers of a letter to king Henry III of England.[164] In 1255 he appended his "vidimus" to several ancient documents,[165] joined in adjudicating a dispute, and approved an important grant to the Hospital.[166] Nothing further is heard of Joscelin, and it is reasonable to assume that he died in the second half of 1255 or some time in 1256.

The last Latin archbishop of Caesarea before the definitive Moslem conquest bore the unusual name of Lociaumes; again, his origin and previous rank are unknown. He was, presumably, the anonymous archbishop who was ordered by pope Alexander IV to settle a dispute in October 1259,[167] who joined in a desperate appeal to Charles of Anjou in April 1260,[168] and who participated in adjudication affecting the Italian merchants in January 1261.[169] He survived the Mamluk conquest of Caesarea in 1265, but not for long, dying in January 1267.[170]

With the fall of Caesarea and Lociaumes' death ends the list of Latin archbishops who actually held that see, but the archiepiscopal title *in partibus infidelium* persisted. In 1277 and 1280, while there still might be a faint hope of recovering Caesarea and other lost portions of Outremer, an archbishop Matthew appears at Acre and Nicosia respectively.[171] Later titular archbishops fall outside our scope; lists may be found in Eubel[172] and in Janin.[173]

3. The Frankish lords and ladies of Caesarea 1101-1265[174]

1101	— 1105/10	king Baldwin I	
1105/10	— 1123	Eustace Granier	wife: Emma
1123	— 1149/54	Walter (I)	wife: Juliana

1149/54 — 1168/74	Hugh	wife: Isabel/Elizabeth Gothmann
1168/74 — 1176/82	Guy	wife: ?
1176/82 — 1189/91	Walter (II)	wife: ?
1189/91 — 1213/6	Juliana	husbands: Guy of Beirut,
		Aymar of Lairon
1213/6 — 1229	Walter (III)	wife: Margaret of Ibelin
1229 — 1238/41	John	wife: Alice of Montaigu
1238/41 — 1264/5	Margaret	husband: John l'Aleman

Great haste was displayed by the victorious crusaders, in May 1101, in providing a Latin archbishop for Caesarea; there would seem to have been at least equal urgency in providing a feudal lord responsible for its defense and rehabilitation, but this step was postponed. King Baldwin I appointed, as commander of the tiny garrison he could spare, Harpin, viscount of Bourges,[175] but there is no indication whatever that this was intended to be permanent, to say nothing of hereditary. A late vague mention of a knight from Horn as commanding at Caesarea[176] must refer to the mid-thirteenth century rather than 1101.

There is little doubt that the first Frankish lord of Caesarea was Eustace Granier, or Garnier,[177] like archbishop Evremar a crusader from the diocese of Thérouannes, where king Baldwin I and his brother Godfrey had also been born.[178] As LaMonte points out,[179] Eustace is first found as lord of Caesarea in [1109 or] 1110,[180] is "among the important barons on an act of the king's" in 1108,[181] and was in Palestine by 1105;[182] his cautious conclusion that the fief was granted "probably between 1105 . . . and 1110," and more specifically by 1108 or "very shortly thereafter" is unexceptionable. There is no apparent basis for the assertion by Delaville le Roulx[183] that he received Caesarea in 1101, or even for Krey's statement[184] that he was prominent from 1102 on, though his conclusion that Eustace may have accompanied Godfrey on the First Crusade is a reasonable guess (it seems just as likely that he accompanied Baldwin, who as king was to enfeoff him).

Nothing is know of Eustace's background; he was obviously a knight but not a member of even the lower nobility prior to receiving Caesarea, but his ability and character led him to the upper ranks of the Outremer barons. Following the Frankish conquest of Sidon in December 1110, Baldwin I granted it too to Eustace in hereditary right, "and throughout his lifetime the two fiefs were part of a single seigneury."[185] Eustace participated in Baldwin's military adventures and in the administration of the kingdom, culminating in his selection as constable and baillie (regent) between Baldwin II's capture on April 18, 1123, and Eustace's death on June 15 of that year, probably from wounds sustained during his successful defense of the kingdom against a strong Egyptian attack at Ramla on May 29. Although he is occasionally termed "count,"[186] or even "prince,"[187] he apparently was entitled only to be called "lord" (dominus; seigneur or sire) of, first, Caesarea and then both Caesarea and Sidon, and he did not use even this title on his documents.[188]

Eustace's marriage presents certain difficulties not explored by LaMonte. His wife, called Emelota by William of Tyre[189] and Aliennor[190] or Ameloz[191] by his Old French translator (Bernard of Corbie?), appears regularly on documents as Emma.[192] She is identified by William as the niece of patriarch Arnulf of Chocques, who is said to have given as her dowry the city of Jericho, a property of the church later worth 5000 bezants a year.[193] Although David is perhaps correct in stating that this identification "appears to rest upon the sole authority of William of Tyre,"[194] this in itself would not invalidate his testimony; much of our knowledge of twelfth-century events in the crusader states rests securely "upon the sole authority" of the admirable archbishop. LaMonte, like Röhricht,[195] accepts William's account here, as elsewhere, without demur.

In the present instance, however, skepticism is warranted on chronological grounds. Arnulf did not become patriarch until April 1112, and would not earlier have been in a position to confer so munificent—though tainted by his lacking title to it—a dowry, even on a favorite niece. We may dismiss the possibility of his having done so during his brief uncanonical "patriarchate" in 1099 (August-December), both because he was in too shaky a position to risk such a misdemeanor and because the then landless Eustace would not have been accorded so grand a dowry. In fact, Jericho never once appears in any documentary association with Eustace, Emma, or their descendants,[196] which alone would justify skepticism.

If Eustace had married Emma after April 1112, his twin sons by her could not legitimately have been more than 10½ years old at his death in June 1123, when they became lords of Sidon and Caesarea respectively. They would still have been under 19 in September 1131, by which time Eustace II "seems to have died, leaving his fief to his minor son Girard under the guardianship of" his uncle Walter I of Caesarea, but Girard's minority "ended sometime before 1135."[197] Since no boy born in 1113 or later could have had a son who attained his majority by 1135 (or 1145), we may reject as impossible any dating of Emma's marriage to Eustace as after April 1112; therefore it occurred in France, or in Syria while Arnulf was an archdeacon unable to give away church property, and the whole Jericho fable collapses, confirming the documentary argument *ab silentio*.

Whether Emma was actually Arnulf's niece cannot safely be hazarded.[198] After Eustace's death she married Hugh II of Le Puiset, count of Jaffa,[199] and last appears alive in 1133; she may have died, gone into exile with Hugh, lapsed into obscurity after his treason and banishment, or remarried after his death.

Meanwhile Emma's twin sons had come into their inheritances. Walter "does not actually appear on any document with the title of Caesarea until March 1128," but I, like LaMonte, "am inclined to believe that both boys entered into the possession of their fiefs in 1123 . . . ."[200] He is on firm ground, too, in deducing from the September 1131 document[201] in which, uniquely, Walter uses "the title lord of Caesarea and Sidon" that Eustace II had "died, leaving his fief to his minor son Girard," for whom Walter "acted as regent . . . during his minority which ended sometime before [December] 1135," when Walter "signs only as lord of Caesarea."[202]

His first important public act was an accusation of attempted regicide hurled against his stepfather, Hugh, in 1132, backed up by a challenge to trial by combat; Hugh's treason, exile, and death in Italy followed. At the time of the challenge Walter was described as "in the full vigor of life, of fine appearance and famous for his strength."[203] He never became a close associate of king Fulk or Baldwin III.[204] He "was one of the barons who participated in the council of Acre in 1148 which directed the Second Crusade to the siege of Damascus and presumably took part in that unfortunate enterprise, though we have no account of his exploits on that campaign."[205] LaMonte notes two sales of property to the Hospital, and deduces that Walter had "financial difficulties which necessitated the alienation of portions of his property . . . to pay off his debts and to liberate from imprisonment in Acre his vassals who had often been held captive as security for his indebtedness."[206]

Walter "last appears . . . in 1149. He died sometime before [July] 1154, when his heir Hugh was in possession of the seigneury."[207] His wife Juliana "is known only from her appearance with her husband on the charter of September 1131."[208]

Their son Eustace "appears with his father on an act of 1149 . . . . He must thus have been older than his brother Hugh who does not appear on that act, but he does not seem ever to have held the seigneury of Caesarea . . . he must have contracted leprosy . . . for . . . his brother Hugh, lord of Caesarea in 1160, . . . grants certain houses and lands to the monastery" of St. Lazarus "for love of his brother" Eustace, "who was a brother in that house. As Hugh had been lord of Caesarea since 1154, and as the brethren" of St. Lazarus "were, at this time, almost exclusively lepers themselves, we may conclude that [Eustace] became infected some time between 1149 and 1154 and entered the order."[209] There is no way of ascertaining when, between those dates, Walter died and Hugh inherited, or even whether Eustace held power for a brief interval between his father and his brother.

Hugh "first appears as lord of Caesarea on an act of 1154. Unlike his father, he seems to have attached himself at once to the royal household, and his appearances as witness of royal documents are as frequent as his father's were rare."[210] He accompanied both Baldwin III and his successor Amalric on military campaigns, and served the latter as ambassador "in his negotiations with the caliph of Egypt in 1167. It was on this occasion that Hugh so shocked the oriental sense of propriety by insisting that the caliph shake hands with his hand ungloved, when he ratified the treaty . . . , a presumption that caused a furor in . . . the Fatimid court."[211] Later in 1167 he was captured by Saladin's uncle Shīrkūh, but was soon released after helping to negotiate an equitable treaty.[212]

Hugh's name appears on several documents[213] between 1154 and 1166, including some sales to the Hospital, but he does not seem to have been in financial straits. Unlike his father, he gave property away, to his brother's order, to the Hospital, and to the church where his father and grandfather were buried.

Hugh's wife joined in several of these acts[214] between 1160 and 1166; she also appears in 1175 as the wife of Baldwin of Ibelin, lord of Ramla,[215] and posthumously in 1207.[216] It is uncertain whether her given name was Isabel or Elizabeth, but she was definitely the daughter of John Gothmann.[217] Their known children are Guy, Walter, and Juliana, each of whom in turn succeeded to the fief.

At some time between Hugh's last appearance in May 1168 and July 1174 he died and was succeeded by his son Guy, who "is known only by his appearance on two charters."[218] We cannot say whether he ever married, but he seems to have died childless, as his brother Walter succeeded him between 1176 and 1182.

Walter II, after his "appearance in 1174 with his brother Guy . . . next appears, with the title lord of Caesarea, on an act of 1182."[219] LaMonte summarizes his brief career: "In the stormy politics of the reign of Baldwin IV," he, like his step-father Baldwin of Ramla, "allied himself with the party of the barons and Raymond of Tripoli against the court party headed by Guy" of Lusignan. Walter "is mentioned by William of Tyre as one of the barons in the army which went out to meet Saladin in 1183 near Bethsan, but refused to fight under the command of Guy . . . . Of his role in the disastrous battle of Hattin we are in ignorance," though he and his knights were there; after it "he was one of the barons who . . . drew up a treaty with the Genoese to secure help in defending Tyre in July 1187."[220] He aligned himself with Conrad of Montferrat and "became one of his staunch partisans, witnessing and approving five of his acts and treaties between October 1187 and May 1188."[221] Walter II "was killed at some time during the siege of Acre which lasted from July 1189 to July 12, 1191, but it is impossible to state at what precise date."[222]

There is, of course, no truth whatever in the scurrilous legend found in the anonymous mid-thirteenth-century *Chronique de Rains*[223] to the effect that an unnamed "marquis" of Caesarea was too miserly to pay his troops, and consequently lost the ill-defended city to Saladin, who thereupon melted down the hoarded gold and silver and poured it down the scoundrel's throat!

As with Guy, so with Walter, we cannot say whether he ever married; he was certainly unmarried in 1182, as no wife's consent appears on his act. "He evidently left no heirs of his body as the fief escheated to his sister. The heritage . . . was, however, sadly diminished as Saladin had overrun the country, and Caesarea and its dependencies had been reduced and occupied by the Moslems in 1187."[224]

When, between July 1189 and July 1191, Juliana became titular lady of

Caesarea, it was in Saladin's possession; before evacuating it after the fall of Acre he had its walls destroyed. They were not rebuilt until 1218, after her death, so she never had secure possession of her fief.

Her first husband was Guy of Beirut, who, like his namesake brother-in-law, "is known only through his appearance on two charters"[225]—one dated October 1179 and witnessed by Walter of Beirut and his brother Guy, the other a charter of Walter II of Caesarea in 1182 to which Juliana and her husband Guy of Beirut consented. "Guy never appears with the title lord of Caesarea, and there can be no assurance that he ever held this title, though he may have done so," says LaMonte,[226] who lists the children of Guy and Juliana as Walter (III), "Bernard, who died without issue," Isabel, who married Reginald of Haifa, and Bertha, who married Reginald of Soissons.[227]

Juliana's second husband was more active than her first in all respects except the procreative—they seem to have had only a single son, named Roger.[228] Aymar of Lairon presumably came to Palestine with Philip II of France on the Third Crusade and remained to become "one of the leading barons of the kingdom, . . . in 1206 acquiring the position of the marshal of the kingdom."[229] He appears as lord of Caesarea from January 1193 through October 1213, often with Juliana and her son Walter, who was already an adult[230] and an active participant in the affairs of the kingdom.

In 1208 Aymar "was one of the barons sent by the High Court to France to secure a husband" for princess Mary, and he was present at the coronation of the chosen bridegroom, John of Brienne, at Tyre in 1210.[231] Juliana and he made liberal grants to both the Teutonic Knights and the Hospital (from which they also borrowed large sums), and she "became a con-soror of the order with rights of burial in the cemetery of the Hospital."[232]

Juliana must have died between October 1213 and February 1216, for in the latter month Aymar appears not as lord of Caesarea but as marshal of the Hospital, which he presumably joined at her death.[233] It was clearly he who was the marshal killed at Damietta in August 1219,[234] for his namesake Aymar is then referred to as nephew of "Aymar de Layron, qui avait esté sires de Cesaire."[235]

Walter III inherited the lordship of Caesarea from his mother between October 1213 and February 1216, as we have seen. By 1216 LaMonte calculates that he "must have been around forty," unusually mature for an heir in Outremer. He had not wasted the intervening years, but had "attached himself to the royal court . . . . In 1206 [error for 1210] he appears with the title of constable of Cyprus, a title which he retained for the rest of his life and . . . regularly employed in witnessing charters."[236] He was active in the Fifth Crusade, "as constable of Cyprus, commanding a company of one hundred knights."[237] It was during his absence in Egypt that Caesarea was sacked by al-Mu'azzam.

Meanwhile Walter had married Margaret of Ibelin, "the sister of John and Philip and widow of Hugh of Tiberias," and had become "one of the most loyal supporters of the Ibelins in the struggle which developed between them and the baillies of Frederick II."[238] He was with John of Ibelin "at the fateful banquet at Limassol when Frederick demanded that John surrender the bailliage of the kingdom [of Cyprus]. When a truce had been arranged between the emperor and John, [Walter] accompanied them to Syria."[239] Although Walter III "profited from Frederick's crusade by the return[240] and rebuilding of his city of Caesarea under the terms of the treaty of Jaffa . . . , he loyally supported the Ibelins when war broke out . . . , and it was in the battle of Nicosia on June 24, 1229 that he lost his life fighting for his brother-in-law" against Frederick's baillies.[241]

By his marriage to Margaret of Ibelin, Walter had one son—John, who succeeded him—and four daughters—Isabel, Alice, Femie, and Helvis (or Heloise). LaMonte deduces that, first, Isabel and then, after her death (at 22) and by special dispensation, Alice were wives of James of La Mandelée; Femie married John of Gibelet (Jubail) and Helvis became a nun.[242]

Although John, called "the young lord of Caesarea" in contrast to his father "the old lord," inherited a newly refortified city whose strengthening might have been considered his primary task, he saw his duty otherwise, and mortgaged his inheritance to secure funds for the Ibelin cause. "He is first encountered as a young page, serving before the emperor at the great banquet at Limassol where Frederick began the trouble by demanding that John [of Ibelin] surrender the bailliage of Cyprus and his city of Beirut. So indignant did young John become . . . that . . . he plotted how to murder Frederick, and was only restrained by the wiser counsel of the lord of Beirut who scorned such violence."[243]

"After the death of his father at the battle of Nicosia, young John stepped in as one of the most trusted of the leaders on the Ibelin side," fighting, raising troops and money, persuading the barons to reject the credentials of Frederick's baillie in 1231, and organizing the pro-Ibelin commune of Acre in 1232. After John of Ibelin "had been received as head of the commune, John of Caesarea remained as his representative in Syria while the lord of Beirut returned to *Cyprus*."[244] Thus, while still in his early twenties, he was second in importance, among the barons of the constricted kingdom of Jerusalem, only to his uncle and perhaps to the constable Odo of Montbéliard. For his intransigent loyalty to the baronial cause, he "was officially declared forfeit of his fiefs by the bailli[e] of the kingdom, Balian of Sidon, in 1231, but the forfeiture remained ineffective, since John was in possession of his lands and able to sell some of them to raise more money."[245]

He joined his uncle and the Hospitallers in besieging Montferrand (Ba'rīn) in 1236, shortly before his uncle's death.[246] In October 1238 he was one of the barons who negotiated with the crusading king of Navarre, Theobald IV of Champagne.[247] LaMonte suggests that John "may have perished during this campaign for he never appears after this on any charters;"[248] but he was probably still alive in April 1239,[249] though definitely dead by 1241.[250]

John of Caesarea married Alice of Montaigu, niece of three distinguished brothers: Eustorgue, archbishop of Nicosia, Garin, master of the Hospital, and Peter, master of the Temple. LaMonte believes that John and Alice "had one son who died a child, and five daughters:" Margaret, Alice, Mary, Isabel, and "Peretine;"[251] I interpret the same account as listing a son Peretin and only four daughters.[252]

In the absence of a surviving son, John's eldest daughter Margaret inherited Caesarea between October 1238 and 1241, though she does not appear on any documents before April 1249.[253] LaMonte is "inclined to believe that John [l']Aleman was already lord of Caesarea, through his wife, in 1243, and that it was to him that [John of] Ibelin referred when he said that his cousin the lord of Caesarea was present at the meeting of the [High] Court which gave the regency of Jerusalem to Alice of Cyprus;"[254] I see no reason to doubt that they were married during John of Caesarea's lifetime, and that their joint tenure dates from his death.

John l'Aleman was a son of Warner of Egisheim (in Alsace), called "the German" (Garnier l'Aleman), twice baillie of the kingdom, and of his wife Pavia of Gibelet; by John's generation the appellation had become a heritable patronym, leading Rey and others to confuse this family with a wholly distinct l'Aleman family from Provence.[255] "Although not one of the most prominent barons of the kingdom, . . . John was active in the political and military life of the realm. In 1254 he was one of a group of barons who wrote to Henry III of England asking for succor for the Holy Land after the departure" of Louis IX of France, and in 1257 he is among those approving a treaty with Ancona.[256] "This act of 1257 is the last on which John actually appears; but," LaMonte adds without logical justification, "that he was still living in 1264 is attested by the fact that his son Hugh who was thrown from his horse and killed in that year, is referred to as the 'heir of Caesarea' at the time of his death."[257] John, of course, might have died between 1257 and 1264; as long as Margaret lived Hugh would still have been only her "heir," whether or not she had remarried. There is no evidence as to when, after 1257, John l'Aleman died, but probably Margaret was still alive in March 1265, when Baybars took Caesarea.[258]

Besides Hugh, John and Margaret had two other sons, Nicholas and Thomas, who both in turn "succeeded to the title, if not to the lands of Caesarea."[259]

Footnotes

1. The orthodox caliphate at Medina   640-656
   the Umayyads at Damascus   656-750
   the 'Abbāsids at al-Anbār and Baghdad   750-877
   the Tūlūnids of Egypt   877-905
   the 'Abbāsids at Baghdad   905-941
   the Ikhshīdids of Egypt   941-969
   the Fāṭimids of Egypt   969-1070
   the Artukids at Jerusalem   1070-1078
   the Selchükids at Damascus   1078-1089
   the Fāṭimids of Egypt   1089-1101

2. Matthew of Edessa (extracts ed. É. Dulaurier in *RHC: Documents arméniens*, I [Paris 1869] 1-150), 16, 18, quotes John's own statement: "from [Acre] we continued on towards Caesarea, which is situated on the coast of the Ocean Sea, and which was reduced . . . . There was no [place], as far as Ramla and Caesarea, which did not submit to us." René Grousset (*Histoire des croisades et du royaume franc de Jérusalem*, I [Paris 1934] xvii) corrects Dulaurier's date from 974 to 975.

3. *Kitāb al-masālik wa-l-mamālik* (ed. and trans. M. J. de Goeje, *BGA VI* [Leyden 1889] 255 (trans., 195). All the Arabic authors cited spell the name Qaisāriyah.

4. *Kitāb al-buldān* (ed. *idem* in *BGA VII* [2 ed., Leyden 1892] 231-373), 329 (trans. Gaston Wiet as *Les pays* [Cairo 1937] 181). 'Umar's caliphate was from 634 to 644.

5. Ibn-al-Faqīh (fl. 902). *Kitāb al-buldān* (*BGA V* [1885]), p. 103; Ibn-Rustah (fl. 922), *Kitāb al-a'lāq an-nafīsah* (*BGA VII* 1-229), 97; al-Iṣṭakhrī (fl. 951), *Kitāb masālik al-mamālik* (*BGA I* [2 ed., 1927]), 66; al-Mas'ūdī (d. 956), *Kitāb at-tanbīh wa-l-ishrāf* (*BGA VIII* [1894]), 43; Ibn-Ḥauqal (fl. 977), *Kitāb al-masālik wa-l-mamālik* (*BGA II* [1873]), 126.

6. *Kitāb aḥsan at-taqāsīm fī ma'rifat al-aqālīm* (*BGA III* [2 ed., 1906]), 174 (extracts trans. Guy Le Strange as part 3 of *PPTS* III [1892] 55). The author's name is also found as "al-Muqaddasī."

7. *Safar nāmeh* (ed. and trans. Charles Schéfer as *Sefer nameh* . . . [Paris 1881]), 18 (trans., 61-62; extracts trans. Le Strange as part 1 of *PPTS* IV [1893] 20: his "fountains" here emended to "springs").

8. Adolf Reifenberg, "Caesarea, a Study in the Decline of a Town," *IEJ* 1 (1950-1951) 29-30.

9. For these pilgrimages see Einar Joranson's monograph on "The Great German Pilgrimage of 1064-1065," in *The Crusades and Other Historical Essays Presented to Dana C. Munro* . . . (ed. Louis J. Paetow, New York 1928), 3-43; Steven Runciman's chapter in *A History of the Crusades* (ed. Kenneth M. Setton) I (Phila. 1955; rev. ed. Madison 1969) 68-78; and *PPTS*, *passim*.

10. Runciman, "The First Crusade: Antioch to Ascalon" (in Setton, *op. cit.* 308-341), 331.

11. Albert of Aachen, *Historia Hierosolymitana* (in *RHC: Occ.* IV [Paris 1879] 265-713), 460 (tr. Herman Hefele as *Geschichte des ersten Kreuzzuges* [2 vol., Jena 1923] 273). See Heinrich Hagenmeyer's edition of *Gesta Francorum et aliorum Hierosolimitanorum* (Heidelberg 1890; cited as *Gesta*), 445, n. 20; *cf.* Raymond of Aguilers, *Historia Francorum qui ceperunt Iherusalem* (*RHC: Occ.* III [1866] 231-305), 291: "we pitched camp beside the marshes which are near Caesarea" (he was chaplain to Raymond of Toulouse, who had obstinately delayed the army for weeks besieging 'Arqah).

12. *Loc. cit.*: "Rex Achon duci Caesareae. Generatio canina per me transivit, gens stulta atque contentiosa, sine regimine, quibus per te et per alios, quantum tuam legem diligis, nocere desidera; quod si vis, facile poteris. Hoc idem et ad alias civitates et castra mandabis."; Reinhold Röhricht, *Regesta regni Hierosolymitani* . . . (Innsbruck 1893, with 1904 (N.Y.) supplement; cited as *Regesta*), #22.

13. *Historia Jerosolimitana* (*RHC: Occ.* IV 1-111), 94 (variant MS).

14. *Gesta Francorum expugnantium Iherusalem*, sometimes ascribed to "Bartolf of Nangis" (*RHC: Occ.* III 487-543), 508.

15. *Gesta* (*RHC: Occ.* III 119-163 [miscalled " . . . Tudebodus abbreviatus"], 305-307) 161, 305 (also ed. and trans. Louis Bréhier as *Histoire anonyme de la première croisade* [Paris 1924] 208-209; ed. Hagenmeyer, 485).

16. Runciman, in Setton, *op. cit.* 341.

17. *Op. cit.* 106 (variant MS). Hagenmeyer (*Gesta*, 485-486, note 24) accepts Baldric's dubious account, and even locates their position as south of the south gate, an odd spot for their

alleged purpose as presumably most of Caesarea's traffic was with ports to the north, especially after the fall of Jerusalem.

18. *Op. cit.* 111 (variant MS); this MS, previously cited, is considered excellent.

19. Fulcher of Chartres, *Historia Hierosolymitana* . . . (*RHC: Occ.* III 311-485), 366 (ed. Hagenmeyer [Heidelberg 1913] 331); Fulcher was with Baldwin. William of Malmesbury, *De gestis regum Anglorum* (ed. William Stubbs, Rolls Series, no. 90), II (London 1889), 441 (trans. J. A. Giles [London 1847], 397-398) adds the hungry pilgrims chewed sugar cane.

20. Albert, *op. cit.* 515 (trans. Hefele, II 13-14).

21. *Ibid.* 519 (trans. Hefele, II 19). Hagenmeyer, ("Chronologie de la première croisade (1094-1100)," *ROL* 8 [1900-1901] 333) dates the banquet about June 10; Godfrey fell ill at Caesarea but continued on to Jaffa and Jerusalem before succumbing.

22. Fulcher, *op. cit.* 377 (ed. Hagenmeyer, 366).

23. Albert, *op. cit.* 541: March; note emends to April (trans. Hefele, II 53). Frederic Duncalf's theory ("Some Influences of Oriental Environment in the Kingdom of Jerusalem," *Annual Report of the American Historical Association for . . . 1914,* I [Washington 1916] 141) that Baldwin renewed treaties with these three emirs but refused tribute from Arsuf because he planned to attack it, overlooks the premeditated attack on Caesarea.

24. Fulcher, *op. cit.* 388 (ed. Hagenmeyer, 400); William of Malmesbury (*op. cit.* II 445; trans. Giles, 405) is indignant: "Thus he impelled them, inconsiderate and blinded, more through lust of gold than love of God, to barter their blood . . . , " but they proved to have made an excellent bargain.

25. Fulcher, *op. cit.* 389; Albert, *op. cit.* 543 (trans. Hefele, II 55); Caffaro di Caschifellone, *Annales Ianuenses* (excerpts in *RHC: Occ.* V [1895] 59-65), 62 (ed. L. T. Belgrano in *Annali Genovesi . . . ,* I [Rome 1890] 9).

26. Fulcher, *loc. cit.;* Albert, *loc. cit.;* Caffaro, *op. cit.* 63 (ed. Belgrano, 9-10).

27. Fulcher, *loc. cit.* (ed. Hagenmeyer, 401).

28. Albert, *loc. cit.*

29. Caffaro, *loc. cit.* Hagenmeyer (Fulcher, 401, n. 2) thinks this was the only embassy.

30. Fulcher, *loc. cit.;* Albert, *op. cit.* 543-544 (trans. Hefele, II 57-58); Caffaro, *op. cit.* 64 (ed. Belgrano, 11).

31. William of Tyre, *Historia rerum in partibus transmarinis gestarum* . . . (*RHC: Occ.* I [1844]) 422 (trans. E. A. Babcock and A. C. Krey as *A History of Deeds Done Beyond the Sea* [2 vol., New York 1943] I 436); William of Malmesbury, on the other hand, says they "resisted with extreme courage" (*loc. cit.*), but the speed of the victory, despite the strength of the fortifications, does not indicate a determined resistance. The capture and massacre are discussed by Ibn-al-Qalānisī, *Mudhaiyal ta'rīkh Dimashq* (extracts trans. H. A. R. Gibb as *The Damascus Chronicle of the Crusades* [London 1932]), 51: end of *rajab,* "by assault, with the assistance of the Genoese, killed the population, and plundered everything in it;" by Ibn-al-Athīr, *Al-kāmil fī-t-ta' rīkh* (extract in *RHC: Or.* I [Paris 1872] 187-744) 208; by Sibṭ Ibn-al-Jauzī, *Kitāb mir'āt az-zamān* . . . (extracts in *RHC: Or.* III [1884] 511-570), 524; and by later Moslem historians like Abū-l-Fidā', *Mukhtasar ta'rīkh al-bashar* (extracts in *RHC: Or.* I 1-165), 6, and Ibn-Taghrībirdī, *Kitāb an-nujūm az-zāhirah* . . . (extracts in *RHC: Or.* III 475-509), 487.

32. *Loc. cit.* (ed. Hagenmeyer, 403-404): "tam pulchras quam turpes."

33. *Op. cit.* 544 (trans. Hefele, II 58): the "Ethiopians" ("Azopart") were Sudanese soldiers in Fāṭimid service. The people of Acre ransomed the qadi of Caesarea for 1000 bezants.

34. *Op. cit.* 64-65 (ed. Belgrano, 12); Hagenmeyer (Fulcher, 403, n. 14) says only 12 merchants survived, which is surely too low an estimate.

35. *Op. cit.* 390: "Feminae . . . impudenter intra se bisantios occultabant; quod et nefas erat sit recondendum et multo turpius mihi ad recitandum."

36. *Historia* . . . (*RHC: Occ.* IV 113-263), 258.

37. *Loc. cit.* (trans. Giles, 406).

38. Caffaro, *op. cit.* 65 (ed. Belgrano, 12).

39. Fulcher, *loc. cit.:* "multi pauperes effecti sunt locupletes."

40. William of Tyre (trans. Babcock, I 437 and Krey's n. 37); there is a considerable literature on this "emerald" chalice. The marginal date "1102" in *RHC: Occ.* (I 422) is an error by an early copyist which has been uncritically followed in several standard works. The date May 17, 1101, was finally established by Hagenmeyer in his chronology ("Chronologie de l'histoire du royaume de Jérusalem," *ROL* 9 [1902] 429-432), correcting Caffaro's "July," von Sybel's "June 7," and his own previous "May 31."

41. William of Tyre (trans. Babcock, I 435). *Cf.* James of Vitry, *Historia orientalis* . . . (trans.

Aubrey Stewart as *The History of Jerusalem, A.D. 1180* [error for circa 1220], part 2 of *PPTS* XI [1896] 5: Caesarea "stands by the seaside, but has not a convenient harbour, but it abounds in gardens, pastures and running waters."

42. *Regista,* #43, 45; the Genoese in 1205 had these privileges inscribed in letters of gold on the walls of the church of the Holy Sepulcher in Jerusalem, at a cost of 2000 gold bezants, according to Caffaro, *De liberatione civitatum orientis liber* (in *RHC: Occ.* V 41-59, 65-73), 72 and note b (ed. Belgrano in *op. cit.* 121 and Pl. VII).

43. Caffaro, *Annales Ianuenses,* 65 (ed. Belgrano, 12). For some reason Camille Enlart, in *Les monuments des croisés dans le royaume de Jérusalem* . . . (atlas, I [Paris 1925]), Pl. VI, refers to the cathedral of "St. Paul," but it was definitely "St. Peter;" archbishop Peter calls it "cathedra Sancti Petri Cesariensis ecclesie" (*Regesta,* #1051, 1066).

44. On him and his successors, see part 2, below.

45. See part 3, below.

46. Albert, *op. cit.* 608-609 (trans. Hefele, II 139-140).

47. Acre fell in 1104, so refugees from Caesarea and Acre, as well as Sidon, Jubail, Beirut, Tripoli, and other conquered ports, were crowded into Tyre when it finally fell in 1124 (William of Tyre, *op. cit.* 563; trans. Babcock, II 9). The absence of a Moslem community was characteristic of towns taken before 1110; after that, the Franks abandoned their policy of extermination or expulsion.

48. Benjamin of Tudela (*Itinerarium* [ed. and trans. Adolf Asher], I [London and Berlin 1840] 65) found ten Jews and 200 Samaritans ("Cuthaeans") there about 1162. Joshua Prawer ("Colonization Activities in the Latin Kingdom of Jerusalem," *Revue belge de philosophie et d'histoire,* 29 [1951] 1088, n. 3) points out that Jews were often dyers of textiles; *cf.* R. B. Solomon, "Twelfth-century Colonies in Palestine," *Jewish Review* 2 (1911-1912) 431-442. The only larger Samaritan colonies were 400 at Damascus and 300 at Ascalon, as reported by Benjamin, *op. cit.* 80, 86.

49. For the Genoese, see William Heyd, (2 vol., trans. F. Reynaud [Leipzig 1885-86] *Histoire du commerce du levant au moyenâge*) and Eugene H. Byrne, "The Genoese Colonies in Syria," in Paetow, *op. cit.* 139-182; for the Franks see E. G. Rey, *Les colonies franques de Syrie* . . . (Paris 1883) and Prawer, *op. cit.* and two other articles: "Étude de quelques problèmes agraires et sociaux d'une seigneurie croisée au XIIIᵉ siècle," *Byzantion,* 22 (1952) 5-61; 23 (1953) 143-170, and "The Settlement of the Latins in Jerusalem," *Speculum,* 27 (1952) 490-503.

50. On him and his heirs, see part 3, below.

51. The definitive work on the fief, as distinguished from the city, of Caesarea is the monograph by Gustav Beyer, "Das Gebiet der Kreuzfahrerherrschaft Caesarea in Palestina" *ZDPV* 59 (1936) 1-91. Auguste Beugnot (*RHC: Lois,* I [Paris 1841] 418, n. a) and Hans Prutz (*Kulturgeschichte der Kreuzzüge* [Berlin 1883] 162) err in terming it subordinate to Sidon; after the death in 1123 of Eustace Granier, who held both, there was no juridical connection between them (see *Regesta, passim*).

52. For agricultural conditions generally, see Prutz, *op. cit.,* Helen G. Preston, *Rural Conditions in the Kingdom of Jerusalem* . . . (Phila. 1903), and Prawer's "Étude" in *Byzantion.* Prawer also makes two excellent points in his "Colonization Activities" (pp. 1065, 1085): the Franks were never able to induce European peasants to immigrate, while the Syrian Christians preferred urban opportunities to rural serfdom. A promising scheme to bring in Armenian peasants foundered because of the authoritarian pretensions of the Latin clergy (see Grousset, *op. cit.* II [1935] 602-604).

53. John of Ibelin, "Livre . . . " (ed. Beugnot in *RHC: Lois,* I 7-432), 422, 426, 427; Gerard of Montreal (ed. Gaston Raynaud as "Chronique du templier de Tyr" in *Les gestes des chiprois* . . . [Geneva 1887] 139-334), 260.

54. "Étude," p. 24. See also John L. LaMonte, *Feudal Monarchy in the Latin Kingdom of Jerusalem* . . . (Cambridge, Mass. 1932) 158, and 189, n. 3.

55. *Op. cit.* 432. Comprehension of the difficulties resulting from the meagerness of Caesarea's population and garrison and its exposure to continual hostile incursions refutes the pejorative implications of C. R. Conder's accurate but misleading comment (in "Samaria", *SWP* II 13) : "The Crusaders settled themselves within the place after their own manner. That is, they made the broad city of gardens and orange-trees into a small cramped mediaeval fortress." Of course they did; they had no alternative.

56. Prawer, "Colonization Activities," pp. 1064, 1067, 1071. On the kingdom's defense system see Paul Deschamps, *Les châteaux des croisés en terre-sainte: Le Crac des*

Chevaliers . . . (Paris 1934) and its sequel . . . : *La défense du royaume de Jérusalem* . . . (Paris 1939). The map of "Palestine of the Crusades" compiled by Cedric N. Johns (3 ed., Jerusalem 1950) is invaluable for visualizing the strategic terrain. R. C. Smail, *Crusading Warfare* . . . (Cambridge 1956) mentions Caesarea only in passing, but is useful for the small forts nearby (p. 229). Ibelin was built in 1141, Blanche Garde in 1142, and Beth Gibelin in 1136.

57. *Nuzhat al-mushtāq* . . . (extracts ed. J. Gildemeister as supplement to vol. 8 [1885] of *ZDPV* 11 (trans. *idem* in *ibid.*, 8 129; excerpt trans. Le Strange in *Palestine under the Moslems* . . . [London 1890] 474).

58. *Ibid.* (excerpt quoted by Abū-l-Fidā' and trans. A. S. Marmardji in *Textes géographiques arabes sur la Palestine* . . . [Paris 1951] 170).

59. F. M. Abel, "Le littoral palestinien et ses ports," *RB* n. s. II (1914) 588.

60. *Liber locorum sanctorum terrae Jerusalem* (ed. Melchior de Vogüé in his *Les églises de la terre sainte* [Paris 1860] 407-433), 430 (trans. James R. MacPherson as part 1 of vol. V [1896] of *PPTS* [erroneously ascribed to "Fetellus"], 47).

61. *Ékphrasis* . . . (ed. and trans. E. C. Miller in *RHC: Historiens grecs*, I [Paris 1875] 527-558), 557; the note in vol. II (Paris 1881) 695 fails to correct ascription to Caesarea Philippi (Banyas) instead of Caesarea Palestinae (trans. Stewart as part 3, *PPTS* V, 35).

62. Conder, *SWP* II 23.

63. Albert, *op. cit.* 676 (trans. Hefele, II 232).

64. Fulcher (ed. Hagenmeyer) 665.

65. William of Tyre, *op. cit.* 754 (trans. Babcock, II 182).

66. *Ibid.* 1108 (trans. Babcock, II 485).

67. J. Delaville le Roulx, *Cartulaire général de l'ordre des Hospitaliers* . . . , I (Paris 1894) 499. This is one of a series of papal letters (1167, 1179, etc.) "demanding the restoration of the privileges granted the Genoese, and the replacement of the inscription in gold letters stating them," which king Amalric had destroyed (LaMonte, *op. cit.* 264), but is the first in which their ejection from their third of Caesarea is specifically mentioned.

68. Bahā'-ad-Dīn Ibn-Shaddād, *Kitāb an-nawādir as-sulṭānīyah* . . . (RHC: Or. III 1-370), 98 (trans. C. W. Wilson and Conder as *PPTS* XIII [1897] 116).

69. Abū-Shāmah, *Kitāb ar-raudatain* . . . (RHC: Or. IV [1898]) 301; Bahā'-ad-Dīn, *loc. cit.* There is no truth in the assertion by T. E. Dowling (*Sketches of Caesarea* . . . [London 1912] 39) that the city's "population was principally Moslem, and welcomed the banners" of Saladin's emirs; this is a flagrant plagiarism from W. B. Stevenson's *The Crusaders in the East* . . . (Cambridge 1907) 250, omitting only the essential ascription to the "country" population, the Arab peasantry.

70. Ibn-al-Athīr, *op. cit.* 690; Abū-l-Fidā', *op. cit.* 56; *De expugnatione Terrae Sanctae libellus* (by an anonymous contemporary, ed. Joseph Stevenson, in Rolls Series, no. 66 [London 1875] 209-262), 229; Roger of Hoveden, *Chronica* (ed. Stubbs, Rolls Series, no. 51), II (London 1869) 341.

71. See part 3, below.

72. The contemporary *Gesta regis Ricardi* (ed. Stubbs, in vol. II of Rolls Series, no. 49 [London 1867]), 192, names only Caesarea, Jaffa, and Ascalon, and dates the hurried destruction in September 1191 after Richard's victory at Arsuf; Ralph of Coggeshall, *Chronicon Anglicanum* (ed. Stevenson in Rolls Series, no. 66. 1-208), 34, adds Haifa, Arsuf, and Gaza, while James of Vitry, *op. cit.* (ed. [Jacques Bongars] in *Gesta dei per Francos* . . . , II [Hanover 1611] 1047-1145), 1122 (trans. Stewart, 113), substitutes Darum for Arsuf; Abū-Shāmah, *op. cit.* IV 462, under A.H. 586 (= 1190/1), lists Tiberias, Jaffa, Arsuf, Caesarea, Sidon, and Jubail. Röhricht (*Beiträge zur Geschichte der Kreuzzüge*, II [Berlin 1878] 180) and Grousset (*op. cit.* III [Paris 1936] 16) clearly err in placing this earth-scorching in 1189, on the approach of the German crusaders, instead of 1191.

73. Ambroise, *L'estoire de la guerre sainte* (ed. Gaston Paris [Paris 1897]), col. 160 (trans. M. J. Hubert and J. L. LaMonte as *The Crusade of Richard Lion-heart* [New York 1941] 244; trans. Edward N. Stone in *Three Old French Chronicles of the Crusades* [Seattle 1939] 85); Bahā'-ad-Dīn (*op. cit.* 250; trans. Wilson, 281) gives the date as the 6th of Sha'bān, 587, two days early. See also Richard of London, *Itinerarium peregrinorum et gesta regis Ricardi* (ed. Stubbs as vol. I [1864] of Rolls Series, no. 38), 256 (trans. [ed. Kenneth Fenwick] as *The Third Crusade* . . . [London 1958] 84): "The circuit of the city of Caesarea is very great, and the buildings are of wonderful workmanship."

74. Trans. Hubert, 244.

75. *Op. cit.* 256 (trans. ed. Fenwick, 84). Al-Maqrīzī, *Al-mawā'iz wa-l-i'tibar* . . . (extracts

trans. Edgar Blochet as "Histoire d'Égypte," in *ROL* 9 [1902]) 51, says the Moslems fled to Beirut.

76. Richard of London, *op. cit.* 286, 288 (trans. ed. Fenwick, 97-100); *cf.* Ambroise, *op. cit.* col. 192-193 (trans. Hubert, 278, 284); the outlying forts (rebuilt October 1191) were Casal des Plains and Casal Maen (or Moyen) southeast of Jaffa. LaMonte cites Roger of Hoveden, *op. cit.* III [London 1871] 174, which says Richard rebuilt Caesarea as well as Jaffa and the casals, and is itself based on *Gesta regis Ricardi*, p. 227, but Richard of London's version, omitting Caesarea, is both more reliable and more plausible.

77. Richard of London, *op. cit.* 322 (February), 405 (July), 413, 425-426 (August) (trans. ed. Fenwick, 111, 145, 150); Bahā'-ād-Dīn, *op. cit.* 336 (trans. Wilson, 374).

78. *Gesta regis Ricardi*, 184, 227 (where Stubbs corrects Caesarea to Ascalon in note), followed by Roger of Hoveden, *op. cit.* III 125, 174; by LaMonte (Ambroise, *op. cit.* trans. Hubert, 211, 30); and by Lionel Landon, *The Itinerary of King Richard I* (London 1935) 52. Ambroise himself (*op. cit.* col. 135; trans. Hubert, 211; trans. Stone, 74) and Richard of London (*op. cit.* 235; trans. ed. Fenwick, 72) are better informed: "Gaufrido . . . cederet comitatus Joppensis, scilicet Joppa et Ascalon." Jaffa and Ascalon were normally combined into a single fief under the count of Jaffa; Jaffa and Caesarea, never.

79. Ernoul's continuation of William of Tyre (ed. as part 2 of "L'estoire de Eracles empereur . . . " in *RHC: Occ.* II [1859] 1-379), versions C (p. 198) and G. (p. 199), and that ed. by Louis de Mas Latrie as *Chronique d'Ernoul et de Bernard le Trésorier* (Paris 1871), 293: "quant li trive fu faite, si ot pité Salehadins des haus homes de le tiere qu'il avoit desiretés qui encore vivoient . . . . Au segnor de Chayphas rendi Cayphas. Al segnor de Cesaire rendi Cesaire. Al segnor d'Arsur rendi Arsur et l'apartenance. Et al conte Henri dona Jaffe." The kernel of fact in this version concerns Saladin's minor concessions to Reginald of Sidon (Sarepta) and Balian of Ibelin (Caymont).

80. See part 3, below.

81. Ernoul, *op. cit.* versions A and B (p. 199) and D (p. 200): "Arsur et Cesaire et Cayphas fussent en cele trive;" Bahā'-ad-Dīn, *op. cit.* 343 (trans. Wilson, 381); Abù-Shāmah, *op. cit.* V (1906) 77.

82. Thomas C. Van Cleve, "The Fifth Crusade," in Setton, *op. cit.* II (Phila. 1962) 394, following Oliver of Paderborn, *Historia Damiatina* (ed. Hermann Hoogeweg in *Bibliothek des Litterarischen Vereins in Stuttgart* 202 [Stuttgart 1894] 159-282), 168-169 (trans. John J. Gavigan as *The Capture of Damietta* [Phila. 1948] 17). *Cf. Chronica regia Coloniensis* (ed. Georg Waitz [Hanover 1880]), 243 (written about 1219), 326, 344; Ernoul, *op. cit.* 325, 332 (ed. Mas Latrie, 421); and especially James of Vitry, *op. cit.* 1130-1131, and letters (ed. R. B. C. Huygens [Leyden 1960]), 101-102, boasting that the work of fortification was accomplished by a few stalwarts, under constant attack by a multitude of Saracens, who were allegedly put to flight. The work at Athlit was directed by Walter of Avesnes; Conder (*SWP* II 14) errs in ascribing to him the 1218 walls at Caesarea, and in thinking that these rather than those of 1228 underlie Louis IX's surviving works.

83. Oliver of Paderborn, *op. cit.* 172 (trans. Gavigan, 19; note dates this March 6).

84. The date, the end of 1219 or beginning of 1220, is established by Oliver, *op. cit.* 244 (trans. Gavigan, 58), and James of Vitry, *op. cit.* 1144; as participants, their testimony outweighs that of Ernoul (*op. cit.* 334, versions A and B), who places it in the summer of 1218. Grousset (*op. cit.* III 212 and n. 4) notes the conflict in dates, and Röhricht's preference for 1219-1220, but accepts 1218, as does LaMonte in his magistral study, "The Lords of Caesarea in the Period of the Crusades," *Speculum* 22 (1947) 155, citing Ernoul and also the chronography of Hetoum of Gorigos (fl. 1307; ed. and trans. Dulaurier in *RHC: Documents arméniens*, I [Paris 1850] 471-490), 484, which, however, dates the rebuilding by king John rather than the subsequent Moslem conquest. Fortunately, there are two independent confirmations for the later date: a letter from Peter of Montaigu to bishop Nicholas of Elne (ed. Röhricht as the 10th of 16 "Epistolae variae" in *Studien zur Geschichte des fünften Kreuzzuges* [Innsbruck 1891] 37-53), 49, dated September 20, 1220, and reporting the fall of Caesarea as a recent event (this letter also appears in Roger of Wendover, *Flores historiarum*, ed. Henry G. Hewlett, Rolls Series, no. 84, II [London 1887] 261); and, more precisely, the chronicle of Abu-Shamah (*op. cit.* V 178), placing this conquest in the hijrah year 616 (March 1219 to March 1220).

85. Ernoul, *op. cit.* 334 (versions A and B, which give more detail than C, D, or G or that ed. by Mas Latrie [p. 423] but do not conflict with them). Oliver, *loc. cit.*, and James of Vitry, *loc. cit.*, say Caesarea was in the king's custody, without explaining why or mentioning the Genoese, but accuse the defenders of negligence. There is nothing in any of these sources to justify three

items in LaMonte's account (*loc. cit.*): that Caesarea had been attacked earlier in 1217-1218 but had been "rescued" by king John (a misinterpretation of "relevèrent" [rebuilt] in Heṭoum, *loc. cit.*), that it was "ably defended" by the Genoese, and that Warner shared this defense effort in person (a confusion resulting from Old French "il" instead of "ils"). He also errs in implying that the Moslems held Caesarea for several years; Ernoul (versions C, D, and G, *loc. cit.*; ed. Mas Latrie, 423) explicitly states—without contradiction by other sources—"il ne le vaurent mie garnir, ains l'abatirent," while versions A and B agree that he "fist abatre le chastel."

86. *Mu'jām al-buldān* (ed. Ferdinand Wüstenfeld as *Jacut's geographisches Wörterbuch*) IV (Leipzig 1869) 214 (trans. in Marmardji, *op. cit.* 169, and in Le Strange, *loc. cit.*).

87. Ernoul, *op. cit.* 365 ("s'en alerent a Cesaire et refermerent le chastel que Coradin [al-Mu'aẓẓam] avoit abatu"), 373 (ed. Mas Latrie, 459, 461). Roger of Wendover, *op. cit.* II 326, says that pope Gregory IX ordered the Germans to refortify Caesarea first, and then Jaffa.

88. Roger of Wendover, *op. cit.* II 367: Jaffa, Sidon, and Montfort could also be refortified, and possibly Jerusalem; see conflicting versions in Setton, *op. cit.* II 455 and 702, with full references. James of Vitry, *op. cit.* 1127, says that the Franks "de novo aedificaverunt optimum castrum" at Caesarea, but not Jaffa, Ascalon, or Gaza.

89. On the participation of Walter and his son John in this war, and the illegal and inoperative "confiscation" of Caesarea, see part 3, below.

90. Matthew Paris, *Chronica majora* (ed. Henry R. Luard, Rolls Series, no. 57), V (London 1880) 257, and VI (London 1882) 205; anonymous continuators of William of Tyre (ed. as "Continuation . . . de 1229 à 1261, dite du manuscrit de Rothelin" in *RHC: Occ.* II 483-639), 628; John of Joinville, *Histoire de Saint Louis* (ed. and trans. Natalis de Wailly [Paris 1874]), 257, 283; Léopold Dressaire, "Saint Louis en Palestine (1250-1254)," *Échos d'orient* 16 (1913) 223-224.

91. Deschamps, *Crac*, 84, n. 2, citing Guillaume de Saint-Pathus, *Vie de Saint Louis* (ed. H. F. Delaborde [1899]), 91: " . . . comme l'on fesait les murs en la cité de Césaire, . . . [le légat] avait donné pardon à tous ceux qui aiderait à faire cele oevre; dont (li benoiez rois) porta plusieurs fois les pierres en la hote sur ses espaules. . . . "

92. See Claude Cahen, "The Mongols and the Near East" in Setton, *op. cit.* II 715-732, and M. M. Ziada, "The Mamluk Sultans to 1293" in *ibid.* II 735-758. The key work on Baybars is Ibn-'Abd-aẓ-Ẓāhir, *Ar-rauḍ aẓ-ẓāhir fī sīrat al-Malik aẓ Ẓāhir* (ed. S. F. Sadeque as *Baybars I of Egypt* [Dacca 1956]), but the extant portion stops before his conquest of Caesarea, which is treated only in the editor's uneven commentary.

93. *Ibid.* 216, 217.

94. Miss Sadeque's commentary in *ibid.* 55 (Feb. 26); Abū-l-Fidā', *op. cit.* 150 (Feb. 27); Mufaḍḍal ibn-Abī-l-Faḍā'il, *An-nahj as-sadīd . . .* (ed. and trans. Blochet as "Histoire des sultans mamlouks" in *Patrologia orientalis*), XII (1919) 474 (Feb. 26); al-Maqrīzī, *Kitāb as-sulūk li-ma'rifat duwal al-mulūk* (ed. Ziada), I, part 2 (1936) 526-528 (trans. Étienne Quatremère as *Histoire des sultans mamlouks*, I [1837], part 2, 7-8) (Feb. 27); Badr-ad-Dīn al-'Ainī, *Kitāb 'iqd al-jumān . . .* (extracts in *RHC: Or.* II, part 1 [1887], 181-250), 219 (Feb. "28", but hijrah date 9/5/663 corresponds to Feb. 27); *Annales de Terre Sainte* (ed. Röhricht and Raynaud in *Archives de l'orient latin*, II [1884], part 2, 427-461), 451 (Jan. 26, "1264", but context indicates 1265); Marino Sanudo, *Liber secretorum fidelium crucis* (ed. Bongars in *op. cit.* II 1-288), 222 (Jan. 26). January is clearly wrong, as the citadel fell early in March after a 6-day siege; February 27 is apparently correct, and is accepted by Röhricht in his "Études sur les derniers temps du royaume de Jérusalem: Les combats du sultan Bibars contre les chrétiens en Syrie (1261-1277)," *Archives de l'orient latin*, II (1884) 1, 377. All these are drawn on for the remainder of this paragraph, as is the letter of pope Clement IV (not Urban IV as in *ibid.* 378, note 52; Urban died in 1264) dated July 26, 1265 (in Delaville le Roulx, *op. cit.* III [Paris 1899] 115), asking help from king Heṭoum I of Armenia: "insolenter irruens in Christicolas, ille proditor, qui soldanus Egipti dicitur, Cesaream violenter optinuit et Azotum, effuso sanguine Christi militum, et nonnullis ex eis, quod est multis morte lugubrius, captivatis . . . . " A letter of Hugh Revel, master of the Hospital, dated May 27, 1268 (in *ibid.* IV [Paris 1906] 291-293; *Regesta*, #1358a), is both inexact and unfair: "castrum Cesaree, quod tam forte fuerat, insultus soldani per duos dies non potuit sustinere . . . , " but it is extremely odd that this "impregnable" fortress fell every time it was vigorously attacked—by the Christians in 1101, by the Saracens in 1187, 1220, and 1265. For details of the defenses, see E. G. Rey, *Étude sur les monuments de l'architecture militaire des croisés en Syrie* (Paris 1871) 221-227 and Pl. XXII; Victor Guérin, *Description géographique, historique et archéologique de la Palestine*, part 2: "Samarie," II (Paris 1875) 321-339; *SWP* II 13-28 (describing the "ditch" as 53 feet broad); Enlart, *op. cit.* II (Paris 1928) 85-89; and the chapter by A. Negev, below. Excellent photographs will be found in *Life*, V, no. 18 (May 5, 1961) 72-82.

95. Al-Maqrīzī (trans. Quatremère) I, part 2, 102.

96. *Ibid.* II (1844) 225, 227; *Regesta,* #1450.

97. *Descriptio Terrae Sanctae* (ed. J. C. M. Laurent in *Peregrinatores medii aevi quatuor* [2 ed., Leipzig 1873] 1-100), 83 (trans. Stewart as part 1 of *PPTS* XII [1896] 94).

98. Runciman, in Setton, *op. cit.* II 598.

99. *Kitāb taqwīm al-buldān* (ed. Reinaud and MacGuckin de Slane as *Géographie d' Aboulféda* [Paris 1840]), 239 (trans. in Marmardji, *op. cit.* 170, and in Le Strange, *loc. cit.*): "today it is in ruins."

100. *De itinere Terrae Sanctae liber . . .* (ed. Ferdinand Deycks in *Bibliothek des Litterarischen Vereins in Stuttgart,* 25 [Stuttgart 1851]) 49 (trans. Stewart as part 3 of *PPTS* XII, 64): "Caesarea of Palestine . . . now . . . is utterly destroyed [funditus nunc eversa]."

101. *Descriptio Terrae Sanctae* (ed. Titus Tobler in *Descriptiones . . . ex saeculo VIII, IX, XII, et XV* [Leipzig 1874] 225-281, 497-522), 261 (trans. Stewart as part 4 of *PPTS* VI [1894] 29): "The city itself is utterly destroyed. [Ipse vero penitus est destructa.] . . . It has an inconvenient harbour, but great abundance of gardens, meadows, and running streams . . . . " For its subsequent woes, see Reifenberg, *op. cit.* 20-32.

102. Caffaro, *op. cit.* 65 (ed. Belgrano, 12). Wilhelm Hotzelt, *Kirchengeschichte Palästinas . . . 1099-1291,* (Cologne 1940) 9, says Baldwin was elected bishop and, discovering that Caesarea had been a metropolitan see, called himself archbishop, but cites no source for this unlikely tale.

103. *Op. cit.* 182-183, 251. H. F. Delaborde (*Chartes de Terre Sainte provenant de l'abbaye de . . . Josaphat* [Paris 1880] 17) asserts that Baldwin could not actually have been abbot, as his successor Hugh is termed "first abbot" of this monastery.

104. Albert, *op. cit.* 599 (trans. Hefele, II 124-126).

105. "B., Caesariensis archiepiscopus" in *Regesta,* #52. Michel Le Quien (*Oriens christianus . . .* [Paris 1740] III, col. 1285), Charles Du Cange (*Les familles d'Outremer* [ed. E. G. Rey, Paris 1869] 756), Pius B. Gams (*Series episcoporum ecclesiae Catholicae . . .* [Regensburg 1873; reprinted, Leipzig 1931] 452), and, less excusably, Raymond Janin ("Césarée de Palestine . . . " in *DHGE* XII [1953] col. 209) all mistakenly place Baldwin's death and Evremar's accession in 1107. Röhricht dates this document 1108; his previous choice of 1108 ("Syria sacra," *ZDPV* 10 [1887] 12) was based, dubiously, on a marginal editorial note in Albert, *op. cit.* 644: February "1108?", corrected by Hefele (II 188) to February 27, 1107 (Ash Wednesday). É. Van Cauwenbergh ("Baudoin Ier, archevêque de Césarée de Palestine" in *DHGE* VI [1932] col. 1417) avoids choosing between 1107 and 1108, but errs in saying that king Baldwin I "designated" his namesake archbishop.

106. Albert, *op. cit.* 659 (trans. Hefele, II 211): "quae nuper pastore viduata erat," at Evremar's election by acclamation.

107. *Regesta,* #49. For the intrigues of Arnulf "Malecorne," also of Chocques (in the diocese of Thérouannes, 19 miles NNW of Arras), patriarch 1112-1118, see the article "Ebremar . . . " by an anonymous Benedictine in vol. X of *Histoire littéraire de la France . . .* (ed. Paulin Paris, Paris 1868) 394-400, and Grousset, *op. cit.* I 288-297; both vindicate Evremar completely.

108. *Gesta Francorum expugnantium Iherusalem* in *RHC: Occ.* III 538: "quidam idiota; sed ampla persona et religiosus;" Guibert, *op. cit.* 233: "virum simplicem et illitteratum;" Albert, *op. cit.* 600 (trans. Hefele, II 125-126): "vir et clericus boni testimonii, praeclarus ac hilaris distributor elemosinarum;" and others.

109. Fulcher, *op. cit.* 413 (ed. Hagenmeyer, 495).

110. *Ibid.* 443 (ed. Hagenmeyer, 625); Walter the Chancellor, *Bella Antiochena* (*RHC: Occ.* V 75-132), 121 (ed. Hagenmeyer [Heidelberg 1896] 103).

111. Albert, *op. cit.* 607 (trans. Hefele, II 138). On the Pisans, see note 42, above.

112. *Regesta,* #40 (late 1102 or early 1103), 42 (April 1104), and 49 (December 1107); *cf.* #50. Spelling variants include Evremarus, Ebremarus, Evermarus, and others, as well as the initial E.

113. *Regesta,* #56a (1109), 65 (July 1112), 69 (late 1111), 76b (1115), 80 (1115), 91 (1120), 96 (unnamed; July 1121), 99 (about 1121), 101 and 102 (1123), 105 (May 1125), 114d and 114e (1126), 117 (unnamed; about 1126), and 126 (1129); *cf.* #89 and 232. The relatively recent articles by Janin ("Césarée") and Tribout de Morembert ("Ebremar, patriarche de Jérusalem") in *DHGE* XIV [1960] col. 1332 unaccountably ignore all after 1123.

114. *Regesta,* #129a; *cf.* #128 (1129, before his elevation). His name usually appears as Gaudentius.

115. *Regesta*, #130. A version cited by Sebastiano Paoli (in *Codice diplomatico del sacro militare ordine Gerosolimitano* . . . , I [Lucca 1733] 471, #12) wrongly identifies him as "Paganus;" this is presumably the source for Rey's nonexistent "Payen" (*Sommaire du supplément aux familles d'Outre-mer* [Chartres 1881] 21).

116. *Regesta*, #133 and 134 (1130),139 (September 1131), 159 (December 1135), 162b (February 1136), 164 (late 1136), 172 (1138), and 174 (February 1138). Janin ("Césarée," col. 209) gives only "1136," ignoring all documents dated either earlier or later.

117. *Op. cit.* 683 (trans. Babcock, II 118). This synod has been variously dated: 1136 (Giovanni D. Mansi *et al.*, *Sacrorum conciliorum* . . . *collectio* . . . , XXI [1776] 503-506, 577-580), 1139 (Röhricht, *Geschichte des Königreichs Jerusalem (1100-1291)* [Innsbruck 1898] 223, n. 5, following Karl J. von Hefele *et al.* [ed. and trans. Henri LeClercq], *Histoire des conciles* . . . , V[2 ed., Paris 1912], part 1, 745; Krey, note in William of Tyre [trans. Babcock, II 118, 19]), 1140 (Hotzelt, *op. cit.* 105, n. 50), 1141 (Beugnot's marginal note in William of Tyre [*RHC: Occ.* I 683]: *Regesta*, #203), and 1142 (Du Cange, *op. cit.* 756, followed by Delaborde, *op. cit.* 56, n. 1); 1139 is now generally accepted. *Regesta*, #232 (January 1145) is posthumous.

118. William of Tyre, *op. cit.* 759, 795 (trans. Babcock, II 185, 218).

119. *Ibid.* 827 (trans. Babcock, II 247).

120. Documents on which he appears as archbishop (as Balduinus, Baldewinus, or B.) include *Regesta*, #210 (1142), 213 (1142/5, mentioning his former chancellorship), 226 (1144), 234 (August 1145), 243 (1146), 262 (1149), 275 (June 1152), 291 (April 1152), 293 (July 1154), and 323 (1156); *cf.* #250. No 1157 document is known for Baldwin, and that of 1162 (*Regesta*, #375) is clearly mistaken in using "B." instead of "E." For documents mentioning him as chancellor of the patriarch, see *Regesta*, 38, 43-46, 51-54.

121. *Regesta*, #215 (1143: "patriarche nepos et cancellarius").

122. William of Tyre, *op. cit.* 854 (trans. Babcock, II 271).

123. *Regesta*, #354 (July 1160), 361 (1160: "Arimis"), 371 (1161: "Ervesius") 377 (about 1162), 418 (1165), 435 (about 1167), 444 (March 1168), 451a (September 1168), 469 (1169), and 492 (about 1171); *cf.* also #375 (1162: "B." for "E.") and 476 (1170: "C." for "E."). His name usually appears as Ernesius or Hernesius; Old French equivalents include Erneys, Erneis, and Herneis (*RHC: Occ.* I 942, 1021, and 960). All those who call him Ernestus (including Gams, *op. cit.* 452) or Ernest (Janin, "Césarée," col. 209) are wrong. For documents mentioning him as chancellor of the patriarch see *Regesta*, 55, 59, 61, 63, and 65.

124. William of Tyre, *op. cit.* 1021 (trans. Babcock, II 412 and n. 19). Janin ("Césarée," col. 209) errs in following Le Quien (*op. cit.* III col. 1288) and Gams (*loc. cit.*) and assigning his death to 1174.

125. William of Tyre, *op. cit.* 942 (trans. Babcock, II 344). The king was not, as usually found, Amalric "I", for "Amalric II" is correctly called Aimery; he appears on documents as Aimericus, Amalric "I" as Amalricus.

126. *Ibid.* 960 (trans. Babcock, II 360); *Regesta*, #464 (Amalric's letter to archbishop Henry of Rheims).

127. Ernoul, *op. cit.* 60 (ed. Mas Latrie, 82): "pour sa biauté l'ama li mere li roi, et si le fist arcevesque de Cesaire."

128. *Regesta*, #528.

129. William of Tyre, *op. cit.* 1068 (trans. Babcock, II 451).

130. *Ibid.* 1049 (trans. Babcock, II 436).

131. Documents include *Regesta*, #458b (date unknown, assigned to "1168-1180" but obviously not before 1175) and 539 (1176), and an undated letter (1177/80, ed. J. P. Migne, in *Patrologia Latina* . . . , vol. CCXI [Paris 1885] col. 355) from Stephen, abbot of St. Genoveta and later bishop of Tournai. The privilege of 1177 in which he is termed patriarch-elect (*Regesta*, #548) is clearly spurious, as both Röhricht and Ernst Strehlke (*Tabulae ordinis Theutonici* . . . [Berlin 1869], #8) indicate. For documents mentioning him as archdeacon or as patriarch, see index of *Regesta* (437, and 115 of supplement).

132. He appears as archbishop in *Regesta*, #618 (November 1182), 619 (1182), 624 (March 1183: "M."), 652a (October 1186), 653-655 (October 1186), 659 (July 1187), and 665 (October 1187). For documents mentioning him as chancellor or as patriarch, see index of *Regesta* (including supplement), *s. v.* "Monachus."

133. *Op. cit.* 1073 (trans. Babcock, II 456).

134. Ernoul, *op. cit.* 203-204; Henry then tried to placate Aymar by a grant to his nephew. For his life and works see P. E. D. Riant, *De Haymaro Monacho* . . . (dissertation, Paris 1865).

135. Ed. Julius von Pflugk-Harttung in *Acta pontificum Romanorum inedita*, II (Stuttgart

1884) 400, #457; this may, however, refer to his predecessor.

136. *Regesta*, #740; "De primordiis ordinis Theutonici narratio . . . , " ed. Max Töppen in *Scriptores rerum Prussicarum*, I (Leipzig 1861) 223. The date March 1190 given for this document by Beda Dudík, *Des hohen Deutschen Ritterordens Münz-Sammlung in Wien* (Vienna 1858) 39, 56, is proved wrong by Töppen, as is March 1195.

137. *Regesta*, #765a.

138. *Regesta*, #757 and 759; *cf.* #233. This "vidimus" procedure, attesting by seal that one had seen a document antedating his elevation, was common practice in Outremer.

139. *Regesta*, #770. Peter is, as was usual in papal correspondence, not named, but Röhricht errs inexplicably in calling him "Gaudentio?"; Gaudens had been dead nearly sixty years, and no namesake is known.

140. *Regesta*, #794; in #797a (July 1204) he appears for the first time as Petrus instead of "P."

141. *Regesta*, #803. Peter's name does not appear in this letter, but he witnessed several documents: *Regesta*, #810 (February 1206), 818 and 819 (February 1207), and 824 (December 1207).

142. Ernoul, *op. cit.* 311 ("Pierre de Limoges"), 323.

143. Letter ed. Mas Latrie in "Histoire des archevêques de l'île de Chypre," *Archives de l'orient latin*, II (1884) part 1, 212-213. Peter witnessed *Regesta*, #866 (October 1213).

144. Letter ed. Migne, *op. cit.* CCXVI (Paris, 1855) col. 974.

145. *Regesta*, #887.

146. Ernoul, *op. cit.* 323; *cf. Regesta*, #901. It was about this time that Thietmar (*Peregrinatio*, ed. Laurent as supplement to *op. cit.*) 53, described him as excessively fat: "qui supra modum pinguis fuit, cum vidi eum."

147. *Regesta*, #937.

148. *Regesta*, #943a (May 15 [not "5"], 1221; Peter, unnamed, is among those designated as acceptable arbiters in a dispute].

149. Letters ed. Mas Latrie in *Histoire de l'île de Chypre sous le règne des . . . Lusignan . . .* , II (Paris 1852) 45, and III (Paris 1855) 618-619; *cf.* LaMonte, "A Register of the Cartulary of the Cathedral . . . of Nicosia," *Byzantion* 5 (1929-1930) 452, #19.

150. Delaville le Roulx, *op. cit.* II (Paris 1897) #1834; *cf. Regesta*, #817.

151. Roger of Wendover, *op. cit.* II 324-327; *cf. Regesta*, #984.

152. *Ibid.* II 351.

153. Letter from Hermann of Salza, ed. Ludwig Weiland in *Monumenta Germaniae historica . . . : Legum, sectio* 4, II (Hanover 1896) 167-168; *cf. Regesta*, #1000.

154. Mas Latrie, *Histoire*, II 49 (July 1229); *Regesta*, #1020 (October 1230), 1021 (December 1230), 1031-1033 (October 1231), 1039 (October 1232), 1051 (March 1234), and 1066 (1235).

155. Lucien Auvray (ed.), *Les registres de Grégoire IX . . .* , II (Paris 1907) #3082.

156. LaMonte, "Register", #43 (September 1236).

157. *Annales de Terre Sainte*, 439: "1237"; his successor had taken office by May 1237.

158. Auvray, *op. cit.* #3639 (May 1237), 3753 (June 1237), 4014 (December 1237), 4129 and 4130 (March 1238), and 4291 (April 1238: *Regesta*, #1079b, and *cf.* #1076: "1237").

159. *Regesta*, #1087 (February 1239).

160. *La règle du temple* (ed. Henri de Curzon [Paris 1886]) 286-287.

161. *Regesta*, #1127 (November 1244); Röhricht's note linking Joscelin to the Templar episode is an error, as the latest possible date for that is 1244, and the prelate in question was obviously a long established friend: "l'arcevesque de Cesaire qui estoit amis de la maison."

162. Élie Berger (ed.), *Les registres d'Innocent IV . . .* , I (Paris 1884) #2026-2028 (July 1246), 2447 (March 1247).

163. *Ibid.* III (1897), #6350 (February 1253), 6490 (April 1253): on the bishopric of Sebastia, sole suffragan see of Caesarea and by 1253 long since *in partibus infidelium*.

164. *Regesta*, #1221 (September 1254).

165. *Regesta*, #39 (1103), 51 (1106), and 69 (1111).

166. *Regesta*, #1226 (unnamed; March 1255) and 1234 (May 1255).

167. Auguste Coulon (ed.), *Les registres d'Alexandre IV . . .* , III (Paris 1953-1959) #2960.

168. *Regesta*, #1291a.

169. *Regesta*, #1298.

170. Anonymous continuation of Ernoul (ed. as part 3 of "L'estoire de Eracles . . . " in *RHC: Occ.* II 380-481), 455; this is the only occurrence of his name: "Lociaumes arcevesque de Cesaire." The marginal date "1266" is corrected to 1267 by Röhricht, *Geschichte*, 935, n. 3.

171. *Regesta*, #1415 and 1417 (August 1277), 1419 (October 1277), and 1437 (October 1280).

172. Conrad Eubel, *Hierarchia catholica medii aevi . . . ab anno 1198 usque ad annum 1431 perducta* (2. ed., Münster 1913), 153, from 1377 to 1413; subsequent years in his later volumes.

173. "Césarée," col. 208-209, with a full list from 1377 to 1936 and a list of Greek bishops from 1645 to 1847, as well as Parthenius (1084), Anastasius (end of 11th [not "12th"] century), Sophronius (13th century), Elias (1281), and "Mélèce,?"; Janin gives details and correct dates for Anastasius in "Anastase, archevêque de Césarée de Palestine . . . " in *DHGE* II (1914) col. 1469-1470.

174. Unlike the archbishops, of whom all existing lists are inexplicably faulty, the lords (and ladies) of Caesarea have been studied with scholarly thoroughness, by John LaMonte, "The Lords of Caesarea in the Period of the Crusades," *Speculum* 22 (1947) 145-161. This article (cited as *Caesarea*) is recent enough to utilize almost all known relevant documents, so the following discussion will summarize LaMonte's findings concerning the city's rulers (but not their family connections, descendants after 1265, and officials), with comments on certain points.

175. Albert, *op. cit.* 544 (trans. Hefele, II 58, with query "Berri?").

176. Ludolph of Sudheim ("Suchem," fl. 1350), *loc. cit.* (trans. Stewart, 64-65): Caesarea, "on the recovery of the Holy Land, came into the possession of a certain knight of these parts named De Horne, whose son-in-law's widow was living even in my own time, for I have often . . . talked upon this subject with her." Deycks (*loc. cit.* n. 7) identifies "these parts" as Westphalia, and suggests the "Städtchen Horn, unweit Detmold." Röhricht (*Die Deutschen im Heiligen Lande . . .* [Innsbruck 1894] 21) notes the presence at Caesarea in 1106 of a Ritter von Horn, but there is no suggestion that he was in command.

177. The spelling of the family name is uncertain. It usually occurs in Latin as Granerius or Granarius, but is also found as Garnerius, Ganerius, Graner, Grener, Graniers, and, in the verses of an anonymous contemporary from his own diocese (ed. Charles Moeller in "Les flamands du Ternois au royaume latin de Jérusalem," *Mélanges Paul Fredericq* [Brussels 1904] 191), Gernirs. In Old French the variants include Grenier, Greniers, Guernier, and Groniers. Extant seals support Granerius (Gustave Schlumberger *et al.*, *Sigillographie de l'orient latin* [Paris 1943] Pl. XVIII, #1 and 2; see "The Sigillography of Crusader Caesarea," in *Studies in Honor of George C. Miles* [in preparation]). LaMonte, *Caesarea*, uses Grenier, but the weight of the sigillographic and documentary evidence favors "a" rather than "e" as the first vowel: Granier, or Garnier. The spellings given by Röhricht in *Regesta* are normalized, not accurately transcribed.

178. Moeller, *op. cit.* 189-202. Eustace apparently came from Herbelles, 35 miles NW of Arras.

179. *Caesarea*, 145 and n. 2.

180. *Regesta*, #57 (September "1109" [Delaville le Roulx, *op. cit.* I #20: "1110"]), with title viscount of Jerusalem. The assertion by Delaborde (*op. cit.* 9) that he was lord of Caesarea "par sa femme" is unfounded and absurd.

181. *Regesta*, #52, the last documentary appearance of archbishop Baldwin and the first of Eustace (usually Eustachius in Latin; LaMonte calls him Eustache).

182. Albert, *op. cit.* 621 (trans. Hefele, II 160).

183. *Op. cit.* I 21, n. 2. This error is repeated by Grousset, *op. cit.* II 482, n. 1.

184. Note in William of Tyre (trans. Babcock, I 541, n. 57).

185. LaMonte, *loc. cit.* For more on Eustace see *idem*, "The Lords of Sidon in the Twelfth and Thirteenth Centuries," *Byzantion* 17 (1944-1945) 185-189. For documents see *Regesta*, #52 (1108), 57 (September 1109 or 1110), 59 (late 1109 or early 1110), 76b (1115), 80 (1115), 82 (May 1116: "et uxor"), 90 (January 1120), 91 (1120), and 101 (1123), and, after his death, #102a, 104, 112, 113, 114b, 139, 147, 237, 293, and 425, and the originals of #309, 354, and 400; *cf.* #89.

186. Guibert, *op. cit.* 262: "Caesareae comes."

187. Moeller, *op. cit.* 191: "princeps Caesariensis Eustachius notus miles, cognomine Gernirs;" "Secunda pars historiae Hierosolimitanae . . . , " sometimes ascribed to "Lisiard of Tours" (*RHC: Occ.* III 545-585), 580.

188. LaMonte, *Caesarea*, 145, n. 2; the assertion that he "never used any title" overlooks "vicecomes de Iherusalem" in *Regesta*, #57.

189. *Op. cit.* 628 (trans. Babcock, II 71).

190. *RHC: Occ.* I 628.

191. Ed. Paulin Paris as *Histoire générale des croisades par . . . Guillaume de Tyr et ses continuateurs . . .* [sic, false], II (Paris 1880) 19.

192. *Regesta*, #102a (1123: already remarried to Hugh), 104 (April 1124), 112 and 113 (January 1126), 114b (1126), and 147 (1133). *Les Lignages d'Outremer* (ed. Beugnot in *RHC: Lois*, II [Paris 1843] 435-474; cited as *Lignages*), 455, calls her Hermeline or Ameline.

193. *Op. cit.* 479 (trans. Babcock, I 489).

194. Charles W. David, *Robert Curthose, Duke of Normandy* (Cambridge, Mass. 1920) 218. It is only "perhaps correct" because the *Lignages* (pp. 455-456) also says "Huistace Garnier fu sire de Cesaire . . . et esposa Hermeline, la niesse dou patriarche Ernoul . . . et ot en marriage Iherico" (later version: "Eustace de Garnier si conquist [*sic*] Cesaire et ot à feme Ameline, qui fut niece dou patriarche . . . et ot Gerico por li."); it is not certain that the *Lignages* here relies solely on William of Tyre. On balance, it probably does not, as the passage in which William gives her name is followed immediately by one giving her sons' names, correctly, as Eustace of Sidon and Walter of Caesarea, while the *Lignages* skips Eustace II and calls his son Girard her son.

195. *Geschichte*, 96, n. 3. Hagenmeyer (Fulcher, 660, n. 7) says "Wahrscheinlich im Jahre 1112 heiratete er die Nichte des Patriarchen Arnulf, namens Emma" and accepts the Jericho dowry story, but cannot be correct in this.

196. *Regesta, passim*. There is, incidentally, no doubt that Eustace II and Walter were Eustace's sons by Emma rather than by a previous marriage, as she is constantly referred to as their mother in the documents. Walter was the last lord of Caesarea to use the family surname Granerius or Garnerius, except for a seal of Hugh's described in "The Sigillography of Crusader Caesarea," in *Studies in Honor of George C. Miles* (in preparation), but the Sidon branch retained it.

197. LaMonte, *Caesarea*, 147; he qualifies this in a footnote: Walter "may have held the regency until 1145 when Girard first employs the title of lord of Sidon." 1135 seems preferable, on the evidence.

198. Since both Eustace and Arnulf came from Thérouannes, it is certainly possible that the former had married a niece of the latter (in view of Arnulf's notorious lechery, it is also possible that "niece" is a euphemism for "daughter") before leaving on Crusade. According to the *Lignages* (p. 456), Eustace and Emma also had a daughter Agnes, who married Henry "le Buffle."

199. On Hugh, see LaMonte, "The Lords of Le Puiset on the Crusades," *Speculum* 17 (1942) 104-106. Despite Krey's doubts (William of Tyre, trans. Babcock, II 71, n. 42), there seems no convincing reason for rejecting the accepted date of 1132 for Hugh's treason and the resulting loss of Banyas (*cf. Regesta*, #147 and 151a).

200. *Caesarea*, 147, citing *Regesta*, #121, as well as #104 (April 1124, with Emma, Eustace II, and Hugh), 112 and 113 (January 1126, with the same), 114b (1126, a grant by Eustace II, with Emma), and 120 (1127). He signs as Walterius or Galterius; LaMonte calls him Gautier.

201. *Regesta*, #139: "G. cognomento Granerius, Cesaree et Sydonie . . . dominus . . . conjux mea domina Juliana."

202. LaMonte, *loc. cit.*, citing *Regesta*, #159. Other documents of Walter I include #162b (February 1136), 174 (February 1138), 237 (1145), 243 (1146), 245 (July 1147), 250 (June 1148), and 256 (1149, with his son Eustace), and the posthumous #309, 354, 400, and 425. LaMonte's suggestion (*Caesarea*, 145, n. 6, based on the 1149 charter) that Bethsan "may have been" subject to the overlordship of Caesarea is unacceptable.

203. William of Tyre, *op. cit.* 629 (trans. Babcock, II 72): "vir toto corpore elegantissimus, viribus insignis, aetate integer."

204. *Caesarea*, 147-148. He may well have been among the lords hated by queen Melisend for opposing her favorite, Hugh.

205. *Ibid.* 148, citing William of Tyre, *op. cit.* 758 (trans. Babcock, II 185).

206. *Ibid.* 148, citing *Regesta*, #162b and 243.

207. *Ibid.* 148, citing *Regesta*, #256.

208. *Ibid.* 148, citing *Regesta*, #139; LaMonte calls her Julianne.

209. *Ibid.* 149, citing *Regesta*, #361.

210. *Ibid.* 149, citing *Regesta*, #293 (July 1154), 299-301 (January 1156), 307 (June 1155), 309 (July 1155), 325 (October 1157), 338 (1159), 344 (March 1160), 354 (July 1160), 355 (November 1160), 366 (July 1161), 397 (April 1164), 400 (July 1164), 412 (March 1165), 413 (April 1165), 416 (August 1165), 422a (April 1166), 448 (April 1168), and 449 (May 1168).

211. *Ibid.* 149, citing William of Tyre, *op. cit.* 909-913 (trans. Babcock, II 319-321). The Fāṭimid caliph was al-'Ādid (1160-1171), last of his dynasty.

212. William of Tyre, *op. cit.* 926, 934, 936 (trans. Babcock, II 322, 339-341).

213. *Regesta*, #298a (1154), 342 (January 1160), 361 (1160), 368 (November 1161), 369

(December 1161, not cited by LaMonte), 373 (1161), 391a and 391b (1163, latter not cited by LaMonte), 425 (late 1166), and 426 (1166), in addition to those previously cited and the posthumous #619, 736, 818, and 819. LaMonte cites one document not in *Regesta*, witnessed by Hugh in January 1166 (ed. Delaville le Roulx in "Chartes de terre sainte," *ROL* 11 [1905-1908], 181-191, #2). His name usually appears as Hugo or Ugo.

214. *Regesta*, #361 ("Ysabel, filie domini Johannis Gothmanni"), 368 and 369 (both: "Helisabeth" daughter of "Iohannes Gothmannus"), 373 ("Helisabeth"), 425 ("Ysabel"), and 426 ("Isabella").

215. *Regesta*, #533 ("Helisabeth").

216. *Regesta*, #818 ("Isabelle") and 819 ("Isabel").

217. Called Goman by LaMonte; he was captured by the Saracens in 1157 and in 1161 raised his ransom by selling several casals for 1400 bezants.

218. LaMonte, *Caesarea*, 151, citing *Regesta*, #517 (July 1174, with Guy's brother Walter) and 539 (1176); Guy (Guido) is only a witness, so we learn nothing useful from them. Rey's suggestion (note to Du Cange, *op. cit.* 279) that this Guy was the first husband of Juliana rather than her brother is rightly rejected by LaMonte (*Caesarea*, 153, n. 49).

219. *Ibid.* 151, citing *Regesta*, #619, and dating it (on the basis of #618, confirming it) November 14.

220. *Ibid.* 151-152, citing William of Tyre, *op. cit.* 1122, and *Regesta*, #659. That he was at Hattin with his men we know from the anonymous *De expugnatione . . . libellus* (ed. Stevenson, 218; not cited by LaMonte).

221. LaMonte, Caesarea, 152, citing *Regesta*, #665-668 (October 1187) and 675 (May 1188); #736 is posthumous.

222. LaMonte, *loc. cit.*, notes, without evaluating, Mas Latrie's assumption that Walter's death occurred on the day of the final assault in July 1191, but rejects Rey's argument (note to Du Cange, *op. cit.* 278) that it occurred before 1189.

223. Ed. Natalis de Wailly as *Récits d'un ménestrel de Reims . . .* (Paris 1876) 109-111 (trans. Stone in *Three Old French Chronicles of the Crusades*, 301-302).

224. LaMonte, *loc. cit.*; Caesarea fell in mid-July. The problematical interlude involving Geoffrey of Lusignan, who was erroneously said to have acquired the shattered fief at this juncture, has already been discussed; LaMonte skips it entirely.

225. *Ibid.* 153, citing *Regesta*, #587 and 619.

226. *Loc. cit.*, noting that the *Lignages* (p. 450) "says that Guy was the lord of Caesarea through his wife;" this evidence is not reliable.

227. LaMonte, *loc. cit.*; the Reginalds were, respectively, chamberlain of Jerusalem and marshal of Cyprus.

228. *Ibid.* 154, citing *Lignages*, 458.

229. *Ibid.* 153, citing *Regesta*, #812 (with his stepson Walter). Lairon is a village about 15 miles east of Limoges, the city associated with Aymar's contemporary, archbishop Peter of Caesarea. For other documents mentioning Aymar (Ademarus or Azemarus in Latin) as lord of Caesarea see *Regesta*, #709 (January 1193), 720 (October 1194), 736 (October 1197, with Juliana), 740 (March 1198, wrongly excluded by LaMonte as corrupt; see note 136, above), 768 (February 1201, with Juliana and Walter), 776 (October 1200), 810 (February 1206, with Juliana and Walter), 818 and 819 (February 1207, with Juliana), 853 (July 1211), 857 (March 1212), 859b (November 1212, with Juliana), and 866 (October 1213, with Juliana).

230. *Ibid.* 154, placing his birth at about 1176, with considerable leeway.

231. *Ibid.* 153, citing (as *"Eracles"*) Ernoul, *op. cit.* 306-312.

232. *Ibid.* 154, citing *Regesta*, #818 and 819, as well as #510 for a gift to the Teutonic Knights before 1243 by an unnamed lady of Caesarea.

233. *Ibid.*, citing *Regesta*, #885a (February 1216). He last appears in March 1219 in a document not cited by LaMonte: *Regesta*, #921.

234. Oliver of Paderborn, *op. cit.* 216-217 (trans. Gavigan, 42-43).

235. Ernoul, *op. cit.* 347, and *cf.* 333, placing him at Damietta with John of Brienne. All subsequent documentary appearances of the name appertain to the nephew, often with his wife Sibyl.

236. LaMonte, *Caesarea*, 154-155. Documents in which he appears include *Regesta*, #721 (January 1195 [or 1194?]), 722a (July 1196), 740b (June 1198), 746 and 747 (October 1198), 768 and 810 (with Aymar and Juliana, cited above), 812 (May 1206, with Aymar), 844 (September 1210, first appearance as constable of Cyprus), 846 (November 1210), 892 (January 1217), 896 (July 1217), 900 (September 1217, executed not "at Nicosia" as LaMonte states, but at Limassol:

"Nimosii"), 903 (October 1217), 912 (July 1218), 938 (October 1220, at Limassol rather than "Nicosia"), and 1003 (April 1229); cf. also #901.

237. LaMonte, *Caesarea*, 155, citing (as *"Eracles"*) Ernoul, *op. cit.* 322, 339-340.

238. *Ibid.* Hugh died in 1205, and Walter probably married Margaret shortly thereafter. Beugnot (*RHC: Lois*, I 109, n. a) errs in calling her (rather than her mother) the widow of King Amalric and in calling Walter "II" instead of "III."

239. LaMonte, *Caesarea*, 156, citing (as *"Gestes"*) Philip of Novara, *Estoire de la guerre que fu entre l'empereur Frederic et Johan d'Ibelin* (ed. Raynaud as part 2 of *Les gestes des chiprois* . . . [Geneva 1887], 25-138), 40 (trans. LaMonte and Hubert as *The Wars of Frederick II against the Ibelins in Syria and Cyprus* [New York 1936], 77, 87), and (as *"Eracles"*) Ernoul, *op. cit.* 369: September 1228.

240. As pointed out above, al-Mu'azzam did not keep Caesarea after sacking and dismantling it during the Fifth Crusade, so no "return" was required. The treaty merely confirmed Frankish ownership.

241. LaMonte, *loc. cit.*, citing Philip, *op. cit.* 67 (trans. LaMonte, 101).

242. *Ibid.* and n. 76, citing *Lignages* (pp. 452, 457). LaMonte's "Helvis" is there spelled "Heloys" (Heloise).

243. LaMonte, *loc. cit.*, citing Philip, *op. cit.* 45 (trans. LaMonte, 82). He was probably about 17 or 18 in 1228.

244. *Ibid.* 156-157, citing Philip, *op. cit.* 67, 83, 96, 101, 113, 116, and 117 (trans. LaMonte, 109, 129-130, 145, 151-152, 163-164, and 167); "L'estoire de Eracles" (*RHC: Occ.* II) 390-394, 398; and other sources including *Regesta,* #1036 (April 1232). LaMonte also lists (*Caesarea,* 157, n. 85) documents John witnessed, with his importance shown by the position of his signature near the top of the list of barons in each: *Regesta,* #1037 (June 1232), 1039 (October 1232), 1046 and 1047 (October 1233), and 1049 (December 1233), and three not in *Regesta* but in his "Register:" #38 and 39 (December 1233) and 42 (August 1234). See also *Regesta,* #1070 (February 1236) and LaMonte, "Register," #43 (September 1236).

245. LaMonte, *Caesarea*, 157, citing "Assises" (*RHC: Lois*) I 528; no such "forfeiture" was valid without the concurrence of the High Court.

246. *Ibid.* 158, citing Philip, *op. cit.* 117 (trans. LaMonte, 194). LaMonte does not mention the *Annales de Terre Sainte* (p. 439), which places John's death in the same year as his uncle's; one version wrongly puts both in 1235, while the other is correct in putting Ibelin's death in 1236, but wrong in adding John's prematurely.

247. LaMonte, *loc. cit.*, citing *Regesta,* #1083. On Theobald's Crusade see Sidney Painter, "The Crusade of Theobald of Champagne and Richard of Cornwall, 1239-1241" in Setton, *op. cit.* II 469-485. *Regesta,* #1233 is posthumous.

248. *Loc. cit.* and n. 90, discussing various ways of dating John's death; in n. 91 he admits his inability to find any basis for Charles Hopf's dates "1228-1251" (*Revue critique d'histoire et de littérature,* V, part 2 [1870] 236), which is understandable as both are demonstrably wrong.

249. *Regesta,* #1089: his sister Alice is called "sororem Johannis de Caesaria," an unlikely phraseology if he were then deceased.

250. LaMonte, *loc. cit.*, citing Philip, *op. cit.* 125 (trans. LaMonte, 171).

251. *Ibid.* and n. 91, analyzing conflicting accounts in *Lignages,* 452, 457. Hopf, *loc. cit.,* calls the son "Eudes" (Odo), but LaMonte finds no basis for this. "Montaigu" is Montaigu-sur-Champeix, a castle south of Clermont in Auvergne.

252. *Lignages,* 452: "Ils orrent quatre filles et un filz: Marguerite . . . et Marie . . . et Ysabiau . . . et Aalis . . . et Peretin mourut petit."

253. LaMonte, *loc. cit.* and n. 92, citing *Regesta,* #1175 (with her husband). They also appear together in #1210 (December 1253), 1233 (April 1255), 1235a (May 1255), and 1238 (June 1255, Margaret's last known appearance): cf. also #510 (before 1243, "domina Margarita" among donors).

254. *Ibid.* 158-159, citing "Assises" (*RHC: Lois*) II 400.

255. Du Cange (ed. Rey) 503-509; the error is the editor's. John appears without Margaret in documents not concerning Caesarea: *Regesta,* #1098b (March 1241, not termed "dominus Caesareae"), 1234 (May 1255), and 1271a (March 1259 or 1260: "cannot be used to prove he was still alive at that date, though the presumption would be to that effect" says LaMonte, *Caesarea,* 159, n. 97).

256. *Ibid.* 159, citing *Regesta,* #1221 (September 1254) and 1259 (August 1257). He was one of the barons who, in 1250, established the laws of the kingdom ("Abrégé du livre des Assises," ed. Beugnot in *RHC: Lois* II 246).

257. LaMonte, *loc. cit.*, citing (as*"Gestes"*) Gerard of Montreal (*op. cit.* 171), "L'estoire de Eracles" (*RHC: Occ.* II 448), and *Lignages* (p. 457).

258. Hopf (*loc. cit.*) says Margaret outlived John, and by 1269 was married to Giles (II) d'Estroem, son of the lord of Haifa.

259. LaMonte, *loc. cit.* For more on Nicholas and Thomas and their wives, on "people called 'Caesarea' [sic] but not members of the house," and on the "grand officers of Caesarea" see *ibid.* 159-161.

Abbreviations

AASOR   *Annual of the American Schools of Oriental Research.*

AJA   *American Journal of Archaeology.*

ALG   *Archiv fuer Lateinische Lexicographie und Grammatik.*

Ath. Mitt.   *Mittheilungen des Kaiserlich Deutschen Archaeologischen Institutes, Athenische Abtheilung.* Vol. XXII, Berlin 1897.

BA   *Biblical Archaeologist.*

Bechtel, HP   F. Bechtel, *Die historischen Personennamen des Griechischen bis zur Kaiserzeit.* Halle 1917.

Berger, BAC   P. Berger, "Inscription Juive ancienne de Volubilis," *Bulletin Archéologique du Comité des Travaux Historiques et Scientifiques.* Paris 1892.

BGA   *Bibliotheca geographorum Arabicorum.*

BIES   *Bulletin of the Israel Exploration Society.* (Hebrew)

BJPES   *Bulletin of the Jewish Palestine Exploration Society.* (Hebrew since 1933)

BLR   *Bulletin of Louis M. Rabinowitz.*

BMCA   R. S. Poole, *Catalogue of the Coins of Alexandria and the Nomes.* (British Museum) London 1892.

BMCB   W. Wroth, *Catalogue of the Imperial Byzantine Coins in the British Museum.* 2 vols. London 1908.

BMCP   G. F. Hill, *Catalogue of the Greek Coins of Palestine.* (British Museum) London 1914.

BMC Ph   G. F. Hill, *Catalogue of the Greek Coins of Phoenicia.* (British Museum) London 1910.

BSAJ   *British School of Archaeology in Jerusalem.*

BZ   *Byzantinische Zeitschrift.*

CH   *Church History*

CIG   *Corpus Inscriptionum Graecarum.* Vol. 3 Berlin 1853.

CIJ   *Corpus Inscriptionum Iudaicarum.* 2 vols. ed. J. -B. Frey, Rome 1936-52.

CIL   *Corpus Inscriptionum Latinarum.* vol. I. Berlin 1902.

CJC   *Corpus Juris Civilis.* 10th ed. ed. P. Krueger, Berlin 1929

CNI   *Christian News from Israel.*

Cod. Theod.   *Codex Theodosianus.* ed. T. Mommsen, Berlin 1905.

CPJ   *Corpus papyrorum Judaicarum.* 3 vols. ed. V. A. Tcherikover & A. Fricks, Cambridge 1957-64.

De Aed.   Procopius, ΠΕΡΙ ΚΤΙΣΜΑΤΩΝ (*De Aedificio*) Text and translation in English by H. B. Dewing, with the collaboration of Glanville Downey (Loeb Classical Library, vol. VII) Harvard University Press, Cambridge, Mass. 1940.

DHGE   *Dictionnaire d'histoire et de géographie ecclésiastiques.* ed. A. Baudrillart, et. al. 15 vols. Paris 1912-63.

DHVG   *Das heilige Land in Vergangenheit und Gegenwart.* ed. V. Cramer & G. Meinertz. Köln 1941.

EEP   L. Robert, *Études épigraphiques et philologiques.* Paris 1938.

Etymol.   *Isidori Hispalensis Episcopi Etymologarium sive Originum.* ed. W. M. Lindsay. 2 vols. Oxford 1911.

Frova, "L'iscrizione"   A. Frova, "L'iscrizione di Ponzio Pilato a Cesarea," *Istituto Lombardo-Accademia di Scienze e Lettere, Rendiconti, Classe di Lettere.* 95 (Milano 1961) 419-34.

Frova, CM   A. Frova, ed., *Caesarea Maritima (Israele).* Rapporto préliminare della I campagna di scavo della Missione Archeologica Italiana. (Istituto Lombardo) (Milano 1959).

Frova, *Scavi*   A. Frova, et al., *Scavi di Caesarea Maritima.* Milan 1965.

GCS   Die griechischen christlichen Schriftsteller der ersten Jahrhunderte (Berlin).

Gloss.   *Corpus Glossariorum Latinorum.* ed. G. Goetz, vol. II, Leipzig 1888; vol. IV Leipzig 1889.

IEJ   *Israel Exploration Journal*

IGLS   *Inscriptions grecques et latines de la Syrie*. ed. L. Jalabert and R. Mouterde, Paris 1929-59.

ILN   *Illustrated London News*

ILS   *Inscriptiones Latinae selectae*. ed. H. Dessau, 2 vols. Berlin 1892-1906.

JA   Flavius Josephus, *Jewish Antiquities*. Text and translation in English by H. St. J. Thackeray, Ralph Marcus and L. H. Feldman (Loeb Classical Library, vols. IV-IX), Harvard University Press, Cambridge, Mass. 1957-65.

JAA   Flavius Josephus, *Against Apion*. Text and translation in English by H. St. J. Thackeray (Loeb Classical Library, vol. I, pp. 162-411), Harvard University Press, Cambridge, Mass. 1956.

JAOS   *Journal of the American Oriental Society*.

JDAI   *Jahrbuch des kaiserlich-deutschen archaeologischen Instituts*.

JE   *Jewish Encyclopedia*. New York 1901-1906.

JEA   *Journal of Egyptian Archaeology*.

JJP   *Journal of Juristic Papyrology*.

JPOS   *Journal of the Palestine Oriental Society*.

JPT   *Jahrbuecher fuer protestantische Theologie*.

JQR   *Jewish Quarterly Review*.

JTS   *Journal of Theological Studies*.

JW   Flavius Josephus, *The Jewish Wars*. Text and translation in English by H. St. J. Thackeray (Loeb Classical Library, vols. II-III) Harvard University Press, Cambridge, Mass. 1956-57.

Kadman, *CC*   Leo Kadman, *The Coins of Caesarea Maritima*. (Corpus Nummorum Palaestinensium, vol. II) Tel-Aviv—Jerusalem 1957.

MAMA   *Monumenta Asiae Minoris Antiqua*. ed. J. Keil and A. Wilhelm, vol. III. Manchester 1931.

MGWJ   *Monatschrift für Geschichte und Wissenschaft des Judenthums*.

MIL   *Flavi Vegetii Renati Epitoma rei militaris*. ed. C. Lang, Leipzig 1885.

Migne, P.G.   J. P. Migne, *Patrologiae Cursus Completus. Series Graeca*.

Migne, P.L.   J. P. Migne, *Patrologiae Cursus Completus. Series Latina*.

Nov.   *Novellae*, in *Corpus Juris Civilis*. (see CJC)

NS   *Nea Sion*.

OA   *Oriens Antiquus*.

OGIS   *Orientis graeci inscriptiones selectae*. ed. W. Dittenberger, Hildesheim 1960.

Onom.   Eusebius, *Das Onomastikon der biblischen Ortsnamen*. (Die griechischen christlichen Schriftsteller der ersten drei Jahrhunderten, vol. 11) ed. E. Klostermann, Leipzig 1904.

Or.   R. Foerster, ed., *Libanii Opera*. vol. III "Orationes. Pro Rhetoribus." pp. 119-46. Leipzig 1904.

Ox. Pap.   *The Oxyrynchus Papyri*. Part XI. ed. B. P. Grenfell and A. S. Hunt, London 1915 (Egypt Exploration Fund. Graeco-Roman Branch. Memoirs. vol. 14).

PAES   *Publications of the Princeton University Archaeological Expedition to Syria in 1904-5 and 1909*. Part III A: Erno Littmann, D. Magie, Jr., and D. R. Stuart, *Greek and Latin Inscriptions*. Leyden 1921.

PBSR   *Papers of the British School At Rome*.

PEFQS   *Palestine Exploration Fund Quarterly Statement*.

PPTS   *Palestine Pilgrims' Text Society*. 13 vols. London 1890-97.

Preisigke, *NB*   F. Preisigke, *Namenbuch*. Heidelberg 1922.

PSI   *Publicazioni della Società Italiana*.

PW   *Philologische Wochenschrift*.

QDAP   *The Quarterly of the Department of Antiquities in Palestine*.

RA   *Revue Archéologique*.

RB   *Revue Biblique*.

RE   Pauly-Wissowa-Kroll *et. al., Realencyclopaedie der classischen Altertumswissenschaft.*

Rec. d'Arch. Or.   C. S. Clermont-Ganneau, *Recueil d'Archéologie Orientale.* vols. IV and VI. Paris 1901, 1905.

REG   Revue des études grecques.

Regesta   R. Roehricht, *Regesta regni Hierosolymitani* . . . Innsbruck 1893, with Supplement, N. Y. 1904.

RHC: Occ.   Recueil des historiens des croisades: Historiens occidentaux. 5 vols. Paris 1844-95.

RHC: Or.   Recueil des historiens des croisades: Historiens orientaux. 5 vols. Paris 1872-1906.

ROL   Revue de l'orient latin.

Rostovtzeff, *Klio.*   M. Rostovtzeff, "Roemische Bleitesserae," *Klio* (Beitraege zur alten Geschichte. Beiheft 3) Leipzig 1905. Pp. 1-131.

Rostovtzeff-Prou,   M. Rostovtzeff and M. Prou, *Catalogue des Plombs de l'Antiquité.* Paris 1900.

RP   Revue de Philologie.

RSR   Revue des Sciences Religieuses.

Schürer, *GJV*   Emil Schürer, *Geschichte des juedischen Volkes im Zeitalter Jesu Christi.* 4 vols. 4th ed. Leipzig 1911.

HJP   Emil Schürer, *A History of the Jewish People in the Time of Jesus Christ.* 5 vols. Trans. J. Macpherson, *et. al.* Edinburgh 1886-90.

SEG   Supplementum Epigraphicum Graecum.

SWP   C. R. Conder and H. H. Kitchener, *The Survey of Western Palestine. Memoirs.* Vol. II. London 1882.

Syl.   Sylloge Inscriptionum Graecarum. ed. W. Dittenberger, 4th ed. 4 vols. Leipzig 1960.

ZDPV   Zeitschrift des Deutschen Palaestina-Vereins.

ZKG   Zeitschrift für Kirchengeschichte.

A Select Bibliography
on Caesarea Maritima

Abel, F. M., "Le Littoral Palestinien et Ses Ports," *RB* N.S. 11 (1914) 556-90.

Albricci, A., "L' Orcestra dipinta del teatro Erodiano di 'Caesarea Maritima'," *Bollettino d' Arte* 47 (1962) 289-304.

Alt, Albrecht, "Stationen der römischen Heerstrassen von Ägypten nach Syrien," *ZDPV* 70 (1954) 154-66.

Avi-Yonah, M., "The Foundation of Tiberias," *IEJ* 1 (1950-51) 160-69.

———, "Jerusalem and Caesarea," *The Twelfth Archæological Convention* (IES) Jerusalem, 1957, 79-84 (Heb.).

———, "The Synagogue at Caesarea (Preliminary Report)," *BLR* 3 (1960) 44-48. Also *IEJ* 6 (1956) 210-2; 13 (1963) 146-8; *RB* 70 (1963) 582-5.

———, *In the Days of Rome and Byzantium.* Jerusalem 1962 (Heb.).

———, "A List of Priestly Courses from Caesarea," *IEJ* 12 (1962) 137-39.

———, "The Caesarea Inscription of the Twenty-four Priestly Courses," *The Teacher's Yoke: Studies in Memory of Henry Trantham.* E. J. Vardaman, J. L. Grant, eds. Waco, Texas 1964, 46-57.

———, "Lucius Valerius Valerianus, Governor of Syria-Palestina," *IEJ* 16 (1966) 135-141.

Barag, D., "An Inscription from the High Level Aqueduct of Caesarea- Reconsidered," *IEJ* 4 (1964) 250-52.

Benvenisti, David, "Auf dem Weg zum Krokodilfluss und nach Caesarea," *Zion* IV (1930) 49-53 (Heb.).

Benzinger, I., "Caesarea Stratonis oder Palästina," (10) *RE* III, 1 (1897) cols. 1291-94.

Beyer, G., "Das Gebiet der Kreuzfahrerherrschaft Caesarea in Palästina siedlungs- und territorialgeschichtlich Untersucht," *ZDPV* 59 (1936) 1-91.

Cadiou, R., "La Bibliothèque de Césarée et la Formation des Chaînes," *RSR* 16 (1936) 474-83.

Calderini, A., "L' Inscription de Ponce Pilate à Césarée," *BTS* 57 (1963) 8-19.

Le Camus, E., "Césarée du Bord de la Mer," *Dictionnaire de la Bible,* F. Vigoroux, ed. Paris 1899, II 456-465.

Chabot, J. B., "Inscription byzantine de Césarée de Palestine," *BZ* 5 (1896) 160-62.

Conder, C. R., and H. H. Kichener, See *Abbreviations, SWP.*

Dalman, Gustaf, "Die Küstenflüsse Palästinas südlich von Caesarea," *ZDPV* 37 (1914) 338-48.

———, *Sacred Sites and Ways.* trans. Paul Levertoff. New York 1935, pp. 4, 11, 222-226.

Degrassi, A., "Sull'iscrizione di Ponzio Pilato," *Linc: Rendiconti di scienze morali* 19 (1964) 59-65.

Dowling, E., *Sketches of Caesarea (Palestine), Biblical–Mediaeval–Modern: from Earliest Caesar to Latest Sultan.* London 1912.

Downey, Glanville, "The Christian Schools of Palestine: A Chapter in Literary History," *Harvard Library Bulletin* 12 (1958) 297-319.

Fritsch, Charles T., and I. Ben-Dor, "The Link Expedition to Israel, 1960," *BA* 24 (1961) 50-59.

Frova, A., See *Abbreviation,* A. Frova, "L'iscrizione"; *CM; Scavi.*

Frova, A., "La Statua di Artemide Efesia a Caesarea Maritima," *Bollettino d'Arte* 47 (1962) 305-13.

———, "Excavating the Theatre of Caesarea Maritima—and the Goddess whom Paul Hated," *ILN* 244 (1964) 524-26.

Galling, K., "Die Syrisch-Palästinische Küste nach der Beschreibung bei Pseudo-Skylax," *ZDPV* 61 (1938) 66-96.

Gelzer, H., "Inschrift aus Kaisareia," *ZDPV* 17 (1894) 180-82.

Germer-Durand, J., "Épitaphe greque de Césarée Maritime," *Échos d' Orient* 7 (1904) 260-67.

Guérin, Victor, "Discoveries at Caesarea," *PEFQS* (1888) 134-38.

——, "Kaisarieh," *Description géographique, historique, et archéologique de la Palestine,* "Samarie," Tome II:2, Paris 1875, 321-39.

Haefeli, Leo, *Caesarea am Meer* (Neutestamentliche Abhandlungen, 10:5). Münster 1923.

Hamburger, Anit, "A Graeco-Samaritan Amulet from Caesarea," *IEJ* 9 (1959) 43-45.

——, "Gems from Caesarea Maritima," *Atiqot* 8 (1968) 1-38.

Hamburger, H., "Minute Coins from Caesarea," *Atiqot* 1 (1955) 115-38.

——, "A New Inscription from the Caesarea Aqueduct," *IEJ* 9 (1959) 188-90.

——, "Nummi Caesarenses et historia urbis," *BJPES* 15 (1950) 78-82 (Heb.).

——, "Caesarea Coin Finds and the History of the City," *BJPES* 15 (1950) 73-82 (Heb.).

Hanauer, J. E., "Two Busts from Caesarea," *PEFQS* (1898) 159-60.

Holland, D. L., "Report of the Joint Expedition to Caesarea Maritima, 1971," *Newsletter* of the ASOR, 1, 1971-72.

——, "Report of the Joint Archaeological Expedition to Caesarea Maritima, 1971," in: Walter J. Burghardt, S.J., "Literature of Christian Antiquity: 1967-1971," *Theological Studies,* 33 (1972) 275-277.

——, "Report of the Joint Expedition to Caesarea Maritima, 1972," *Newsletter* of the ASOR, 1972-73.

Iliffe, J. H., "A Copy of the Crouching Aphrodite," *QDAP* 2 (1932) 110.

——, "A Portrait of Vitellius (?) in Rock Crystal (from Caesarea)," *QDAP* 1 (1932) 153-54.

Israel Department of Antiquities, *Short Guide to the Ruins of Caesarea.* Jerusalem 1955. (Also editions in Hebrew and French).

Janin, R. P., "Césarée de Palestine," *DHGE* 12 (1953) 206-9.

Jeremias, J., "Der Taraxippos im Hippodrom von Caesarea Palestinae," *ZDPV* 54 (1931) 73-81, 279-89.

Jones, Arnold H. M., *The Cities of the Eastern Roman Provinces.* Oxford 1937, pp. 273-74, 276, 278, 280-81.

Josephus, F. *Jewish Antiquities.* See *Abbreviations, JA.*

——, *The Jewish Wars.* See *Abbreviations, JW.*

Kadman, L., *The Coins of Caesarea Maritima.* See *Abbreviations, Kadman, CC.*

Kallner-Amiran, D. H., "A Revised Earthquake-Catalogue of Palestine," *IEJ* 1 (1950-51) 223-46; 2 (1952) 48-65.

Kedar Y. and Y. Ziv, "The Water Supply of Ancient Caesarea, i. a. aquaeductus," *Yediot* 28 (1964) 122-31 (Heb.).

Kindler, A., "A Seventh Century Lamp with Coin Decoration," *IEJ* 8 (1958) 106-9.

Klein, S., "Antipatris-by-Caesarea; Tripolis-by-Caesarea," *BJPES* 2 (1934) 10-13 (Heb.).

Knight, O. H., "Notes on Caesarea and Neighborhood," *PEFQS* 52 (1920) 79-81.

Krauss, S. "Caesarea," *JE* III 485-89.

——, "Das Tetrapylon in Caesarea," *ALG* 14 (1906) 281-82.

——, "Zur Topographie von Caesarea," *JQR* 14 (1902) 745-51.

Kubitschek, Wilhelm, "Zu Münzen von Caesarea in Samaria," *Numismatische Zeitschrift* 44 (1911) 13-20.

La Monte, J., "The Lords of Caesarea in the Period of the Crusades," *Speculum* 22 (1947) 145-61.

Lazega, M., "Ponce Pilate a écrit son nom (interview of L. Semkowski)," *Ecclesia* 16 (1963) 87-90.

Lees, G. Robert, "Antiquities from Caesarea, etc.," *PEFQS* 25 (1893) 137-41.

Lehmann-Hartleben, K., "Die antiken Hafenanlagen des Mittelmeeres," *Klio*, Beiheft XIV (N.F., Heft 1) Leipzig 1923, *passim*.

Levy, S., "A Hoard of Abbasid Coins from Caesarea," *Eretz Israel* 7 (1964) 47-68 (Heb.).

Lieberman, S., *The Talmud of Caesarea*. (*Tarbiz Supplement* II:4) Jerusalem 1931 (Heb.).

——, "The Martyrs of Caesarea," *Annuaire de l'Institut de Philologie et d'Histoire Orientales et Slaves* VII (1939-44) 395-446.

Lifschitz, B., "Une inscription byzantine de Césarée en Israël," *REG* 70 (1957) 118-32.

——, "Timbres amphoriques trouvés à Césarée de Palestine," *RB* 70 (1963) 556-58.

——, "Inscriptions de Césarée en Palestine," *Latomus* 22 (1963) 783-84.

——, "Einige Amulette aus Caesarea Palestinae," *ZDPV* 80 (1964) 80-4.

——, "La nécropol juive de Césarée," *RB* 71 (1964) 384-87.

Linder, E., and O. Leenhardt, "Recherches d'Archéologie sous Marine sur la côte Mediterranean d'Israël," *Revue Archéologique* 1 (1964) 47-51.

Link, E. A., *Survey Trip to Israel. (a) The Port of Caesarea*. New York 1956.

MacLeish, K., "Sea Search in the History of Caesarea," *Life* (May 5, 1961) 72-82.

Moulton, Warren J., "Gleanings in Archaeology and Epigraphy: 4. A Caesarean Inscription," *AASOR* 1 (1919-20) 86-90.

Negev, A., "Caesarea Maritima," *CNI* 11 (1960) 50-59.

——, "Césarée Maritime, la ville des procurateurs romaines," *BTS* 41 (1961) 6-15.

——, "Where Vespasian was proclaimed Emperor: Caesarea Maritima on the Coast of Israel—A Summary of Recent Excavations. Part I: The Crusader and Arab Cities; Part II: Excavations Herodian and Byzantine," *ILN* 243 (1963) 684-86; 728-31.

——, "The High Level Aqueduct at Caesarea," *IEJ* 14 (1964) 237-49.

——, *Caesarea on the Sea*. Tel Aviv 1965.

Neubauer, Adolphe, *La Géographie de Talmud*. Paris 1868, pp. 11, 91-96.

Oestreicher, B., "A Contemporary Picture of Caesarea's Ancient Harbor," *Israel Numismatic Bulletin* 2 (1962) 44-47.

Picard, L. and Avnimelech, M., "On the Geology of the Central Coastal Plain," *JPOS* 17 (1937) 255-99.

θωκυλίδης Ἰωάννης, "καισρεια," *NS* 29 (1934) 534-38.

Reifenberg, A., "Caesarea, A Study in the Decline of a Town," *IEJ* 1 (1950-51) 20-32.

Ricciotti, Giuseppe, "Die Ruinen von Caesarea," *Il Cantiere di Hiram*. Torino 1936, 189-95.

Rim, M., "Sand and Soil in the Coastal Plain of Israel," *IEJ* 1 (1950-51) 33-48.

Röhricht, Reinhold, ed. *Bibliotheca Geographica Palestinae: Chronologisches Verzeichnis der auf die Geographie des heiligen Landes bezüglichen Literatur von 333 bis 1878*. Berlin 1890. New ed. Jerusalem 1963. *Passim*.

Rosenzweig, A., *Jerusalem und Caesarea*. Berlin 1890.

Runciman, Steven, *A History of the Crusades*. 3 vols. Cambridge 1953, *passim*.

Saulcy, Louis F. J. C. de, "Premièr Palestina—Caesarea," *Numismatique de la Terre Sainte*. Paris 1874, 112-41.

Schalit, A., *King Herod. Portrait of a Ruler*. Jerusalem 1962.

Schemmel, F., "Die Schule von Caesarea in Palästina," *PW* 45 (1925) 1277-80.

Schneller, Ludwig, *Jerusalem und Cäsarea*. Köln am Rhein 1919.

Schumacher, G., "Recent Discoveries at Caesarea, Umm el Jemal, and Haifa," *PEFQS* 20 (1888) 134-40.

——, "Researches in the Plain North of Caesarea," *PEFQS* 19 (1887) 78-90.

Schwabe, M., "Two Jewish-Greek Inscriptions Recently Discovered at Caesarea," *IEJ* 3 (1953) 127-30; 233-38.

Spee, Placidus von, "Ein Ausflug nach Caesarea Maritima," *Nachrichtenblatt f. d. Teilnehmer und Förderer des Deutschen Vereins vom heiligen Lande* 8 (1934) 27-30.

Smith, Simon E., S.J., "Césarée", *RB*, 78 (1971) 591-93 + Pl. XXIX.

Σπυριδωνίδης, Χριστόδουλος Κ., "Καισάρειαή τῆς Παλαιστίνης." *NS* 17 (1922) 586-92.

Stauffer, E., *Die Pilatusinschrift von Caesarea*. (Erlanger Universitätsreden. Neue Folge-Sonderreihe der "Erlanger Forschungen") Erlangen 1966.

Sukenik, E. L., "Three Jewish Inscriptions," *Zion* 1 (1926) 16-20 (Heb.).

——, "More About the Ancient Synagogue of Caesarea," *BLR* 2 (1951) 28-30.

Thomsen, P., *Die Palästina-Literatur*. 6 vols. (1895-1939) Leipzig & Berlin 1908-56. Band A (1878-94) Berlin 1960.

——, *Loca Sancta*. Halle 1907. 74-75.

Turner, C. H., "The Early Episcopal Lists," *JTS* 1 (1900) 181-200; 529-53; 18 (1916-17) 103-34.

Vardamann, E. J. M."Introduction to the Caesarea Inscription of the Twenty-Four Priestly Courses," *The Teacher's Yoke: Studies in Memory of Henry Trantham*. E. J. Vardaman, J. L. Garrett, eds. Waco, Texas 1964, 42-5.

——, "A New Inscription which Mentions Pilate as 'Prefect,'" *JBL* 81 (1962) 70-71.

Weippert, M., "Caesarea Maritima," in "Archäologischer Jahresbericht", *ZDPV* 80 (1964) 156-58.

Wolf, C. U., "Eusebius of Caesarea and the Onomasticon," *BA* 27 (1964) 66-96.

Yeivin, S., "Excavations at Caesarea Maritima," *Archaeology* 8 (1955) 122-29.